P9-DWJ-942

The Journalist's Handbook on Libel and Privacy

The
Journalist's Handbook
on
Libel and Privacy

Barbara Dill

THE FREE PRESS
A Division of Macmillan, Inc.
NEW YORK

Collier Macmillan Publishers
LONDON

Copyright © 1986 by Barbara Dill

All rights reserved. No part of this book may be reproduced or transmitted in any form or by any means, electronic or mechanical, including photocopying, recording, or by any information storage and retrieval system, without permission in writing from the Publisher.

The Free Press
A Division of Macmillan, Inc.
866 Third Avenue, New York, N.Y. 10022

Collier Macmillan Canada, Inc.

Printed in the United States of America

Printing number

1 2 3 4 5 6 7 8 9 10

Library of Congress Cataloging-in-Publication Data

Dill, Barbara.
  The journalist's handbook on libel and privacy.

  Includes index.
  1. Libel and slander—United States. 2. Privacy,
right of—United States. 3. Mass media—Law and
legislation—United States. I. Title.
KF1266.D55 1986   346.7303'4   86-551
ISBN 0-02-908070-3   347.30634

Credits

"*Mercy, it's the revolution and I'm in my bathrobe,*" Nicole Hollander, St. Martin's Press, Inc., New York. Copyright © 1982 by Nicole Hollander. The generosity of Ms. Hollander is gratefully acknowledged.
Richmond (Va.) *News Leader,* copyright © 1982. Reprinted with permission. Translation by Hu Ping.
Paul Conrad, 1968, *The Los Angeles Times.* Reprinted with permission.
Paul Szep, 1972, *Boston Globe.* Reprinted with permission.
Frank Evers, 1976, New York *Daily News.* Reprinted with permission.
James Morin, 1980, *The Miami Herald.* Reprinted with permission.
Timothy Newcomb, 1985, Barre-Montpelier, Vt., *Times Argus.* Reprinted with permission.
Cullman, Ala., *Times Democrat,* copyright © 1961. Reprinted with permission.
Copyright © 1978 Gianfranco Gorgoni/Contact. Reprinted with permission. The generosity of Robert Pledge, president of Contact Press Images, is gratefully acknowledged.
Publishers' Auxiliary, the journal of the National Newspaper Association. Copyright © 1985. Reprinted with permission.

For Joseph B. Treaster

Contents

With Appreciation

THIS is fun to write—the part thanking people who helped me.

General Arthur B. Hanson, a diminutive former Marine and intrepid old-time press lawyer, helped launch my libel seminars with The Mutual Insurance Company of Bermuda as sponsor. The seminars are the foundation of this book.

George Wilson's optimism buoyed me, and his jazz energized me.

Julian Bach, my agent, believed in my book and in me and gave unstintingly of time and advice. Through Julian, I met Grant Ujifusa, my editor. A warm and determined idealist, Grant is perversely attracted to eggplants and elephants and, being from Wyoming, never tires of hollering "pronto!". Still, I'm going to miss our conversations and laughter so much, I may have to propose another book. It must be beginner's luck that delivered me Julian and Grant, the best in the business.

Lawyers all over the country took time to talk with me about their cases and sent materials. I am especially grateful for thoughtful critiques from David J. Branson, Andrew L. Hughes, and Katherine R. Trager, and for advice and assistance from Pamela J. Brown, Marjorie T. Coleman, David E. Kendall, Slade R. Metcalf, and Paul L. O'Brien.

Friends' enthusiasm glowed even when my own resolve flickered. Marjorie and Roy Bonsnes, Jay Bushell, Charlene Canape, Margarett Loke, Anne Stovell, and my sister Maureen Dill cheered me on. Chris Riso's talent and skill made onerous tasks manageable. Philip C. Oxley's and Chris Hu's generosity saved the day—many, many days.

There would be no book without Joe Treaster, who urged me to write but forgot to say how hard it would be. Some days I was anything but grateful, but now I am.

Introduction

THIS book is a comprehensive newsroom handbook on libel and privacy. It is designed to be a practical book that explains the law and answers the questions journalists most often ask about their legal rights and responsibilities.

The book approaches the topic two ways. The first six chapters recount case stories that highlight problems journalists have confronted. The seventh chapter responds to common questions posed by journalists around the country: Should I keep my notes? If someone sues for libel, who pays the costs—me or my news organization? Can the publisher settle a case when I'm sure my story is not libelous and I want to prove it in court? Can I countersue someone who takes me to court on a groundless claim, trying to shut me up or punish me?

I begin with a short history of libel law. Then stories, cartoons, reviews, and editorials that have led to libel suits are analyzed. The purpose is to allow journalists to see the statement that provoked the suit, understand how the reporting measured up to legal requirements, and identify journalistic steps that would have strengthened the defense.

On the subject of privacy, the book deals with embarrassing truths, both in words and pictures, that must be evaluated for public interest and legitimacy as news. The book then treats false light suits, those which arise from embellishments or distortions that create a false impression. I go on to talk about how far a journalist physically can go in pursuing a story without risking arrest for trespassing. Finally, I look at claims of misappropriation by people whose names or photographs have been used in advertising without their consent.

The stories here are drawn from complaints against the press; they have been brought by people who said they had been injured and were judged by their fellow citizens, which is the way the law develops and is passed down. I have chosen cases for their dramatic appeal. Some are amusing, others are touching, but above all they illustrate recurring problems and dangers for journalists. Some of the stories may seem extreme or bizarre, but they were selected precisely because they would hold readers' interest. I hope readers will not be tempted to dismiss the more unusual stories as atypical, but will absorb the principles of reporting and editorial decision-making which they embody. The principles apply equally to the quirky and the mundane.

This book grew out of my experience giving seminars to reporters and editors around the country on how to prevent libel and privacy suits. Over the course of two years I met hundreds of journalists from both large and small news organizations, all with the same questions and all fearful of making a mistake, getting sued, and causing big damages.

I developed the seminar in the belief that journalists wanted to know more about libel and privacy law from a practical standpoint: how to spot problems and avoid them. Many recent court cases had been widely publicized, but only rarely did the publicity provide the exact words that the plaintiff claimed were libelous or any insight into the reporting and editing involved. Emphasizing instead the multimillion-dollar demands and awards, the publicity mainly succeeded in scaring without enlightening journalists.

From my study of hundreds of the latest decisions, I came to believe that the cases held lessons which would interest and help journalists. One lesson was that some suits are purely political; not caused by any journalistic error, those suits could not have been avoided. However, from many cases there emerged a pattern of common errors and pitfalls, replete with lessons that could help journalists avoid recurring complaints.

The state of the law, and of the climate in which it was evolving in the 1980s, begged for explanations. Journalists need to know what the law permits, what it punishes, and where it is murky. I wanted to clearly lay out the basic principles and show how they work, to isolate the areas of confusion, and with as much order as possible, show how they could be dealt with. The law and its milieu—always inseparable—looked ominous and intimidating.

A jury had voted recently to give a million dollars of a newspaper's money to a horse breeder as damages for libel because a reporter had misread a mortgage. When an intermediate appeals court refused to overturn the verdict, the publisher's lawyer filed a new appeal. He said he expected to win in the end, but not everyone was as optimistic. Newspapers had fallen on hard times in the courts.

For one thing, confusion about who is a public figure has made many cases unpredictable. The Supreme Court has ruled that the press must be accorded extra protection from libel suits by public officials and public figures in order to encourage critical discussion and debate of public issues. But twenty years after *New York Times Co. v. Sullivan* unveiled the double standard for public and private libel plaintiffs, it has become difficult to say who will be classified as a public figure. The uncertainty has bred timidity and to a large extent nullified the extra freedom supposedly guaranteed by the law.

Taking the example of the horse breeder, it had been anybody's guess which way the courts would rule. Locally, he was a celebrity. A rich and powerful man who had founded and run the hometown bank, he owned real estate and successful businesses, influenced politics, and had frequently been in the community news.

The New Jersey court's decision to classify this community leader as a private plaintiff in his libel suit was part of a nationwide trend of choking back on protections for the press. Classifying him as a private figure virtually guaranteed his victory because it freed his complaint from the "actual malice" standard imposed on public plaintiffs as a result of the *New York Times Co. v. Sullivan* decision. If he had been recognized as a public figure, he would have had to prove that the paper had deliberately lied or had published its story despite serious doubts that it was true. That heavy burden of actual malice has caused most public libel plaintiffs to lose. As a private figure, the horse breeder carried the much lighter burden of showing simply that the newspaper had made a careless mistake.

At around the same time as the horse breeder's victory, another newspaper had lost a million-dollar case. The newspaper, a small one, had run an editorial accusing a politician of lying. The paper said the politician had reneged on a campaign promise. The politician told the court he had kept his promise, that he had been working secretly and behind the scenes. When the verdict was announced, the publisher and the editor said they would appeal because they had thought they had editorial freedom to criticize official performance. They said they were shocked.

Their predicament, and their shock, were shared by many other journalists who had learned the hard way that courts can't always distinguish protected opinion from libel. One black realtor took out a couple of advertisements to air his opinion that his white opponent in a zoning fight was "racist." Courts found it libelous and ordered the developer to pay $350,000 in damages. On appeal, the damages were reduced by one-third, but the judgment was upheld. Two columnists denigrated a professor's scholarly reputation and disappeared into the swamp of libel litigation for years as courts seesawed—one calling it libel, the next calling it protected opinion. Every few seasons, press watchers would spot the columnists' heads struggling to the surface for a fleeting cheer or moan. But then there would be an appeal of the latest reversal, and the heads would disappear again, sucked into the swamp. Back before the suit, the columnists had thought the law protected their right to an opinion. That thought finally prevailed, but a lot of people were shocked at how flimsy the protection turned out to be.

Theirs was not the only shocking libel case. A small town Georgia school bus driver and part-time baby-sitter had collected $100,000 in damages from her local newspaper because she said it had misreported her experience as a juror in a murder trial. She had told a reporter that she had made up her mind to vote for acquittal three days before the trial ended—after the prosecution had rested, but before the defense had finished its case, the newspaper reported. In her libel suit, she denied making the statement and claimed that it had ruined her reputation.

The jury believed her. It chose to believe not only that the reporter and his interview notes were lying, but also that the report was damaging, even though there is absolutely nothing wrong with deciding to acquit after the prosecution rests, since the government bears the entire burden of proving guilt beyond a reasonable doubt. The jury chose also to "compensate" her with $100,000 even though the only actual loss she claimed was a temporary hiatus in baby-sitting.

The universal problem of awards being out of sync with losses was the most frightening trend in press law. A Richmond jury had voted $1 million to "compensate" a city teacher for her suffering caused by an article that criticized her performance. The jury award was reduced to $100,000 on review, but even at that, it far outstripped any proven losses.

If big compensatory awards were unrelated to loss, punitive damages were likely to be even more outlandish. A Texas newspaper columnist accused a prosecutor of cheating and lying, based on the journalist's misunderstanding of rules of evidence. The jury voted a $3.5 million award, $3 million of which was punitive, to punish the paper for its mistake. Later, all but $600,000 was canceled by the judge, and the newspaper was appealing. Even with the huge reduction, it was a big ticket, especially when the plaintiff's reputation and career had shown no signs of damage and had continued to flourish. The prosecutor's situation was like that of Carol Burnett, who had persuaded a jury to punish the *National Enquirer* for implying that she was drunk in public. Her award of $1.6 million, of which $1.4 million was punitive, and which ultimately was cut to $200,000, reflected the loss of not a single job, fan, or friend. In a suit against the *Washington Post*, Mobil Oil president William Tavoulareas won more than $2 million, of which $1.8 million was punitive.

The suits kept coming. In the 1980s, suit-happy Americans went to libel court more than ever before. Some had been genuinely hurt by the press and were looking for a way to fight back. Some wanted publicly to back up their claims of being right or pure or not guilty as charged. Some hoped to intimidate and silence political enemies. Undoubtedly, some just took a gamble for money.

And for some people the suits were profitable. Occasionally, plaintiffs danced away with remarkable prizes: Synanon collected settlements of $1.25 million from ABC and $600,000 from the *San Francisco Examiner*; $800,000 was paid to two prosecutors maligned by the *Wall Street Journal*; $510,000 to a consulting firm libeled by the *New York Post*; and there were numerous low six-figure payoffs to private and public people complaining of untrue and unfair publicity. Of those who stayed through the whole dance, more plaintiffs than not lost the prize in the last step and left with empty pockets, but their lawyers, good ones and bad, came away with pockets bulging. They billed clients for hours and days, even years, of "discovery" and motions and trials and appeals. Insurers lost money; adjusted, restructured, and raised rates; and lost more money, with no end in sight.

Visionaries talked about putting an end to it. Press crusaders suggested adopting the English system of charging all costs to the losing side and, in frivolous libel suits, allowing countersuits for damages besides. Outlaw punitive damages, outlaw all damages, outlaw lawyers on contingency, outlaw libel claims by public officials, they urged. Crusaders on the opposing side said the government should finance libel suits by judges and other public officials so more could be brought.

They said corporations should buy plaintiffs' libel insurance to cover executives' actions, and political syndicates should take over and force the arrogant media to serve the "public interest."

The media didn't exactly cower in a corner while the sky was falling, but often, when they came out into the open, they trailed or tripped on their dirty laundry or shot themselves in the foot. "The media," of course, were not a monolith, but a motley beleaguered crowd of everything from giant conglomerates to mom-and-pop shops. Still, the distinctions blurred and the public began thinking "the media" were all alike—all rascals and knaves.

The big media guys looked just terrible, and they did everything imaginable to make sure everyone noticed. *Time* did a cover story on a trend of the eighties it had espied: public hatred for the press. For anybody who missed that, *Time* followed with its own hateful case, brought by Israeli general Ariel Sharon, and brought about by dismal journalism and a haughty refusal to retract an invented scoop. CBS's and ABC's libel and privacy cases revealed jump-cut interviews of gross unfairness, films of innocents in false contexts, and instances of ruthless disregard for people, litigated to the hilt and publicized to the world.

While the big guys kept busy reporting on one another's dirty laundry and foot-shootings, the little guys held panel discussions about why the public hated them and the chilling effect of libel suits. The public continued to feel whatever it always felt toward journalists, if anything, and the chilling effect turned some newsrooms into virtual meat lockers. The climate was fear.

Hollywood capitalized on libel fever with *Absence of Malice*, a smash hit about dumb and dirty journalism, and even threw in a cameo of a sleazy press lawyer. Numerous films portrayed journalists as moral cripples and frauds, morons and locusts—*Year of Living Dangerously, The Right Stuff, Jagged Edge,* and *Flash of Green* to name a few. Whatever became of Clark Kent?

But these film portrayals might have been a welcome relief when you considered that reality included a Pulitzer winner who made up her material, a reporter who staked out financial rights in the story of a potential suicide she had been assigned to cover, and a *Wall Street Journal* writer who was sentenced to jail for using advance knowledge of *Journal* articles to make illicit profits in the stock market. No one knew just when it happened, but finally, the public's only unsullied newsroom hero was Les Nessman of radio station WKRP in Cincinnati.

To my many newsroom heroes, this book is offered as a guide through troubled waters and hard times and a reference for information and advice on everyday legal problems. It does not pretend to take the place of the good press lawyers in towns and cities around the country who are the authorities on what the law is and isn't in their own regions. Legal solutions depend heavily on the particular facts presented, as well as on local precedent, so a guide like this can only be an adjunct to on-the-spot legal advice. The intention is to paint an overview that captures the general shape and color of these human stories and highlights the lessons they teach.

My goal here is to help journalists do their jobs. This book is offered with respect and affection for journalists, who inspire me with their curiosity about people and their drive to make society better for all of us.

1

Libel Law and How It Developed

AMERICA'S libel law is in transition. From English roots, the law shaped by the United States Supreme Court and the individual states over the years is continuously developing, being threatened and trimmed, nourished and refined.

The difficulty with a changing libel law is that journalists, the people most affected by it, must cope with unpredictable rulings and shifting standards, yet somehow make sense of the confusion. Some of the crucial formulas are murky: Who is a public figure? When is it safe to report on public debate? How can opinion statements be separated from libelous fact statements? Another quandary is how to control the size of awards where juries seem prone to huge verdicts despite the absence of proof of any actual injury.

The Supreme Court libel decisions that set the law on its present course left basic questions to be solved.

GOOD OLD DAYS

In early times, libel law was much simpler. In primitive Icelandic society, it was libelous to accuse a man of being a coward. To get re-

8

venge, and, incidentally, prove the accusation false, the libel victim was allowed to kill his accuser.

As civilization advanced, libel and slander suits developed as a deterrent to murder, and legal penalties replaced the older right of private vengeance. Under Norman law, anyone who falsely accused another person of being a thief was ordered to pay money and publicly confess. For the confession, the libeler had to stand in the middle of the town square holding his nose and loudly proclaiming, "I'm a liar! I'm a liar!" This was a precursor to the modern newspaper's correction box.

In ninth-century England, under Alfred the Great, the Anglo-Saxon libeler had to forfeit his tongue. The seventeenth-century English libeler had his ears lopped off.

Early libel was primarily treated as a criminal matter. The function of libel statutes was to punish criticism of the government and the Church as well as statements that might incite rioting or cause a breach of the peace. Early English defamation law was enviably succinct. It recognized only three types of insults as libelous on their face:

1. Bad morals (accusing someone of being a criminal)
2. Bad health (in those days, accusing someone of having syphilis, leprosy, or plague)
3. Bad workmanship (accusing a professional or tradesman of incompetence)

These types of insults were presumed automatically to be damaging. In order to sue over an insult outside of these three categories, the complainer had to prove actual monetary loss.

Libels were rare as long as few people were literate and there was not much to read. But when the printing press was introduced in England in 1476, the government recognized its potential for spreading treasonous words and inciting revolution, and responded by enacting stiff censorship and libel laws that quickly became instruments of suppression.

Formal English libel law, born in 1609, and its successor statutes in England and America, were criminal codes that outlawed verbal insults. The law reserved the harshest jail terms and corporal punishments for defaming a public official or nobleman—the public figure of the day. These penalties were exacted whether the offensive statements were true or false.

In America, libel law gradually evolved state by state. Many states came to recognize the defense of truth and carved out privileges for fair comment on public issues and for accurate reporting on judicial proceedings. Several states enacted retraction statutes to bar punitive damages if a prompt retraction was published on demand. And ten states developed a special rule immunizing honest misstatements about officials and candidates. These states ruled that public officials criticized for their performance or fitness could not win a libel suit unless they could prove the information was deliberately false. The states that had fashioned a defense of honest mistake against public official libel suits by 1964 were Arizona, California, Iowa, Kansas, Michigan, Minnesota, New Hampshire, North Carolina, South Dakota, and West Virginia. Then the United States Supreme Court, which had previously left the tinkering almost exclusively to the states, got into the libel business with *New York Times Co.* v. *Sullivan.*

New York Times and other cases I discuss are listed in a table of cases at the end of the book. The table gives the legal volume and page where the opinion may be found, the court, and the year of the decision.

For those unfamiliar with legal research, an explanation of the nomenclature is in order. A case title consists of opponents' names; the order of their names may vary on appeal. The original title will be the name of the initiator (the plaintiff) against ("versus," abbreviated "vs." or "v.") the name of the person being sued (the defendant). If the losing party appeals, that person's name assumes the lead, and the title of the appeal becomes appellant against appellee. In the United States Supreme Court, the nomenclature is petitioner (the one seeking review) against respondent. Hence, a jury considered the case of *Sullivan* v. *New York Times Co.*; the Supreme Court ruled on the appeal, *New York Times Co.* v. *Sullivan.*

Judges' formal opinions and orders are generally published in a series of books called state and federal legal reporters, which are found in law libraries. But events in litigation that do not produce judge-written decisions, such as jury verdicts or settlements, go unreported in these volumes. Therefore, tracking a suit may require contacting a participant to find out whether and how the case ended.

NEW YORK TIMES CO. V. SULLIVAN

Forced racial desegregation in the 1960s turned much of the American South violent with bloody rioting over court-ordered school integration and deadly battles over blacks' seating at lunch counters and on public buses. Segregationists blamed the strife on Rev. Dr. Martin Luther King, Jr.'s, preaching against unequal treatment of blacks. They also blamed "outside agitators," liberal civil rights activists from the Northeast and the northern-based newspapers, magazines, and television networks.

One of those perceived agitators, *The New York Times*, was being punished in the South with libel suits. Eleven suits by southern state and local officials claiming a total of $5.6 million in damages were pending against *The Times* in 1964 when *New York Times Co. v. Sullivan* was decided by the United States Supreme Court, and five suits had been brought against CBS, another perceived agitator, claiming $1.7 million in damages.

Montgomery, Alabama, city commissioner L. B. Sullivan sued *The Times* over a full-page advertisement, entitled "Heed Their Rising Voices," that espoused racial equality and sought donations for the Committee to Defend Martin Luther King and the Struggle for Freedom in the South. Appearing on March 29, 1960, over the signatures of celebrities and noted religious and civic leaders, the ten-paragraph advertisement said that protesters had been met with "an unprecedented wave of terror by those who would deny and negate" their rights. It began:

> As the whole world knows by now, thousands of Southern Negro students are engaged in widespread non-violent demonstrations in positive affirmation of the right to live in human dignity as guaranteed by the United States Constitution and the Bill of Rights.

The advertisement continued:

> In Montgomery, Alabama, after students sang "My Country, 'Tis of Thee" on the State Capitol steps, their leaders were expelled from school, and truckloads of police armed with shotguns and tear-gas ringed the Alabama State College Campus. When the entire student body protested to state authorities by refusing to re-register, their dining hall was padlocked in an attempt to starve them into submission. . . .
>
> Again and again, the Southern violators have answered Dr. King's peaceful protests with intimidation and violence. They have bombed his home almost killing his wife and child. They have assaulted his person. They have arrested him seven times—for "speeding," "loitering" and similar "offenses." And now they have charged him with "perjury"—a felony under which they could imprison him for ten years . . .

Commissioner Sullivan, as the official in charge of Montgomery's police department, contended that the accusations against "Southern violators" and "police" were false, and that they all referred to his police force and, thus, to him personally. He brought suit in Alabama state court against *The New York Times* and four black clergymen named as sponsors of the advertisement. Under Alabama law at that time, as in most states, *The Times* was "strictly liable" to Sullivan for statements that tended to hurt his reputation unless it could prove they were true. Under strict liability, truth was the only defense.

A few statements in the advertisement were untrue. Students on the capitol steps had sung the National Anthem, not "My Country, 'Tis of Thee," and the expulsions had been not for singing but for demanding service at the Montgomery County Courthouse lunch counter. The school dining hall had never been padlocked and the police had never literally "ringed" the campus. King had been arrested four times, not seven, and the police denied ever having assaulted him. *The Times* could have caught several of the errors merely by checking its own news stories on the incidents, but it had relied on the trustworthiness of those who had endorsed the advertisement and had not questioned the copy.

Sullivan had demanded a retraction, as required by Alabama law, as an antecedent to a claim for punitive damages. *The Times* had answered in a letter that it was "puzzled as to how you think the statements in any way reflect on you" and invited Sullivan to elaborate. Instead, he sued.

An Alabama jury voted to award Sullivan $500,000 in damages. It found the statements to be "libel per se," meaning libelous in themselves, without reference to extraneous facts—the sort of insults that are regarded as inevitably harmful to reputation and which entitle the person to "presumed" damages, or automatic compensation. No one at the trial testified that he or she actually believed the statements or had lost respect for Sullivan. But Sullivan did not need to prove injury to his reputation—that was presumed under Alabama law from the bare fact of publication. Sullivan did have to prove "malice" (meaning maliciousness or bad faith) as a basis for punitive damages, but he received an undifferentiated award—not broken down into general and punitive damages—so it was impossible to know whether the jury had found malice.

The Alabama Supreme Court affirmed on the basis that the advertisement reflected on the police, of which Sullivan was in charge, and therefore imputed misconduct to him. Having published false statements that were libelous per se, *The Times*'s only recourse was to pay an award the court considered not to be excessive. The verdict might well have been partly punitive because in failing to check for accuracy and to retract, *The Times*, under Alabama law, had been guilty of malice.

The United States Supreme Court disagreed. In a fifteen-page opinion written by Justice William J. Brennan, Jr., the Court swept aside more than two hundred years of libel law in Alabama and most other states. Justice Brennan called the old law "constitutionally deficient for failure to provide safeguards for freedom of speech and of the press that are required by the First and Fourteenth Amendments in a libel action brought by a public official against critics of his official conduct."

In its place, the Court constructed a new law to insulate honest criticism of official conduct from libel judgments. It was not enough for the states to permit the press to try to prove truth, the Court said. Now every state had to also excuse a good faith mistake made in criticism of government officials.

Under the new law, a public official had to prove not only that the statements were false, but also prove convincingly that the press published them while knowing them to be false or with reckless disregard to whether they were false or not. Without proof of such deliberate or reckless lying—conduct the court called actual malice—the public official would lose the case.

The actual malice defense was needed to protect the press from intimidation and harassment and to encourage the most valuable kind of speech in a democracy, criticism of government, the Supreme Court said. "The difficulties of legally proving truth may deter critics of official conduct from voicing their criticism even though it is believed to be true and even though it is in fact true, because of doubt whether it can be proved in court or fear of the expense of having to do so," the Court said.

The facts in *Sullivan* did not constitute actual malice, the Court said. At most, it was negligence, not actual malice, for *The Times* to have relied on the reputation of the sponsors and not to have discovered the misstatements. The Court, furthermore, failed to see "even an oblique reference" to the police commissioner in the advertisement by name or position, and noted that nobody had testified that he had read the advertisement as referring to Sullivan. (Alabama governor John Patterson had demanded and received a *Times* correction on the same advertisement because as "the embodiment of the State," the statements referred to him—this according to the somewhat feeble testimony of *The Times*'s corporate secretary in the *Sullivan* trial.)

As "an expression of protest on one of the major public issues of our time," the advertisement represented the kind of public debate that the Court said "should be uninhibited, robust, and wide-open" and which should not be vulnerable to attack if published in good faith, with a belief in its truth. The Court ruled that Sullivan's half-million-dollar libel judgment could not stand because "[W]hether or not a newspaper can survive a succession of such judgments, the pall of fear and timidity imposed upon those who would give voice to public criticism is an atmosphere in which the First Amendment freedoms cannot survive."

The actual malice concept did not meet with unanimous approval, not even on the Supreme Court itself. First Amendment absolutist, Justice Hugo L. Black, an Alabaman, joined by Justice William O. Douglas, voted with the majority but wrote a separate opinion. He attacked the malice standard as a weak and elusive abstraction that would not work. In its stead, he proposed absolute immunity for criticism of the way public officials do their public duty.

Justice Black, who always carried a copy of the Constitution in his vest pocket, believed the First Amendment guaranteed freedom of speech and of the press and, at a minimum, an "unconditional right to say what one pleases about public affairs." To him, the actual malice standard not only fell far short of the minimal guarantee, but, even worse, was just a legalistic formula incapable of protecting the press. He saw no indication that the *Sullivan* jury would have voted differently if they had been told of the actual malice requirement. He warned: "'Malice,' even as defined by the Court, is an elusive, abstract concept, hard to prove and hard to disprove. The requirement that malice be proved provides at best an evanescent protection for the right critically to discuss public affairs and certainly does not measure up to the sturdy safeguard embodied in the First Amendment."

Justice Arthur J. Goldberg also voted with the majority, but he expressed concern that the right to speak out about public officials and affairs "should not depend upon a probing by the jury of the motivation of the citizen or press."

EXTENDING THE *NEW YORK TIMES* RULE TO PUBLIC FIGURES

Having dived into libel and made waves with its 1964 decision in *New York Times Co.* v. *Sullivan*, the Court explained in *Rosenblatt* v. *Baer* that while actual malice was not to apply to every government employee, it would reach all those with "substantial responsibility for or control over government affairs."

In determining which officials would have to prove actual malice, the Court said that one factor should be whether an official's position or conduct of government business legitimately invited public scrutiny of the officeholder. The Court also said that status—whether of public official or private person—should be determined as of a time preceding the unfavorable publicity. In other words, if the plaintiff would not have been ruled a public official beforehand, the alleged libel and surrounding publicity could not turn him into one. In addition, the Court noted, even after leaving office a person would remain a public official for libel purposes, at least as long as the public legitimately had an interest in appraising his or her performance.

Just three years after *New York Times*, the Court extended the rule to "public figures." Justifying the extension, it noted that public figures were involved in issues in which the public had an interest, and that they had therefore voluntarily exposed themselves to an increased risk of being libeled.

Two more suits from the Deep South were the vehicle for this sweeping declaration. The first involved Major General Edwin A. Walker, U.S. Army retired. Having resigned from the army over criticism of his right-wing political activities, Walker technically was no longer a public official and therefore was treated as a private plaintiff at trial even though he was famous throughout the South for his radio and television campaigns against integration.

Walker, whose headquarters were in Dallas, Texas, had arrived in Jackson, Mississippi, on the evening of September 29, 1962. The next day, Sunday, James H. Meredith, twenty-nine, was to be escorted onto the University of Mississippi campus and registered as the school's first black student. Three attempts to register Meredith in accordance with court-ordered integration had been blocked by state troopers; a fourth attempt had been called off because a mob of 2,500 threatened violence. Now, over 3,000 federal troops were amassed for the showdown.

Walker told reporters that he had come to town for the game between Ole Miss and the University of Kentucky. While there, however, he read a speech, which was filmed by NBC, in which he urged citizens to "Rally to the cause of freedom in righteous indignation, violent vocal protest and bitter silence under the flag of Mississippi at the use of Federal troops." He blamed the "anti-Christ conspirators of the Supreme Court" for their "betrayal of a nation."

The next evening, Walker was on campus during rioting in which two men were killed and fifty injured; six U.S. Marshals were shot, one critically; and sixteen automobiles were destroyed. A twenty-one year-old reporter for the Associated Press, Van Savell, telephoning dispatches from the campus, reported that Walker had "assumed command" of a crowd of about a thousand students and "led a charge" against federal marshals. (Claude Sitton reported in *The New York Times* that Walker had not advocated violence but had harangued a crowd, shouting "Protest! Protest! Keep it up!," and had walked toward the marshals with a hundred students following him.) Walker later claimed he had only been an observer and had not incited, directed, or participated in any way in the violence. Walker was arrested and charged with insurrection and leading a charge against United States forces, but the charges were dropped.

Almost two years afterward, a Fort Worth, Texas, state court jury heard Walker's libel complaint against A.P. and believed him. It awarded $500,000 in actual damages and $300,000 in punitive damages. The trial judge canceled the punitive damages, finding that no malice had been proved, as required by Texas law. The Court of Civil Appeals agreed. The United States Supreme Court accepted the case.

Joined with Walker's case for Supreme Court review was a suit by University of Georgia's football coach, Wallace Butts, against the *Saturday Evening Post*. "The Story of a College Football Fix," subtitled "A Shocking Report of How Wally Butts and 'Bear' Bryant Rigged a Game Last Fall," told how Butts threw the September 1962 game in Birmingham to the University of Alabama by betraying his team's strategies to the opposing coach.

The story, purchased by the *Post* from writer Frank Graham, was based entirely on the sworn statement of an Atlanta insurance salesman on probation for passing bad checks. The salesman, George Burnett, said that he had accidentally overheard Butts and Bryant conspiring to fix the game when, trying to telephone another man in Butts's office, Milton Flack, he had intercepted the coaches' conversation due to some electronic mix-up. The story prompted an investigation by the Southeast conference and Coach Butts resigned, citing personal and business reasons.

Because Butts was not technically a state employee, he was not a public official; despite great fame in national football, he was still merely a private libel plaintiff. An all-male jury sitting in federal district court in Atlanta found the *Post* story false and malicious.

Malice, necessary as a basis for punitive damages, was proved in part by the *Post's* self-proclaimed intention of engaging in "sophisticated muckraking . . . to provoke people, make them mad," in the words of its editor, Clay D. Blair, Jr., as quoted in a *Newsweek* interview. An in-house memorandum from Blair at about the same time, which was introduced at the Butts trial, said, "We have about six lawsuits pending, meaning that we are hitting them where it hurts, with solid, meaningful journalism."

The Butts story did not strike the jury as solid, meaningful journalism. Even though the source had been of doubtful integrity given his criminal record, the *Post* had scarcely bothered to check the shocking claim that archrival football giants had fixed a match. The source, Burnett, had notes he had taken while overhearing the call and had discussed it with his friend, John Carmichael, but the *Post* did not check the notes (which turned out to be nonincriminating), interview Carmichael, consult with football experts, or look at films of the game to corroborate Burnett's claim.

Graham testified that he had recognized from the start that his story would ruin Butts's career. In fact, he had ended the story with the statement, "Wally Butts will never help any football team again," and the prediction, "careers will be ruined, that is sure." Still another sign of callousness, in the jury's eyes, was that the *Post* had published the story even after Butts, who had not been interviewed, had got wind of the story and had told them it was false. After the story appeared, Butts, who had been negotiating for a coaching position with a professional team, demanded a retraction. The *Post* refused.

In addition to a lack of sympathy for the *Post's* hard-heartedness, the jury may have felt some sympathy for the local hero. A passionate oration by Butts's lawyer, the late Allen E. Lockerman of Atlanta, suggested a rousing play for home-team prejudice. Lockerman, a friend of Butts since their student days at Mercer University, urged the twelve Georgian gentlemen to send a message to New York that "we don't have that kind of journalism down here and we don't want it down here." He told the jurors:

> I am looking to you for my protection. Heaven knows, if you let them out of this case for $5 million or less, and boy, it's been worth it to them, I may be next, because they are not going to stop with that. You may be next; my wife, my children, yourself. We have got to stop them now, and you are the only twelve in the world that can stop them. . . .
> I say, Gentlemen, this is the time we have got to get them; $100 million in advertising, would 10 percent of that be fair to Wallace Butts for what they have done to him? Would a 50-cent assessment on each of the

23 million issues which they wrote about him there, would that be a strain or a burden on them? I think it would teach them that we don't have that kind of journalism down here, and we don't want it down here, and we don't want it to spread from 666 Fifth Avenue any further than that building right now [a reference to Curtis Publishing Company's headquarters in New York City]. . . .

You know, one of these days, like everyone else must come to, Wallace Butts is going to pass on. No one can bother him then. The *Saturday Evening Post* can't get at him then. And unless I miss my guess, they will put Wallace Butts in a red coffin with a black lid, and he will have a football in his hands, and his epitaph will read something like this: "Glory, Glory to old Georgia."

The jury assessed $60,000 in general damages against the *Saturday Evening Post* and $3 million in punitive damages. But trial judge Lewis R. Morgan of the Federal Court for the Northern District of Georgia ruled that the punitive award was excessive and cut it to $400,000. The Fifth Circuit Court of Appeal affirmed.

The Supreme Court ruled that both Walker and Butts were public men whose positions and involvement in public affairs had made them legitimate subjects of press coverage. Therefore, as libel complainants, they, like public officials, would be made to prove more than just falsity in order to win. They would have to prove "highly unreasonable conduct constituting an extreme departure from the standards of investigation and reporting ordinarily adhered to by responsible publishers." They would not be permitted to win by proving merely that journalists had made honest mistakes in the course of reporting on their public activity.

Public activity was to be one key to recognizing and classifying a libel plaintiff as a public figure. A public figure was a person like Butts, whose position alone made him publicly important, or one like Walker, who had mounted a rostrum to influence public events or opinion.

A second key to recognizing a public figure was whether the person had means of self-defense against negative publicity—that is, access to channels of communication to present rebuttal and counterargument. In the Court's view, both Butts and Walker were able to use the media to make their views known.

Applying the "highly unreasonable conduct" standard to the facts of each case before it, the Supreme Court found no evidence of such irresponsibility in the Associated Press's "hot news" deadline-story and reversed Walker's victory. By contrast, it found irresponsibility in the

Saturday Evening Post's "grossly inadequate" reporting and affirmed Butts's $460,000 combined award. The magazine's unquestioning acceptance of a sensational claim from a source with a reputation for dishonesty without an attempt to verify it, despite time and resources to do so, seemed to the Court to be an extreme departure from good investigative practice.

The decision in *Butts* and *Walker*, written by Justice John M. Harlan, represented a further shielding of the press from liability for good faith errors in reporting about people in public life, both government officials and public figures. Chief Justice Earl Warren voted for the result but objected to the creation of another new standard—"highly unreasonable conduct"—and urged the use of the actual malice standard for public officials and figures both. Justice Black, of course, bemoaned the further sinking into a "quagmire" and wrote a concurring opinion urging the Court to abandon *New York Times* "and adopt a rule to the effect that the First Amendment was intended to leave the press free from the harassment of libel judgments."

Instead, the Court briefly and abortively stretched the actual malice standard further, to private citizens caught up in events of public concern.

SHORT-LIVED SUBJECT-MATTER TEST

The public figure doctrine articulated in the *Butts* and *Walker* decision was one of several approaches that the Supreme Court was tinkering with in an effort to maximize freedom of discussion of public issues.

One approach—the ruling in *Butts* and *Walker*—was to vary the level of constitutional privilege with the status of the plaintiff. Public officials would have to show actual malice on the part of the journalists. Public figures would have to show highly unreasonable journalistic conduct—an extreme departure from the standards of investigation and reporting ordinarily adhered to by responsible publishers.

Another approach was to extend the *New York Times* actual malice standard to an expanding variety of situations. At its outer boundary, for a brief moment before being reeled back in, actual malice had been declared by the Supreme Court to be the standard not only for public plaintiffs, but also for ordinary citizens in cases in which the focus of the libel claim was an issue of public concern.

It was that approach that the Court employed in 1967 in *Time*,

Inc. v. *Hill,* a suit by a private man against *Life* magazine for misrepresenting a fictional play as a reenactment of the nineteen hours he and his wife and their five children had spent as hostages of three escaped convicts in their home in Whitemarsh, Pennsylvania, near Philadelphia. The Court ruled that because the play was of public interest, in order to win James J. Hill would have to prove that *Life* acted with actual malice.

The Hill family had made news when they were freed unharmed by three heavily armed desperados who had fled the federal penitentiary in Lewisburg, Pennsylvania, by scaling a 30-foot wall. On leaving the Hills' sumptuous home, the men, all convicted bankrobbers in their twenties, led police on a wild five-state chase that ended eight days later on Manhattan's Upper West Side, where they were cornered in a rooming house and two were killed.

The Hills, besieged by the press, gave an interview and posed for photographs immediately after the incident. Hill, a sales manager for a hosiery company, said that the convicts had been polite and not violent. Later, the Hills avoided further publicity, declined talk show offers, and finally moved to Connecticut.

Life magazine reported on the Broadway opening of *The Desperate Hours,* a play about a family held captive and terrorized in their home by escaped convicts. Joseph Hayes, who had based the play on his novel of the same name, told *Life* that the drama had been "triggered" by the Hill event three years earlier. The major difference between the play and real life, which was brought out in court, was that while in the play the convicts were threatening and violent, the three men who had held the Hill family hostage had, by the Hills' own account, been not at all violent, or even rude.

In heralding the play with an article entitled "True Crime Inspires Tense Play," *Life* reported that the drama was an enactment of the Hills' experience and characterized it as a "heart-stopping account of how a family rose to heroism in a crisis." An editor had deleted the words "somewhat fictionalized" from the final copy. Several *Life* photographs of scenes from the play actually had been staged at the scene of the crime—inside the Hills' former home. One picture showed an actor playing the part of the son being roughed up by a convict and another showed an actress playing the daughter biting a convict to get him to drop a gun.

Hill at first won $50,000 in compensatory damages and $25,000 in punitive damages from a New York jury. Hill's complaint was in the nature of a "false light" claim—that is, he had been portrayed falsely, although not necessarily in a negative way. The state Appellate Division ordered a new trial to assess the damages. In the second trial, the compensatory damages were reduced to $30,000 and the punitive damages eliminated. The New York Court of Appeals affirmed, and Hill had lawyer Richard M. Nixon argue his case before the Supreme Court.

The United States Supreme Court ruled that *Life* magazine's report concerned a subject of public interest and therefore qualified for the protection of the actual malice standard, even though Hill was a private citizen. This sweeping extension of the actual malice principle commanded just five votes from the nine-member Court. Three dissenters—Justice Abe Fortas, Chief Justice Warren, and Justice Tom C. Clark—called it "not only an individual injustice but an encouragement to recklessness and careless readiness to ride roughshod over the interests of others."

Justice Harlan's separate concurring opinion warned that it would be "ultimately harmful to the permanent good health of the press itself." Justice Harlan saw no justifying reasons for the actual malice burden when Hill had no public position and no forum for refuting the false publicity. In his view, the public had no independent interest in the subject of his suit—Hill's relationship to the play.

While a deeply divided Supreme Court in *Time, Inc.* v. *Hill* imposed the actual malice standard when the subject of the publication was of public interest, the Court was strained to the breaking point by the next test: *Rosenbloom* v. *Metromedia.*

In that case, the Court applied the actual malice standard to a nudist magazine distributor's libel suit against a Philadelphia radio station, which had broadcast news reports about his run-ins with police. George A. Rosenbloom had been arrested while delivering magazines to a retailer who was at that moment being visited by the vice squad. Police captain Clarence Ferguson was dedicating himself to wiping out obscenity, which he defined as "any time the private parts is showing of the female or the private parts is shown of males." With a warrant, Ferguson later raided Rosenbloom's home, arrested him again, and confiscated his inventory. Rosenbloom brought a suit against the police to enjoin them from interfering with his business. Later he was acquitted of obscenity charges.

Radio station WIP, in reporting on Rosenbloom's arrests, used the terms "smut literature racket" and "girlie book peddlars" and failed at least once to say "allegedly" obscene. The Court ruled that even though Rosenbloom was a private figure, he would have to prove actual malice in his libel suit because the reports concerned a public issue.

The eight Justices who participated in the *Rosenbloom* decision (Justice Douglas did not) wrote five separate opinions, none of which commanded more than three votes. The main opinion of twenty-five pages was written by Justice William J. Brennan, Jr.; Justices Black and Byron R. White had separate opinions, as did Justice Harlan, who counseled leaving the states to work out their own laws, and Justice Thurgood Marshall, who recommended restricting all libel plaintiffs to proved actual losses.

The lack of consensus on how to balance press freedoms with reputational interests set the stage for another experiment, and *Gertz* v. *Robert Welch, Inc.* offered itself.

DIFFERENT RULES FOR PUBLIC AND PRIVATE PLAINTIFFS

While the Supreme Court was wrangling over the public interest doctrine of *Hill* and *Rosenbloom*, Elmer Gertz, a Chicago lawyer, was suing the magazine of the John Birch Society for calling him a Communist. Elmer Gertz's libel suit was destined to arrive at the Supreme Court at a historic turning point. The Court had become "fractionated," as one Justice described it, over how far the actual malice standard should stretch, and its latest extension—to a private plaintiff in a public interest story—had reached too far too fast to suit several Justices.

Taking a new position in *Gertz* v. *Robert Welch, Inc.*, the Court disavowed the subject-matter test and proclaimed a double standard based only on the plaintiff's status. In its 1974 decision, the Court held that public officials and public figures would have to prove actual malice, but it left states free to determine the rules for private citizens claiming libel. In addition, the Court laid down the governing principles of compensatory and punitive damages in libel.

The story in the John Birch Society's magazine, *American Opinion*, that led to the suit, "Frame-Up: Richard Nuccio and the War on Police," warned of a national conspiracy to discredit local police and replace them with officers who would support a Communist regime. The story had been built around the case of a Chicago policeman, Richard Nuccio, who had been convicted of second-degree murder in the death of a seventeen-year-old criminal suspect. Gertz had represented the youth's family in a civil suit against Nuccio, but had nothing to do with his criminal prosecution and, except in his work on the civil suit, had made no public statements about the policeman.

The magazine article, written by Alan Stang, a New York freelance and longtime ardent anti-Communist, labeled Gertz a "Leninist" and a "Communist-fronter" and said that he had a police file so heavy it would take a "big, Irish cop to lift it." The eighteen-page article also said that Gertz had been a member of the Marxist League for Industrial Democracy and the National Lawyers Guild, and went on to say that the Lawyers Guild had been responsible for a Communist attack on Chicago police officers during the 1968 Democratic National Convention. The article was illustrated with a photograph of Gertz captioned, "Elmer Gertz of Red Guild harasses Nuccio." Gertz said that all the statements about him were false except that he had belonged to the Lawyers Guild from 1930 to 1950.

The *Gertz* case, caught in the stream of Supreme Court rulings from *New York Times* onward, had become snagged on the question of whether Gertz had to prove actual malice. A jury initially awarded him $50,000, but the federal trial judge set it aside saying that while he considered Gertz to be a private figure, the issue in the case was of public concern and required proof of actual malice, which Gertz had not provided.

The federal appeals court said it regarded Gertz as prominent enough to be ruled a public figure because of his law practice, lectures, and publications. The appeals court affirmed the lower court without reclassifying Gertz, agreeing that proof of actual malice was lacking, whatever his status. The United States Supreme Court, however, took a different view. In a ruling that created the double standard for libel plaintiffs, it said that private plaintiffs deserved to be treated differently from those in the public spotlight because they had not volunteered for public scrutiny, were more vulnerable to injury, and less able to defend themselves.

Having different rules for public and private plaintiffs, the Court said, would help journalists avoid self-censorship when writing about prominent figures and, at the same time, would not impose such severe restrictions on suits by private individuals that they would be unlikely to receive compensation for damage to their reputations. Henceforth, the actual malice standard developed in *New York Times Co.* v. *Sullivan* would apply only to public libel plaintiffs—government officials and others who had made themselves prominent outside of government. The states would still be free to set their own standards for private libel plaintiffs so long as they did not choose strict liability—the old rule allowing only truth as a defense: "We hold that, so long as they do not impose liability without fault, the States may define for themselves the appropriate standard of liability for a publication or broadcast of defamatory falsehood injurious to a private individual."

With *Gertz v. Robert Welch, Inc.*, the Court ushered in the negligence rule for private libel cases in a large majority of the states and also announced two radical new rules on damages.

"Presumed" damages, a time-honored remedy, were now forbidden as unconstitutional. Since injury from libel had been "presumed" by law in most states, there had been no need to prove actual loss. Now, however, libel plaintiffs seeking general or compensatory damages would have to prove injury. A jury could decide the dollar-value of such elements of injury as out-of-pocket loss, "impairment of reputation," humiliation, mental anguish and suffering.

Second, libel plaintiffs seeking punitive damages would be required to prove actual malice—and this applied to both public and private plaintiffs. The Court cautioned that punitive damages should be "reasonably" related to actual injury and not "excessive." Gertz himself, in a subsequent new trial, won $460,000 in compensatory and punitive damages because he convinced a jury that the John Birch Society magazine had acted with actual malice in failing to verify accusations made by a writer with a history of virulent anti-Communism.

An enticing fillip in the *Gertz* decision concerned opinion: The Court said that opinion statements, as distinct from fact statements, may be considered nonlibelous and exempt from the law no matter how mean or rude. The Court failed to lay down guidelines for distinguishing fact from opinion. Nevertheless, its brief reference to the opinion privilege is today without doubt the most often-quoted passage on the subject of privileged opinions: "Under the First Amendment there is no such thing as a false idea. However pernicious an opinion may seem, we depend for its correction not on the conscience of judges and juries but on the competition of other ideas."

The Supreme Court in *Gertz v. Robert Welch, Inc.* settled some questions, raised others, and scattered the seeds of many of today's major problems in press law.

As with Elmer Gertz himself, the plaintiff's status often was debatable, and the Supreme Court's fuzzy guidelines made a lottery of this single most significant question in many libel cases. The goals of the Court were admirable—giving the press more leeway to report on government officials and others in the public spotlight while ensuring a measure of protection for the reputations of private citizens—but in practice, the formula proved elusive.

Gertz—active in civic, professional, and community affairs— seemed a private man to the trial court and a public figure to the appeals court. The Supreme Court ruled him a private figure because he was neither generally known (the jurors, for instance, had not heard of him before the trial) nor an activist who had voluntarily "thrust" himself into the limelight to influence people's thinking about the particular controversy that had caused him to sue (Communist frame-ups).

The problem of distinguishing public from private figures remained after *Gertz* and bewilders courts to this day, consuming disproportionate hours of litigation time and substantially contributing to the high cost of seeing libel cases through. The Supreme Court refined its definition of public figures in 1979 and created two subcategories:

1. "Pervasive public figures" are celebrities who are so widely known that virtually all facets of their lives are considered legitimate for public discussion, such as movie stars, sports heroes, and former presidents. They are public figure libel plaintiffs for all purposes and their libel suits are governed by the actual malice standard.

2. "Limited-purpose public figures" are primarily citizens who have become known publicly for engaging voluntarily in particular events or causes for the purpose of influencing their outcome. They are "limited" public figures because that status is limited to libel cases arising from criticism of their public role. Those cases would be governed by the actual malice standard. But suits that might arise from publicity about their private lives would be governed by the lesser standard, usually negligence, because they would be considered to be private plaintiffs.

Illustrating the narrowness of the limited public figure category in one case, the Court declared that a research scientist was a private figure for purposes of criticism of his publicly funded research; in another decision, it ruled that a person convicted of a crime was a private figure for purposes of comment on the crime or conviction.

In the first case, Michigan scientist Ronald A. Hutchinson had sued Senator William Proxmire for awarding him the Golden Fleece of the Month Award and stating that his federally financed $500,000 studies of why monkeys clench their teeth were worthless and had made a "monkey" out of the taxpayer. Proxmire contended that the scientist was a public figure for the limited purpose of discussing his use of a public grant.

Proxmire won a grant of summary judgment and an affirmance from the Court of Appeals for the Seventh Circuit on the ground that Hutchinson was a public figure and was lacking any proof of actual malice (the same court had suspected Gertz of being a public figure because of his professional prominence).

The Supreme Court reversed, ruling that Hutchinson, like Gertz, was a private figure. Although the scientist had lectured and written numerous articles in his field, he was primarily known only within his profession, so he was not a "pervasive public figure." He was not a limited public figure, either, the Court ruled, because he had not voluntarily entered into the controversy over wasted public funds. The Court said it disapproved of automatically turning everyone into a public figure who accepted a government grant.

In a companion case, the Supreme Court ruled that Russian-born Ilya Wolston was a private figure in his suit against Reader's Digest Association, the publisher of a book that mistakenly identified him as a convicted Soviet agent. A nephew of Myra and Jack Soble, who had both pleaded guilty to spying in 1957, Wolston had also been investigated at that time. He failed to appear before a grand jury on one occasion and was charged with contempt, to which he pleaded guilty. He was not, however, convicted of espionage, as stated in a 1974 book by John Barron, *KGB, The Secret Work of Soviet Agents*.

The federal trial and appeals courts in New York ruled that Wolston was a public figure for the limited purpose of discussing espionage investigations in which he had been involved. The Supreme Court took the opposite tack. It stated that Wolston's brush with the grand jury had not been voluntary conduct motivated by a desire for publicity or influence over public events, and found him to be a private figure. The Court did not address the lurking question about the effect of the passage of time. If Wolston were indeed a public figure at the time of the spy case—as the lower courts found—did he retain that status sixteen years later when the book was published? The Supreme Court simply determined that Wolston had been a private figure at all times and left it at that. But this is a question that may well be regarded as crucial in some future case and will demand an answer.

Gertz v. *Robert Welch, Inc.* bequeathed not only a confusing formulation of public figure status but also a frightening legacy about the awarding of damages. Even while conceding that actual injury might not be quantifiable when the stated harm is as intangible as injury to an individual's reputation, and even while conceding that punitive damages pose ominous threats to First Amendment expression, the Justices gave only vague admonitions and no useful guidance on awarding damages against the press.

Allowing compensation for embarrassment, humiliation, and suffering has invited juries to spend in accordance with their sympathies. Allowing punitive damages, uncontrolled but for a nebulous caveat that they be reasonably related to the harm and not excessive, has invited vengeful, crippling punishment of the press. The looming liability and risk of massive losses, and the resultant cost and scarcity of insurance for publishers, are among the biggest problems facing publishers today. They threaten the existence of a free press.

JURISDICTION, DISCOVERY, AND APPEAL

In this decade the Supreme Court has dealt mostly losses to the press. Besides narrowly defining the limited public figure, it has expanded state jurisdictional power over journalists, endorsed examination of their state of mind, and allowed litigants to prevent publication of some of the information turned up in the pretrial investigation known as "discovery." The only decision favoring the press reaffirmed the broad power of appeals courts to overturn libel judgments when it appeared that First Amendment protections had not correctly been applied.

The Court unanimously decided two jurisdictional issues against the press in 1984. In one of the cases, *Keeton* v. *Hustler Magazine*, which had grown out of a feud between two nationally circulated nudist magazines, the Court held that Kathy Keeton, a New York resident and the vice chairman of *Penthouse* magazine, could bring suit in New Hampshire against the Ohio corporation that published *Hustler* magazine.

Previously, publishers had believed that they were vulnerable to libel suits only in the plaintiff's home state or in states with which they had "substantial" contacts—where they had business offices, were incorporated, or had major distribution. Both a federal district court and an appeals court had ruled that neither Keeton, an out-of-stater, nor *Hustler*, which had no office in New Hampshire and sent only 15,000 copies to that state monthly—less than one percent of its circulation—had sufficient contacts with the state to justify jurisdiction. But the Supreme Court said that New Hampshire did have sufficient contacts with *Hustler* to take jurisdiction over the case. Besides, it said, a state should have the power to protect its citizens from libelous publications—an alarming comment that struck some Court-watchers as an endorsement of government censorship. The effect of the ruling was to make publishers of nationally distributed newspapers and magazines vulnerable, for the first time, to libel suits in every state where they had even a small volume of circulation.

Hustler magazine, a relative newcomer to the field of men's magazines featuring nude photographs of women, and decidedly more brazen in its presentation than the pioneers of the genre, *Playboy* and *Penthouse*, had published a centerfold picture and cartoon that Keeton, who was also the girlfriend of the founder and publisher of *Penthouse*, Robert C. Guccione, claimed had libeled her—neither the photograph not the cartoon could be described in a family newspaper.

Keeton's lawyers had gone to New Hampshire because the statute of limitations had run out in every other state. (At the time, New Hampshire gave a person six years in which to sue for libel. It has since changed to a three-year limit, making Florida's four-year statute the most generous in the nation. For other states' time limits on libel filings, see Appendix A.)

The libel suit is back in New Hampshire awaiting trial, but the jurisdictional decision from the Supreme Court represented a setback for all publishers.

Simultaneously, in *Calder* v. *Jones*, the Court held that the chief executive of the *National Enquirer*, which has its main office in Lantana, Florida, and an *Enquirer* reporter could be ordered to go to California to defend a libel suit. Previously it was thought that individual journalists who had worked on a story that resulted in a suit could not be compelled to travel to distant states to participate in court proceedings. The *Enquirer* had acknowledged that it was responsible for responding to the suit in California, the home state of the plaintiff, entertainer Shirley Jones. But Iain Calder, the president and editor of the *Enquirer*, and the reporter, John South, contended that all their work on the story had been done in Florida. Therefore, they said, they should not be subject to the jurisdiction of the California courts.

The Supreme Court ruled that the involvement of the two journalists in a story that Jones claimed had intentionally libeled her by stating she had a debilitating drinking problem was sufficient to warrant including them in California's jurisdiction. The Court said they could not avoid testifying in the state in which their work—as they must have appreciated—was bound to have had its greatest impact on the plaintiff, both because it was her residence and because the state had 600,000 *Enquirer* readers, more than any other state. This decision puts writers and editors on notice that they may be forced to appear and defend libel charges in distant courts.

In *Herbert* v. *Lando*, the Supreme Court in 1979 allowed broad-ranging pretrial investigation into the editorial process and journalists' newsroom conversations, saying that since *New York Times Co.* v. *Sullivan* required plaintiffs to prove state-of-mind, it certainly entitled them to ask about it. In a decision that really broke no new ground, the Court rejected CBS's argument for a First Amendment shield to prevent retired army colonel Anthony Herbert from continuing to question producer Barry Lando and correspondent Mike Wallace about a "60 Minutes" segment, "The Selling of Colonel Herbert," which accused Herbert of lying about an army cover-up of Vietnam atrocities.

The Court ruled in *Seattle Times Co.* v. *Rhinehart* that libel defendants do not have an automatic First Amendment right to publish plaintiff's secrets unearthed in the course of a suit. Plaintiffs Keith Milton Rhinehart and his religious group, the Acquarian Foundation, had revealed confidential membership and donor lists to the *Seattle Times* under a protective order that prohibited their publication. The *Times* challenged the order, but the Supreme Court ruled the protective order constitutional because it was limited to discovery materials and did not restrain the *Times* from publishing whatever it might obtain elsewhere.

The decision does not mean that the press has no right to pretrial proceedings or discovery materials. On the contrary, the Court assumed access to the fruits of discovery, absent a clear need to shield information from the public before trial. Such a need was what defeated the *Times*'s demands; the controversial religious society argued its own strong First Amendment interest in protecting the confidentiality of its members and supporters. Despite the apparent narrowness of the ruling, press lawyers with a penchant for crepe hanging predicted that it would lead to more secrecy in all types of discovery and would also invite more libel litigation, as soon as potential plaintiffs learned that they could use protective orders to avoid exposure to adverse pretrial publicity. It's too early to know whether they're right.

In a gloomy decade of press losses, the bright spot was *Bose Corp.* v. *Consumers Union of the United States, Inc.*, in which the Court in

1984 reiterated that appellate courts must judge First Amendment issues in cases de novo (as if trying them anew). This contrasts to the ordinarily narrow scope of review of most civil court decisions, which generally cannot be reversed unless they are "clearly erroneous." In the *Bose* case, *Consumer Reports* had reviewed some stereo speakers manufactured by the Bose Corporation, which had advertised that the speakers produced highly directional sound from which the listener could pinpoint the location of individual instruments of an orchestra. The review said the sound actually was distorted, "seemed to grow to gigantic proportions," and "tended to wander about the room." The reviewer testified that he had meant that the sound had crossed "along the wall" between the speakers. A Massachusetts federal court found that the statement was deliberately false, and Bose, a public figure, won $115,296 in compensatory damages.

A federal appeals court, exercising its power of independent de novo review, determined that evidence of actual malice was lacking and reversed. The Supreme Court endorsed that decision and the process. The Court's reaffirmation of the constitutional importance of de novo review to ensure that the actual malice standard has been correctly applied was of enormous value to journalists, who lose heavily with juries but see 70 percent of the verdicts reversed on appeal.

The latest Supreme Court decision, *Dun & Bradstreet v. Greenmoss Builders, Inc.*, offers a glimpse of the continuing lack of consensus among the justices as to how and how much to shield journalists from liability for mistakes. The high Court bickering over *New York Times Co. v. Sullivan* and its extensions, noted throughout this chapter, escalated in 1985 to a cacaphony. Perhaps *Dun & Bradstreet* is the alarum, our warning of drastic cutbacks on press protections in the future.

In twenty years, the Court had swept away the libel law of most states and imposed the actual malice standard on public officials and public figures, and finally on every libel plaintiff seeking punitive damages—significantly enhancing a journalist's position in court. But the bench had feuded over every move and, in *Dun & Bradstreet*, some justices fumed that they were ready to recall and redo history. Perhaps, they contended, the Court had gone too far in its support of the press.

The suit had erupted over a mistaken report that Greenmoss was bankrupt, circulated by Dun & Bradstreet to five subscribers. The mistake was made by a seventeen-year-old high school student paid by Dun & Bradstreet to check on bankruptcy filings. Dun & Bradstreet refused to tell Greenmoss who had received the report and waited a week before correcting it. In its libel suit Greenmoss was declared a private figure and voted $350,000 by a jury sitting in Vermont state court.

The United States Supreme Court approved the award even though it violated the rules laid down in *Gertz* v. *Robert Welch, Inc.*: *Gertz* had outlawed presumed damages and prohibited punitive awards unless actual malice was proved. Greenmoss's award included $50,000 in "presumed" damages without proof of actual injury and $300,000 in punitive damages without proof of actual malice. The jury had been told to presume damage automatically from a false report of bankruptcy and to add punitive damages if Dun & Bradstreet had acted maliciously or in bad faith—instructions based on Vermont common law.

The Supreme Court held that *Gertz* rules did not apply because the credit report concerned a private plaintiff and a "purely private" matter, not an issue of public concern. In separate concurring opinions, Justice Burger advised overruling *Gertz* as "ill-conceived" and Justice White counseled doing away with both *Gertz* and *New York Times Co.* v. *Sullivan,* which he said allowed the press to "pollute" society with lies and then overpower people who sued to clear their names. Justice White proposed giving back to the states the freedom to fashion their own libel laws with perhaps only a mandatory cap on damages.

Nobody knows yet just what *Dun & Bradstreet* portends, but it does show that the Supreme Court laboratory is still experimenting with libel law and the First Amendment. Younger journalists, brought up on *New York Times* and *Gertz* rules, which the Court said had sprung from the Constitution, might have thought them immutable. Yet it appears the Court may gouge holes in the malice shield by circumscribing its duties until a majority of the Court agrees to banish it altogether.

Important questions remain. The courts will struggle to refine the formulas for distinguishing public from private plaintiffs, select appropriate standards for private libel and privacy suits, and analyze the effect of the passage of time on the publication of old embarrassing facts and on the status of onetime public figures who have retreated from the limelight. Courts will continue to wrangle with individuals' control over promotional uses of their names and pictures, even beyond the grave. Some of these questions may be addressed in the future by a substantially changed Supreme Court because five of the nine Justices on the Court today are between the ages of seventy-seven and eighty.

In addition, legislatures will be lobbied to change the rules for the trial of libel suits and to put a ceiling on damages. Journalists and educators, press lawyers and the courts will be called on to resolve these and other fundamental questions about libel and privacy, some of the most controversial issues of our time.

2

Actual Malice:
A Deliberate or
Reckless Libel

BEFORE the Supreme Court adopted the actual malice standard, public officials and public figures in a large majority of states could win a libel suit whenever the publisher failed to prove truth. *New York Times Co.* v. *Sullivan* in 1964 radically changed all that. For the first time, all states were to require public official libel plaintiffs to prove that the challenged statement was not only false, but that it was published by people who knew that it was false or didn't care one way or the other. Actual malice was thus strictly defined as a deliberate lie or reckless indifference to truth and elevated as a principle of constitutional stature. It meant that even if a story eventually proved to be false, if a reporter had, in the court's view, acted in good faith and done his or her best to verify the facts, the reporter was cleared of the charge of libel.

The Court's intention was to encourage what it called the most important type of expression: criticism of official conduct published in the belief that it was true. Extending the actual malice requirement later to public figures, the Court reasoned that information about celebrities and opinion leaders was equally deserving of constitutional protection.

The actual malice concept has proved somewhat unwieldy. Since a

Nicole Hollander, from *"Mercy, it's the revolution and I'm in my bathrobe."*

private plaintiff's burden of negligence is far easier, big fish have big incentives to avoid having actual malice apply to their cases. So they argue that they are mere private citizens, not important officials or influential leaders of society. Except with a famous few, public figure status is more often than not debatable, the rulings unpredictable and irreconcilable, and the category shrinking, as discussed in the preceding chapter. And whether the plaintiff is ruled to be a public figure or not, there's plenty of room left to argue that whatever steps were taken or skipped in the editorial process are proof of actual malice—that is, a deliberate or reckless indifference to the truth.

ELEMENTS OF ACTUAL MALICE

The two main questions asked of journalists in attempts to establish a case of actual malice deal with sources and verification:

1. What made you believe the accusation?
2. Did anything cause you to doubt it?

The most important requirement for a reporter in defeating a claim of actual malice is to produce a report based on sources in which he or she believed. In theory, just one reliable source is enough, and there's not even any requirement for a reporter to verify the information if there's no reason to doubt the source's truthfulness. This was the operating principle in a Nashville case of a citizen's account of police brutality.

Technically, as basic as it may seem to good journalism, trying to confront the subject is optional. However, with other lapses, the failure to confront can look sneaky, and if the prime source is weak, it can seem reckless. When *Look* magazine's secret and shady informants linked San Francisco mayor Joseph Alioto with the Mafia, failure to verify and failure to confront the mayor were ruled actual malice. The biased reporter and slanted story are not evidence of actual malice, but they help to supply a motive for defamation, which may hurt the defense if the story contains libelous mistakes. Lawyers for Israeli general Ariel Sharon and Mobil Oil Company president William Tavoulareas showed how digging up the dirt on the reporter can complicate the issue of actual malice.

Finally, relying on confidential sources poses a potentially fatal dilemma for defense, as CBS found when it was sued for libel by a Long Island diet doctor.

Believable Source: A Trucker's Word Against a Trooper's

The state highway patrol helicopter had set down along a main road and the pilot was answering the call of nature. A passing trucker described the scene over his Citizens Band radio: "We've got a Smokey here choking his chicken! You know, if that was one of us out there, we'd be taken down for indecent exposure." The Highway Patrol pilot, Michael Dover, had the radio in his helicopter tuned to the C.B. band. Hearing the trucker's remarks crackling over the radio, Dover jumped into his aircraft.

"Smartass," the trooper said into his microphone as he gave chase and buzzed the truck as it rumbled up Interstate 95 outside Nashville. Three other troopers joined in and chased the truck driver down.

The driver, Aubrey Roberts, later said the troopers had pulled him over for no reason and had kept him prisoner in a locked patrol car all afternoon, with the windows rolled up and the heater on. Roberts, overweight and asthmatic, said he had been afraid he was going to die. When he was freed, Roberts told his story to the *Tennessean.* After the story ran, the driver sued several troopers, including Dover, for false arrest. Trooper Dover countered by suing the trucker for slander and accusing the *Tennessean* and its reporter of libel.

Reporter Albert Cason, Jr. was on the *Tennessean's* night city desk when Roberts had telephoned. After about an hour's conversation with the trucker, Cason sent a photographer to get a picture of Roberts, thus putting the trucker more firmly on the record. Later this was seen by the court as an element of good faith, going a step further than merely accepting over the phone that the caller was indeed a trucker named Roberts.

When the *Tennessean* reporter telephoned the Highway Patrol the next day, Dover said he'd stopped Roberts for speeding but he had no explanation as to why he had not issued a ticket, and he simply denied the rest of Roberts's accusations.

Cason went back to Roberts with the trooper's version, but the trucker stuck to his story. Cason found the trucker's detailed account convincing. Some of the details were corroborated. Cason felt that the way the trooper glossed over the question of the ticket and wouldn't elaborate suggested he was not telling the truth. In the end, Cason made a subjective judgment on credibility and went with a story he believed.

In the discovery phase of the libel suit, Dover's lawyers found that the *Tennessean* reporter had a history of traffic violations and questioned him about them. Cason acknowledged one arrest for driving under the influence of alcohol and five or six other citations, at least one of which he said was undeserved. The lawyers' objective was to suggest that Cason's motive for the damaging trooper story lay in his hostility toward troopers, although technically a reporter's prejudices are not evidence of actual malice.

Here, the *Tennessean*'s lawyers contended that the reporting was sound and that, even assuming the reporter hated troopers, there was no evidence that the investigation had been affected. The court concluded that after careful checking, the paper had relied upon a believable man's serious accusations of police misconduct. The story, obviously of interest to the public, had included a fair report of Dover's denial. The *Tennessean* had asked the judge to listen to the evidence and grant summary judgment. The judge ruled that the trooper, a public official by virtue of his job as a uniformed law enforcement officer, had failed to prove actual malice. The *Tennessean*'s reporting was found to have been careful and in good faith, which is just the opposite of actual malice, and the newspaper was dismissed from the suit without a trial.

In the second phase of the case, Roberts and Dover, a local hero, slugged it out before the jury. Dover had become a celebrity around Nashville over the years for some dramatic, televised helicopter arrests he had performed by swooping down on marijuana fields and rounding up the surprised growers and dealers.

The jury decided that the trucker had made everything up. Even the judge was convinced that he had intentionally lied about the initial incident. Trooper Dover's lawyers had presented evidence showing that the helicopter had been parked at the top of a steep cliff and that the trooper could not possibly have been seen from the truck. (This same showing had been attempted unsuccessfully at the newspaper's summary judgment hearing.)

This case is an example of the actual malice standard working properly. A credible source and no conflicting facts to cast the story in doubt presented an adequate basis for publishing accusations against the public official, even in the face of his denial. Even though the story was later found to be false, the newspaper was not held responsible for libel because it reported what it believed, which is to say without actual malice.

The case also exemplifies the value of summary judgment—permitting a judge to rule on a paper's defense of lack of actual malice—in advance of a jury trial. Had the newspaper gone to court along with Roberts, the jury might have found it difficult, convinced that Roberts lied, to excuse the reporter for believing him.

Verifying and Confronting: A Mayor and the Mafia

Proving that a journalist used unreliable sources without verifying them and ignored doubts about the truth of a story is the requirement for sustaining a claim of actual malice. That was the challenge facing San Francisco mayor Joseph L. Alioto when *Look* magazine enraged him with its report on his relationship with organized crime. It must have infuriated him that he had given *Look* an interview but had not been asked the direct question: Did you meet with certain underworld figures at the Nut Tree Restaurant?

The story, entitled "The Web That Links San Francisco's Mayor Alioto and the Mafia," ensnared *Look* in eleven years of libel litigation, with four trials and two appeals, ending with a verdict of $350,-000 plus $50,000 costs to Alioto. Relying on one unconfirmed source for crucial material, while refusing to confront the main subject, proved to the court that *Look* must have doubted the story.

Alioto's so-called links with the underworld were illustrated by a full-page diagram that showed his picture in the center of a web connected to Mafia leaders. "A lengthy investigation by LOOK reveals that some of these links . . . go back almost a quarter of a century," the article stated, describing relationships with "at least six leaders of La Cosa Nostra."

"He has provided them with bank loans, legal services, business counsel and opportunities and the protective mantle of his respectability," *Look* said. "In return, he has earned fees, profits, political support and campaign contributions."

Look bought the article from two KGO-TV reporters in San Francisco for $10,000 plus $4,000 in expenses. The reporters, Lance Brisson and Richard Carlson, started with a tip from a law enforcement official that Alioto had helped members of the Mafia get loans from the First San Francisco Bank, which he and some other investors had founded and of which he had served as chairman.

James Fratianno, who was described by federal authorities as the West Coast Mafia's "chief executioner" and was widely known as "Jimmy the Weasel," was said by the article to have been a particularly good friend of Alioto. Fratianno, the magazine said, had obtained five loans for his trucking company from Alioto's bank.

The accusation held to be the most ruinous was that before winning the city hall job, Alioto had met several times with a crowd of known mafiosi at the Nut Tree restaurant on the highway between San Francisco and Sacramento to plan the opening of his bank.

When the *Look* story was published, Alioto had been mayor of San Francisco for two years. He was a bright light in the national Democratic party and had been mentioned as a possible vice presidential candidate in 1968. He spoke at the Chicago convention in support of Hubert H. Humphrey's nomination for president.

In his suit, Alioto denied having relationships with the Mafia, interceding with the bank on behalf of Fratianno, and meeting gangsters at the Nut Tree. Alioto said *Look's* financial peril had caused it to publish sensational lies about him, without verification, in a desperate bid to increase circulation. (*Look*, in fact, was losing circulation and advertising, and within two years was dead, at thirty-four, a victim of television, postal rate hikes, and changing tastes.)

Relationships with the Mafia, never easy to prove, tended to be elusive in the *Look* case. The magazine proved that the mayor's brother-in-law had business dealings with a known hood, but it mistakenly identified Alioto as a director of the brother-in-law's meat-packing company. Alioto admitted representing two or three clients who had been cited in various "listings" as mafiosi, but he denied any relationship with Fratianno. He had not befriended Fratianno, he said, and the one and only time they had met, he had given him the cold shoulder.

To contradict Alioto, *Look* produced a Fratianno pal as a surprise witness who testified that Fratianno had taken him to Alioto's law office to discuss a trucking deal. The witness, Frank E. Greenleaf, said the mayor greeted Fratianno familiarly with, "Jimmy, how are you?" and that Fratianno asked, "Joe, have you been having any luck with our contract?," referring to a hauling contract.

But Alioto testified that he had never laid eyes on Greenleaf. Then a uniformed Yolo County deputy sheriff took the stand and testified that he knew Greenleaf's reputation for truthfulness was "very low" in Clarksburg, California. Greenleaf's 1945 juvenile record and his wife's unsuccessful attempt to commit him to a mental institution were not admitted in evidence, but were hinted at.

Brisson testified that he and Carlson made judgments about the Alioto-Fratianno relationship based on the mayor's other Mafia friendships. "Guilt by association, is that right?" asked Alioto's lawyer.

As proof that Alioto had pressed for Fratianno's loan, *Look* relied on a state investigator's report of an interview with a bank officer who processed the loan. But contrary to the state investigator's report, the bank officer testified that Alioto had "never put any pressure on me to make any loan from the bank." *Look*'s managing editor, Martin Goldman, conceded that no one had specifically told *Look* that the mayor had forced the loans through.

Carlson and Brisson, who is the son of Rosalind Russell and producer Frederick Brisson, said they had relied on confidential law enforcement sources. Their secretiveness might have made the writers seem sneaky to the court, particularly when several of their named sources were not paragons of virtue. But then, a corporate lawyer inside Cowles Communications, *Look*'s parent, who had spotted the name of a secret FBI source in the authors' notes while previewing the story, revealed it in pretrial testimony. The agent's name was Mudd.

By the time of the trial, Herbert Mudd had left the FBI, retiring rather than taking a disciplinary transfer for having talked to *Look*. Mudd testified that, as he had told Carlson, he knew nothing about Alioto's pressuring the bank or dining with gangsters at the Nut Tree, and that it was highly improbable that he would not have known about the meetings if they had occurred.

The Nut Tree allegations were now the focus of the trial and regarded as the crux of the libel, despite *Look*'s efforts to move the spotlight, and the magazine needed to prove it had reliable sources.

The sole source for the Nut Tree story, Tommy Lee Thomas, Fratianno's former son-in-law and business associate, did not show up at the trial and evaded subpoenas from both sides. Thomas, who had cooperated with a government prosecution of Fratianno for underpaying his truckers and had been regarded as reliable in that matter, had seemed "incredibly believable" to Carlson when he interviewed him. Carlson testified that he had been surprised at the breadth of Thomas's knowledge about Fratianno.

According to Carlson, Thomas had told him in the interview that a few years back Fratianno had talked about dining several times at the Nut Tree with Alioto and some mobsters to plan the opening of Alioto's bank. Thomas never claimed to have attended any of the meetings himself. His was a secondhand, dated account that was never corroborated. According to Carlson, Thomas first said that Fratianno had told him about the meetings five years earlier, but in a second interview, which was taped, Thomas became hazy about dates and details, saying, "I'm just guessing, because it's so long ago. . . ."

FBI agents responsible for investigating organized crime in northern California told the reporters they thought Thomas's story sounded ridiculous.

One of the people Thomas said had been at the Nut Tree meetings was Jack Goldberger, a Teamsters official. In a brief telephone interview, Goldberger denied meeting Alioto at the Nut Tree. He did not want to say any more on the phone, the reporters recalled, but offered to meet with them personally. They never followed up with the man whom the court later called the "most obvious available source of possible corroboration." Brisson later testified in court that they were nearing the end of the investigation and the entire story was practically "in the can."

In an interview with Alioto, the writers didn't even bring up the Nut Tree meetings. They did mention two hoodlums—Frank Laporte, a Chicago *capo*, and Frank "Bomp" Bompensiero, a San Diego gangster—who supposedly had been at the restaurant, but only to ask if Alioto knew them. Alioto denied knowing them and nothing more was asked. Afterward, Alioto learned what the article was going to say and demanded a meeting. *Look* said the story was already at the printers.

The authors said they had had no reason to disbelieve Thomas. Editor Goldman said he didn't remember how he had come to believe the Nut Tree allegation, except that he had "solid confidence" in the authors and "absolutely believed" them, even in the face of the FBI's characterization of the story as ridiculous. Goldman, however, also said that he personally regarded Fratianno as a notorious liar and name-dropper. Indirectly, of course, Fratianno had been the source, since Thomas had gotten the Nut Tree vignette from Fratianno.

The court found actual malice in the Nut Tree report. Judge William W. Schwarzer said that "ambitious young men, anxious to sell a sensational story to a national magazine," had taken Thomas's word without confronting Alioto or Goldberger, despite doubts they must have had. As the judge saw it, such failure to investigate could only mean that they didn't want to learn that the story was false.

Editor Goldman, the court said, had had "obvious reasons to doubt, if not Thomas's veracity, certainly the accuracy of his report, given its hearsay nature, the time which had passed since the alleged events had taken place, and the general tenor of the Thomas interviews including the farfetched claims of Fratianno and the vague state of Thomas's memory."

Alioto, a millionaire lawyer specializing in antitrust law, said that *Look*, with its 6.5 million worldwide circulation, had ruined his reputation and deserved harsh punishment for accusing a man of Sicilian descent of having Cosa Nostra ties. Former California governor Edmund G. Brown, a friend and political ally of thirty years, testified as a witness for Alioto. He told the court that the news media "put your entire life through a microscope." He said that "it means a public official has to be very careful, but it also ought to mean that the publications, like *Look* and the newspapers, must be very careful what they print is true."

Alioto won far less than the legal fees of $600,000 he had sought and no punitive damages, which California reserves for victims of proven ill will. The first trial ended with a hung jury: They believed Alioto had been defamed but split on actual malice. The second trial also ended in a hung jury: they found the story false but voted 9–3 in favor of *Look* on the actual malice issue and could not reach agreement. The presiding judge then held that actual malice had not been proved and dismissed the case, but an appeals court found that he had overstepped his bounds and ordered another trial. After a third hung jury, a final nonjury trial was conducted by Judge Schwarzer, who ruled in favor of Alioto.

The Alioto case typifies the concentration on sources that can be determinative of actual malice. *Look* went ahead with the Nut Tree report based on a single, unbelievable, unverified source.

Even if Tommy Lee Thomas had testified, his lack of firsthand knowledge, hazy memory, and bad reputation probably would not have saved *Look*. It is always a risk to base a libelous accusation on one source. *Look* needed to confirm the Nut Tree anecdote with Goldberger or other Nut Tree diners or to drop it from the story, particularly in light of the disbelief of law enforcement officials who had cooperated with other information.

Not confronting the mayor would not, by itself, have been evidence of malice. Nor would printing the story along with the mayor's denial have made it safe, because the key was whether the reporters believed—or had doubts about—the tale they had learned from a disreputable man. And unless they were entertaining doubts and didn't want to be blown out of the water, why wouldn't they have asked the mayor about the meetings at the restaurant? The judge inferred malice, not from lack of confrontation alone, but from that omission and other investigative lapses despite what he regarded as obvious reasons to doubt.

"Proof" that reporters or editors had doubts and ignored them need not be direct, as the Alioto case demonstrates. Quite naturally, journalists usually swear that they "absolutely believed" their story and never doubted it. But if the editorial process looks weak and wobbly enough, judges or juries may deduce doubts, just as the Alioto judge calculated that *Look* "must have doubted" the word of Jimmy the Weasel and must have refused to meet Goldberger and confront Alioto in order to preserve a good story.

THE SLANTED STORY

Portraying the reporter as a villain and the story as a hatchet job does not prove actual malice, but it does complicate a libel defense. A reporter's evil deeds, enmity toward the subject, sloppy methods, and careless remarks may hurt credibility, just as a one-sided story may offend juries' notions of fairness.

While "fairness" does not appear in the Supreme Court's definition of actual malice and technically is not a factor in the strict equation—knowing or reckless falsity—the fairness of a story always influences a jury's feelings for the journalist and, consequently, its appraisal of reporting. Juries prefer stories that present both sides of an issue, and they resent reporting that seems to have been stacked in support of a journalist's preset thesis.

Balanced reporting comports with the jurors' belief that journalists' proper function is to give people the facts and let them make their own judgments about them. And when journalists are on trial for libeling a person and ruining a reputation, an evenhanded report with comment from the other side may be perceived as less damaging to the plaintiff than a one-sided attack. The concept of journalistic fairness, already present in jurors' minds, is naturally never far off-stage in a libel trial, and it may even play a starring role with some skillful directing by lawyers for the plaintiff.

Bias Against the Subject as Motive to Defame

In a widely publicized case in which General Ariel Sharon, the former defense minister of Israel, sued *Time* magazine for libel, the general's lawyers argued that America's best-selling newsweekly and one of its correspondents had long harbored biases against him. This attitude, the lawyers contended, had fueled what the general described as a deliberate lie: that he had tacitly sanctioned the massacre of over 700 Palestinians in Beirut in September 1982 by Lebanese Christian Phalangist troops allied with the Israeli armed forces. The general's lawyers contended that *Time* had known that its report was incorrect but had published it anyway, heralding the story on the cover of its issue of February 21, 1983, and featuring it in advertisements on radio and television. This, the general's lawyers said, was definitely a case of actual malice.

It took twenty months of legal battling, testimony from forty-nine witnesses, depositions of thirteen *Time* staffers, the production of 17,000 documents, and a two-month trial; the legal fees were estimated at over $3 million. In the end, *Time* conceded its report on General Sharon had apparently been false. As one senior editor testified, the story had no basis other than "sheer thumbsucking." The *Time* correspondent who filed, David Halevy, a forty-three-year-old Israeli who had been locally hired fifteen years earlier, conceded he had deduced the information, based on years of analyzing and reporting on officials of the Israeli government. He testified that he had never doubted the truth of his report, which had become one paragraph of *Time's* eight-page story, and the jury of two men and four women indicated that they believed him. The jurors also believed Halevy's testimony, brought out by the general's lawyers, that he thought of the general as a symbol of what he called the "fascism" that was tyrannizing Israel. He also confirmed, in response to questions from the general's lawyers, that he had been reprimanded previously by *Time* for a story about former Prime Minister Menachem Begin that did not check out and had to be retracted.

The general's lawyers called Halevy "a Humphrey Bogart playing Ernie Pyle" at the trial and succeeded in convincing the jurors that Halevy was incompetent, but not that he had intentionally gone ahead with a false story—a fundamental requirement in sustaining a claim of actual malice. Thus, the jury found the correspondent and *Time* magazine had not acted with actual malice.

The Sharon jury had been advised by the presiding judge, Abraham D. Sofaer, that evidence concerning the question of whether *Time* had doubted the accuracy of the report before publishing would be circumstantial. The judge explained that the standard for their decision would not be whether a reasonably prudent person would have investigated further before publishing, but whether *Time* had clearly entertained doubts about the truth and published anyway.

Time had based its story, entitled "The Verdict Is Guilty," on a 108-page report issued by an Israeli commission which had investigated the massacre that took place at a time when Beirut and the southern half of Lebanon were occupied and controlled by Israeli forces under General Sharon's command as minister of defense. The Israelis, 60,000 strong, had invaded Lebanon in June 1982 in an operation that General Sharon called Peace for Galilee. The objective of the campaign, the Israelis said, was to root out members of the Palestine Liberation Organization who for years had been planning and launching attacks on Israel from neighboring Lebanon.

By September most of the fighting was over and Beirut was quiet. On September 14, Bashir Gemayel, the thirty-four-year-old charismatic leader of the Phalangists and the president-elect of Lebanon, was assassinated by a 200-pound bomb. His followers suspected the P.L.O. Two days after Gemayel's funeral, at which mourners made speeches vowing to avenge his death, Phalangist soldiers entered the stark Palestinian camps of Sabra and Shatilla on the southern edge of Beirut and systematically slaughtered hundreds of refugees, mostly men, but also some women and children.

The world was stunned, and Israelis shuddered with shame and humiliation. The three-man Israeli commission of inquiry that was headed by supreme court president Yitzhak Kahan, concluded that Israel had been responsible for the deaths. It charged that General Sharon had ignored warnings that the Phalangists would attempt to avenge the death of their leader, and that he could have prevented the killings. Finally, it called for his resignation.

Time reported all that, but went one step further. Based on material filed by its correspondent in Jerusalem, *Time* said that according to a secret appendix to the Kahan Commission's report, a few hours before Bashir Gemayel's funeral General Sharon had paid a condolence call to the family in the cool, mountain village of Bikfaya, the 400-

year-old ancestral home of the Gemayels, one of Lebanon's most powerful Maronite Christian families. According to *Time*, Sharon had "discussed with the Gemayels the need for the Phalangists to take revenge." The magazine added: "the details of that conversation are not known."

General Sharon, fifty-four, who had resigned as defense minister two days after the commission's report was made public, admitted meeting with the Gemayels in their pink stone house overlooking the olive groves on the day of the funeral, but he denied that the conversation *Time* reported ever took place and demanded a retraction. *Time* refused. General Sharon filed suit against the magazine in Israel within days. Four months later, he sued in New York, where the magazine has its main offices, demanding $50 million in damages.

As in most claims of actual malice, the first line of attack by General Sharon's lawyers was to examine the editorial process, step by step, trying to evaluate the quality of the sources to see whether any of them might have provoked doubts. When that was exhausted, they moved on, as is also common, to examine the "state of mind" of those on the magazine who worked on the story, trying to expose personal traits that might undermine credibility in the eyes of judge and jurors and raise questions about abilities to act fairly. The inquiry into Halevy's state of mind became the centerpiece of General Sharon's case.

Under questioning by the general's lawyers, Halevy described his disillusionment with General Sharon, a hero from his youth and a *Sabra*, like himself—the name given native-born Israelis. Halevy drew parallels between Israeli society today and pre-Nazi Germany. The lawyers also introduced a letter from Halevy to one of his editors in which he said he regarded General Sharon and the Peace for Galilee operation as symbolic of what he called the "mysticism, fascism and radicalism" that he said was engulfing Israel.

When asked at trial if he thought General Sharon had encouraged, instigated, or condoned the massacres at Sabra and Shatilla, Halevy answered, "Encourage the massacre—no, sir. Instigate—no, sir. He turned his back. If this means condone—yes, sir. Yes, sir, he turned his back." Halevy continued, "I think he knew that there were some atrocities, that some atrocities might take place in the camps."

After reading the Kahan Commission report, both Halevy and *Time*'s Jerusalem bureau chief, Harry Kelly, suspected that the commission knew more about the massacre than it had put in its public report. The condemnation of General Sharon, both journalists testified, was harsher than seemed justified by the material in the report. They both knew that the commission had compiled an appendix to its report, which had been labeled "Appendix B" and classified secret.

Months earlier, Halevy testified, a confidential informant had told him that at the condolence meeting General Sharon had used nonverbal signs to indicate acceptance of the Gemayels' plan for revenge. Halevy had reported this tip in a December 6 "World-Wide Memo," a weekly internal communication among *Time* correspondents and editors. The memo, headlined "Green Light for Revenge?," said that General Sharon "gave them the feeling after the Gemayels' questioning, that he understood their need to take revenge for the assassination of Bashir and assured them that the Israeli army would neither hinder them nor try to stop them."

Now Halevy suspected that this information was at the heart of the commission censure of Sharon and figured that it must be in the secret appendix. Kelly wanted confirmation before he included it in their story on the commission's report.

Halevy testified that he contacted two confidential sources. The first, Halevy testified, did not mention Appendix B, but said cryptically: "It all started at Bikfaya. Watch Bikfaya. Learn the story of Bikfaya."

The second source, Halevy testified, characterized the secret appendix as "an index," "a reference book" containing the names of witnesses who had appeared before the commission along with references to the documents and testimony they had provided. Halevy testified that he did not ask whether the appendix contained information about Sharon's prefuneral meeting in Bikfaya or pose his theory on the contents of the appendix to the source.

After those two brief conversations, Halevy testified, he made a thumbs-up gesture to *Time*'s Jerusalem bureau chief to indicate, "Okay, all clear." His hunch had been confirmed, he signaled. He had an exclusive.

Kelly then telexed his file to New York, including the findings on Appendix B and a clearance for Halevy's "World-Wide Memo" report. "We understand," he wrote, that "some" of the appendix dealt with "Sharon's visit to the Gemayel family to pay condolences," as reported in Halevy's "World-Wide Memo." "Certainly in reading the Report," he continued, "there is a feeling that at least part of the Commission's case against Sharon is between the lines, presumably in the secret portion."

In New York, the magazine's writers and editors, following standard *Time* procedures, incorporated Halevy's copy into the story on the commission report, which they were preparing with contributions from several bureaus. In rewording Halevy's information, the New York writers and editors also strengthened it.

The paragraph that appeared in the magazine said:

> One section of the report, known as Appendix B, was not published at all, mainly for security reasons. That section contains the names of several intelligence agents referred to elsewhere in the report. Time has learned that it also contains further details about Sharon's visit to the Gemayel family on the day after Bashir Gemayel's assassination. Sharon reportedly told the Gemayels that the Israeli army would be moving into West Beirut and that he expected the Christian forces to go into the Palestinian refugee camps. Sharon also reportedly discussed with the Gemayels the need for the Phalangists to take revenge for the assassination of Bashir, but the details of the conversation are not known.

Before publication, Halevy's reworked material had been routinely "played back" to him in Jerusalem by telex for "comments and corrections," and he had raised no objection.

After the story appeared, the magazine heard not only from General Sharon, who had not been asked for his comments before publication, but also from a member of Israel's parliament, the Knesset, who sat on the Committee for Defense and Foreign Relations and who therefore had been given access to the secret appendix. Ehud Olmert testified that he had met Kelly at a dinner party in Tel Aviv immediately before Sharon's suit was filed in Israel and had told him that the magazine had been wrong. At Kelly's request, Olmert testified, he had reread the appendix and had telephoned Kelly a few days later with the news, "I just think you have no case. There is nothing in this that resembles your story."

General Sharon demanded a retraction, but *Time* refused for almost two years. As the New York jury was close to decision, the magazine published "A Statement by *Time*." Based on the examination of the secret appendix, which a *Time* representative was afforded during the lawsuit, it said, "*Time* now issues a correction: Appendix B does not contain further details about Sharon's visit to the Gemayel family. *Time* regrets that error."

The statement continued: "*Time* stands by the substance of the paragraph in question."

Time could easily have lost the case. It was clear that it had published a sensational scoop without possessing any information that it was true. The evidence showed that Halevy had made up a theory, had tried to find support for it from unnamed confidantes, and had represented that it had been confirmed, all without ever asking any one of his sources the crucial question: Is my theory right or not? The jury could have concluded from this failure to confront either the sources or the general that Halevy deliberately chose not to test his theory for fear that it would be undermined. In other words, that he was intent on seeing it published, true or not.

Halevy's disillusionment with General Sharon and bitterness over what he saw as the government's vindication of him could have been perceived by the jury as proof of a motive to defame, or of a state of mind that propelled his illogical process. Halevy's use of sources not only in the story on the general but earlier, in the Begin tale, presented evidence of reckless indifference to truth.

Beyond Halevy, there was a bureau chief with a desire to provide *Time* with a scoop. He and the succession of editors in New York did not question the story, despite an obvious puzzle: They all had read the entire public commission report and were aware that, in a text dotted with citations, its one-sentence mention of Bikfaya carried no citation to Appendix B or to exhibits or testimony. This might have prompted any of the editors to question how *Time* had ferreted out the invisible link to the appendix, but no one asked.

From all of the evidence, the jury could have interpreted *Time*'s conduct as evidence of a reckless disregard for truth, but it didn't. At the time that Halevy and Kelly prepared the story, they had not possessed any information that conclusively proved it was false. The facts they did know seemed consistent with the story and gave them no reason to doubt it. Halevy maintained that he had had several sources and that he had believed them. The New York team relied on the representations in Kelly's file and Halevy's memo, seeing no contradictions or reason to question.

As Judge Sofaer had remarked before the trial, the concept of actual malice is "deceptively simple." Whether actual malice is finally proved or not in any case depends upon subjective judgments about what the journalists knew and didn't know at the time they wrote the story. The jury that tried the case analyzed the steps which led *Time* magazine to print a story the jury found to be false and damaging to the general. They found a reporter who despised General Sharon had had a hunch and then had assured *Time* that it had been confirmed. But even though the jury concluded that an unconfirmed and false suspicion had been the sole basis for the story, they found that the journalists had believed it and had never doubted its truth. The jury sifted the evidence, the politics, the bias, the rancor, the sourcing, all of which had been poured out to them over eight weeks of trial. They found *Time* guilty of careless, irresponsible journalism, but not of actual malice.

What lesson does *Sharon* v. *Time, Inc.* hold for other journalists? It would seem to be an object lesson in how not to do reporting and editing. Although Sharon failed to penetrate the actual malice barrier, he poked holes in *Time*'s editorial process big enough to drive a tank through. The *Time* correspondent ignored some fundamental reporting procedures.

The simple rule is to report only what you know and to let the reader know how you know it. If you say flatly that the material is in the document, the implication is that you have seen it. If you haven't seen the material, tell the reader how you learned about it: you were told by someone or you read about it in a report or another document.

If you are relying on a secondary source—someone else who has read the document in question—it is preferable to identify the source with full name and position. At the very least, you must make it clear that your report is based not on the primary document but on the report of someone who has seen it. By providing full or even partial identification of the secondary source, such as "a close aide to the President," you give readers the opportunity to make their own evaluation of the source's credibility. It is assumed, of course, that you will not report information from a source whose credibility you question.

Actual malice tests aside, a responsible journalist confirms any story, but especially an accusatory story, and it is basic to check the information with the person who is likely to be damaged. When more than one journalist is working on the same story, everyone involved should review the final copy to make sure that the language is precise: that the story is neither overblown nor oversimplified nor distorted in any other way. Finally, when it is clear that a published story is in error, a correction should be published.

Reporters can do little about mudslinging and other assaults on their personal integrity by people who bring libel suits. But this is only a secondary line of attack: the primary offensive is against the journalistic process, not the journalist. The best insurance for success in defeating a libel suit is thorough investigation, accurate reporting, and responsible editing.

Notes as Weapons Against the Reporter on Trial

Sharon's defeat signaled that neither carelessness, even of stupefying magnitude, nor contempt for the subject was enough to prove actual malice without there also being deliberate lying or publishing with doubts about truth.

The efforts by the general's lawyers to show the *Time* correspondent in the worst possible light unquestionably damaged the reporter's credibility with the jury and his magazine's reputation with the people who followed the trial in the news. Sharon's strategists must have admired the hoist-with-his-own-pitard maneuvers in a *Washington Post* trial where reporters' notes supplied almost all the weapons the plaintiff needed.

One of the ironies of the *Washington Post's* duel with Mobil Oil was that the multimillionaire president of the second largest oil company in the world managed to play the embattled little guy up against the ruthless, powerful, arrogant, big newspaper corporation.

William P. Tavoulareas (he pronounces it Tah-voo-lah-REE-yes) won the sympathy juries naturally express for the Davids of the world, and the *Post* was handed a Goliath's punishment of over $2 million. A devoted husband and father who began his career pumping gas, Tavoulareas cried on the stand when he described to a packed courtroom how his family was humiliated by a story that he had set his son Peter up in an oil shipping business and steered exclusive, no-bid Mobil contracts his way. "It was devastating," he testified. "I had a career, an unsullied career. . . . My wife was devastated. Peter was devastated. Here is an article that made my son look like a fool or an idiot."

Peter told the jury what a blow the article had been to him. "I perceived that this exceptional man here [his father] was being ridiculed; being called a perjurer, a thief, a liar; was being accused of criminal wrongdoing, and I knew how much it would upset him. . . . At the same time I was being called a bogus businessman and a rogue and a playboy."

The whole family felt better as soon as father and son sued the *Post*, the reporters, and an ex-son-in-law who had been a source. Tavoulareas thought some people who had been suspicious or pitying stopped cringing then and started believing his side of the story.

The case did not end with the award of $2 million to Tavoulareas. For four more years the oil company executive and the powerful newspaper struggled on in the courts. The presiding judge canceled the jury verdict on the ground that there had been no proof of actual malice. Then Tavoulareas appealed and won a reinstatement of the verdict by a three-judge panel of the District of Columbia federal appeals court. The vote was 2–1. Next, the *Washington Post* urged that the decision be reconsidered by all ten District of Columbia federal appeals court judges. The result of that *en banc* rehearing was being awaited as this book went to press.

The case was fascinating for several reasons. It was a spectacular contest in the nation's capital: one of the world's most powerful business magnates pitted against a great and influential newspaper, with editors made famous by Watergate. There had been marathon pretrial skirmishing: Which documents had to be turned over? Which would be designated confidential? Would sources be shielded? Dozens of witnesses on both sides had been examined by high-powered champion lawyers, in one corner the prestigious old-line New York Wall Streeters, in the other corner Washington's premier litigators.

John J. Walsh, a partner in New York's 190-year-old Cadwalader, Wickersham & Taft, who represented Tavoulareas, had never tried a libel case. He contended that the story was false and had sprung from the reporters' arrogance and ambition, fueled by the *Post's* willingness to use its raw power to hurt people. Walsh told the jury that this was proof of actual malice, even though actual malice, of course, is something quite different.

Irving Younger of Washington's Williams & Connolly, a jury trial expert and an immensely popular and renowned lecturer on evidence and jury persuasion, represented the *Post.* Younger did not try to teach the jury about actual malice or even impress upon them that they must vote for the *Post* unless they found convincing proof of actual malice. He did not even mention reckless disregard in his final speech to the jury. Instead, he argued that the story was true and thoroughly researched. He said the *Post* stood by the story.

The judge painstakingly instructed the jury about actual malice and reckless disregard before they went out. But with what they had heard from the lawyers, together with the speech from the judge, they must have been confused. Four jurors interviewed by *American Lawyer* after the trial said they had not understood the judge's instructions and had not based their verdict on any finding of malice. When they came back, after three days, with a verdict for Tavoulareas, the judge said it could not stand because there had been no evidence of actual malice. The multimillion-dollar, nineteen-day trial was over, but the suit was not.

Of course Tavoulareas had helped his son, had given him "a little nudge" when the opportunity arose, the executive acknowledged in court. But he had not done anything wrong or in any way abused his position or Mobil assets, he testified, and his outrage over the *Post's* insinuations continued to boil for a whole year as he pressed for a correction and met a stone wall. The business relationship was open and aboveboard, he said. It had been fully disclosed to Mobil directors and to the Securities and Exchange Commission, and there was nothing wrong with it.

Mobil issued a news release on the day the *Post* published the first in a series of two articles, calling it "twisted with innuendo and inaccurate statements." Tavoulareas wrote the *Post* a letter demanding a retraction four days later, and shortly after that he met with the *Post's* executive editor, Benjamin C. Bradlee, complained about mistakes he wanted corrected, and threatened to sue. He got no satisfaction.

"The Mobil statement was fun. We laughed at it. We blew [Tavoulareas] out of the water. He left with his tail between his legs." That was how *Post* reporter Patrick ("Sandy") Tyler was said to have described the results of the Bradlee-Tavoulareas showdown in a telephone conversation with Sandy Golden, a Maryland writer who had worked with him on the Mobil story. Golden's notes of this conversation, along with his other notes and tapes on the whole course of the investigation were to become acutely embarrassing to the *Post* and useful to the prosecution's argument that imperiousness had driven the two journalists to malice.

Golden had been a staff reporter for the *Montgomery Journal* in Rockville, Maryland, angling for a job on the *Post*. He passed the *Post* a tip from his dentist that the son of Mobil's president was getting rich from Mobil's contracts with his shipping management firm. In return for the contact with the Baltimore dentist, Philip J. Piro, who was still smarting from his nasty divorce from William Tavoulareas's daughter, Golden wanted to team up with a *Post* staffer and share the byline. Tyler, who had had previous leads on this story that he had not yet pursued, didn't particularly relish a team effort and said Golden was trying to shake down the *Post*, but he finally agreed to work with Golden in order, he said later, to keep Golden from pursuing the story without him.

Tyler and Golden testified that they worked doggedly, poring over public records and transcripts of official hearings, interviewing numerous people acquainted with the Tavoulareases, Mobil, and the shipping business, and trying for personal interviews at Mobil, which were denied. Golden told the jury that he had referred to potential sources as "possible enemies." By that he meant people who would have a reason to talk about the father and son and how the twenty-four-year-old trainee making $16,500 a year had leaped to partnership in a firm that prospered on Mobil's business.

"The *Post* is ruthless going after a story. The *Post* has no ethics," Golden had told the dentist who was Tavoulareas's former son-in-law during a telephone call warning him against talking to Tyler without him. Golden's tape of their conversation was produced as evidence at trial. He had continued taping even after Piro asked him not to. Golden had told the dentist in one of their taped conversations that the article would be so strong that Mobil chairman Rawleigh Warner, Jr., would have to get rid of Tavoulareas.

The Tavoulareases' lawyer argued that these remarks and tactics showed actual malice. Walsh repeatedly told the jury that the reporters' haughty demeanor and the newspaper's persistent striving to "get" his client amounted to actual malice. Both the reporters' and the *Post*'s aggressive style gave him a lot of ammunition for the argument, even though that is not the way the courts have defined actual malice.

Tyler, only twenty-seven and rather new to the *Post*, had a reputation for aggressiveness on a staff that metro editor Bob Woodward had organized into "swat teams" and had trained to bring in what he called "holy shit" stories. At trial, Woodward explained he meant stories that were "unusual, and perhaps surprising, and relevant, and of consequence."

Bob Woodward is, of course, *the* Woodward of Woodward and (Carl) Bernstein fame, whose Deep Throat source and Watergate sleuthing brought down President Richard M. Nixon in 1974. The *Post* lawyer didn't have Woodward or Bradlee tell the jury about their daring Watergate days, or the books and movies that had made them stars, on the assumption that there in the nation's capital surely everybody on the jury knew automatically that Woodward had lived the part that Robert Redford later played in *All the President's Men*. And that Bradlee was Jason Robards.

As it turned out, no Watergate bells rang in the jurors' heads, they said later, and so the only things they absorbed about the *Post* heroes were what was brought out at trial. What Tavoulareas's lawyer brought out about Bob Woodward was his lust for finding out about whatever was not right with the world.

"It's almost a perverse pleasure," Woodward had said by way of explaining the thrill he got out of newspapering to another writer who was working on a book about the *Post*. "I like going out and finding something that is going wrong, or something that is not the way that other people say it is, then putting it into the newspaper." Tavoulareas's lawyer read this aloud to the court.

Perverse pleasure, it was implied, was what Woodward and Tyler got from the Mobil story, at least in its early phases, before it became too much of a good thing. Tyler saw it as giving a rare glimpse of big-time corporate "nepotism and favoritism" atop one of the world's most powerful industries.

It required four months of serious reporting, but Tyler had a few laughs in the process. The jury learned about them at trial because Golden kept notes, not just on names and leads, but also on Tyler's wisecracks. Walsh said they showed that the *Post* was "out to get" his client.

Once Tyler jokingly asked Tavoulareas's former son-in-law if he knew someone who could rifle a safe in Tavoulareas's home. And he gloated that the *Post* was about to "knock off one of the Seven Sisters," a reference to the seven major international oil companies. That statement was made to Representative John D. Dingell (D.-Mich.), whose subcommittee later called upon the Securities and Exchange Commission to reexamine the roles of Mobil and its president in the shipping firm. (The SEC investigation cleared Mobil and Tavoulareas.)

As if this wasn't bad enough, Tyler suggested that the Customs Service look into whether either Tavoulareas was taking cash out of the country illegally—on Piro's report that he once saw Peter Tavoulareas's briefcase filled with cash. Repeating that accusation to Customs caused the Service to detain the Tavoulareases at various airports throughout the world. Piro's tip did not make the story and nothing came of the surprise inspections.

Through the reporters' notes and testimony, Walsh led the jury through the reporting process right up to deadline, where a copy editor, according to an internal memorandum introduced in court, pronounced the story "impossible to believe." Walsh cited the memo of the copy editor, Cass Peterson, again and again to the jury as proof that someone at the *Post* had voiced serious doubts about the truth. He downplayed the subsequent memo that had answered her point by point. Peterson wrote that either the angle was wrong or the story was meaningless.

> I've read the Mobil story several times, and while I'm impressed with the amount of work the reporter obviously did, I'm still left with an overwhelming sense of So What? Is there any way to give this story of high-level nepotism a dollars-and-cents angle? Did Mobil's shareholders lose anything? Mobil's customers? Parts of Tyler's case against Tavoulareas seem tenuous, and the whole—a $680,000-a-year plaything for an indulged son, at worst—just seems like a withered peanut in an 84″ gilded shell [a reference to the story's length].

A far more interesting angle, it seems to me, is Mobil's concern about Saudi preference shipping—a concern so profound that it led to the formation of an entire . . . corporation. It's impossible to believe that Tavoulareas alone could put together such a scheme for the sake of his son's business career, or that he would want to. . . . [The memo ends with specific queries.]

Peterson's complaints foreshadowed many of Tavoulareas's. The story simply never said whether the business arrangement was good or bad for Mobil, and Peterson wanted to know, if it didn't cheat the shareholders or violate the law, what was the big deal? Tavoulareas, too, emphasized that the reason for setting up the corporation in the first place was worry over Saudi laws and not Peter's future.

Peterson's memo brought a response from Tyler professing to be disturbed that the copy editor wasn't captivated and blaming the "turgid, investigative tone" of a lot of paragraphs added on the advice of the *Post*'s lawyers "in anticipation of litigation." Tyler defended the story:

> The reasons for running the story haven't changed.
>
> Mobil undertook some incredibly fancy corporate footwork in the wake of the embargo to apparently accomplish two things: ingratiate itself with the Saudis by spinning off shipping equity to the royal family and others and set up the son of Mobil's president in a shipping business when business was bad and the business, therefore, stood little chance of prospering without Mobil's help.
>
> Mobil did both of these things with a minimum of honesty to its shareholders. . . .
>
> This is a rare occasion when our readers can get a peek at how decisions are sometimes made at the top of the largest and most important industry in the world.

Tyler replied to each of Peterson's objections, and two days later the story went to press.

Post lawyer Irving Younger found his loss "incomprehensible." He had been pleased with his smooth, engaging opening statement, and everybody, jurors included, agreed that he had outshone Walsh in style, polish, and "charisma." Younger, who later left the firm to teach at the University of Minnesota Law School, "talked past" the jurors while brilliantly mesmerizing the journalists and lawyers in court, according to one critic. Steven Brill, recapping the trial in the *American Lawyer*, found that jurors considered Younger more "exciting" but called Walsh "direct" and "straight."

Why did the jury find actual malice and vote $2.05 million in damages for the elder Tavoulareas? Younger had neglected to explain that responsible, careful, detailed reporting about a public figure is not punishable in the absence of actual malice—that is, intentional lying or recklessly disregarding some doubt about the truth of the story.

Younger's tactic cleared the way for Walsh to teach actual malice, his way. He pointed to inaccuracies, especially to a misstatement about securities law. Even more basically, he preached that his clients had suffered not so much from lies actually expressed as from the gross, implied lie that Mobil's president had abused his position of trust and power to enrich his son. He also told the jury that the *Post's* arrogance was proof of actual malice. Two competitive young reporters were out to "knock off" an oil company with skuttlebutt, all to feed the boss's appetite for "holy shit" stories.

Actual malice is not what Walsh argued—hostility or callous behavior, an aggressive drive to investigate, or questioning of angle and emphasis where the questions are analyzed and resolved before publication. There was no evidence of actual malice, no evidence that the *Post* had published a deliberate lie or had recklessly disregarded doubts about the truth of its story. For that reason the jury verdict was reversed and ultimately the case should be won by the *Post*. But the battle, estimated to have cost several million dollars in fees and hundreds of hours of staff time, was made infinitely bloodier by "state of mind" evidence: editors portrayed as pressuring reporters for sensationalistic stories; reporters depicted, from evidence of their conversations, as reveling in their power to shake up a company and bring down its president, all the while cracking jokes and looking for more enemies.

Tavoulareas v. *Washington Post* is much more a lesson on style than on substance: The image that journalists project of themselves and of their attitude toward people and stories can become a factor in a lawsuit where reporters' and editors' personal credibility, as well as the quality of reporting, will be examined. It is a great asset in a libel case for a newspaper to be able to present reporters and editors whose work has been thorough and whose personal dignity has been demonstrated in their handling of a story with seriousness and evenhandedness.

Secret Sources Cripple the Defense

Since the quality of sources may be determinative, as the Alioto case shows, confidential sources can hamstring the defense. To excuse a libel from a secret source flies in the face of the American belief in the fairness of accuser openly confronting accused.

Without being able to observe and test the credibility of a source the jury and judge may believe the worst: that there is no source and the story is invented. The lawyer for the plaintiff may skillfully turn the absent source to the plaintiff's advantage, inviting speculation on who the source really is and questioning whether the source really exists. If the information is true, the lawyer parries, what's to be ashamed of? Why hide?

A journalist's privilege to protect source identity does not solve the quandary. Many jurisdictions recognize this privilege and some states have formal shield laws permitting journalists to maintain source confidentiality and forbidding their being held in contempt for refusing to identify a source (see Appendix B). The scope of the privilege varies widely from state to state, however. Some shield laws are inapplicable to libel cases where the journalist is the defendant. Others are designed flexibly to yield to the "interests of justice," such as the plaintiff's crucial need for evidence of malice. A few shields are absolute, but even the most absolute privilege cannot eliminate the prejudice against a libel derived from a nameless, invisible source.

Confidential sources told CBS's "60 Minutes" about a Long Island diet doctor who freely prescribed amphetamines as treatment for obesity.

In a "60 Minutes" segment about the dangers of the drugs and their potential for abuse, entitled "Over the Speed Limit," a former patient, her face obscured in heavy shadow, said that Dr. Joseph C. Greenberg had prescribed between four and six amphetamine-type drugs a day for her, and that under his direction she had been taking up to *eighty pills a day*. The woman, who had agreed to go on the air after being promised confidentiality, told correspondent Mike Wallace that drugs had ruined her life. Here is part of the colloquy between Wallace and the woman:

Q: You eventually came to Dr. Joseph Greenberg?
A: Right, in Great Neck.
Q: And what did he do for you?
A: I was taking eighty pills a day.
Q: Under his direction?
A: Under his direction.
Q: Eighty pills?
A: Eighty pills a day. Eight zero.
Q: And how many of those were amphetamines or amphetamine related or amphetamine substitutes?
A: I would say between four and six a day were amphetamine-

type drugs. I had a very, very strange experience, and this is perhaps why I finally left him: I could not determine where I ended and where you began.

Q: What?

A: I could not determine where I ended and where you began for two years after that time. I walked around holding my hands because I did not know that they were attached to my body.

Q: And when you said that to Dr. Greenberg, he said what to you?

A: Nothing. He said everyone feels that way. . . . I had my daughter after ten years of marriage. She was born with some birth defects.

Q: Do you think as a result of amphetamines?

A: Let me put it this way to you, Mike, okay? We're real healthy people. My husband's family is real healthy people. My daughter comes along ten years after our marriage. She's got a kidney involvement. She's born with a . . . virtual nil antibody level. She has all kinds of allergies. For the first three years, we thought she was hyperactive. She looked like strung-out on medication. I feel that there has to be a connection between what I have done to my body, because of the medications that were given to me because I wanted to be thin.

Greenberg called those and other accusations lies and in his libel suit demanded to know CBS's sources. CBS replied that they were numerous but confidential, all protected by New York's shield law. Nevertheless, to demonstrate absence of malice on its summary judgment motion, CBS persuaded one source, the woman in shadow, to reveal her identity.

The woman, Barbara Goldstein, swore that Greenberg's prescriptions for massive quantities of amphetamine-type pills for her "diet" turned her into a "speed" addict. But Greenberg's old patient records showed that she had visited him for only a brief period ten years back, during a time in which she was seeing at least four other doctors, including one who treated her as an in-patient in a hospital. "60 Minutes" had not indicated that she was recalling an old experience, but gave the impression that it was current. What was more disastrous to CBS's case was that Greenberg's prescription records showed that he had not given her amphetamines but a milder diet pill, Tenuate Dospan, which is not an amphetamine and is regarded by the health department as less dangerous. With Goldstein's credibility in question, CBS needed to show what it had done to verify her story.

Except for confidential sources, CBS had no corroboration of Goldstein's accusations against the doctor. Producer Grace Diekhaus had interviewed about twelve people, including members of Overeaters Anonymous and former and present drug abusers in Greenberg's community, but half hadn't met him and the other half, all former patients, wished to remain anonymous.

One of those, Goldstein, was chosen to be interviewed on camera when she told Diekhaus over the telephone and in their first meeting that she had taken diet pills prescribed by Greenberg. No one involved with the broadcast asked about Goldstein's medical history, how long or how long ago Greenberg had treated her, or whether she could document her claims.

Diekhaus said she verified Goldstein's statements in the usual way: "Unless it is a very specific incident, you would talk to a lot of people who have done similar types of things, and you try and get a feeling for who says what, and whether these things seem to check out." Wallace asked Goldstein at the taping if she was telling the truth. She said she was.

Diekhaus talked only to other confidential sources about Greenberg. She did not interview pharmacists or other doctors in the vicinity. [An investigation of Greenberg by the New York State Department of Health, prompted by "Over the Speed Limit," included interviews with local druggists, reviews of prescription duplicates filed with state authorities, and lengthy talks with Greenberg. It turned up nothing.] CBS broadcast its exposé without documentation and without confronting Greenberg.

After Goldstein's segment was taped, Mike Wallace had telephoned Greenberg, but had asked simply about the merits of amphetamines for dieting, without warning the doctor that the program would refer to him. Greenberg had no comment but referred Wallace to the American Bariatric Society for expert comment. CBS later called this Greenberg's "ostrich" approach.

As a standard first step in defeating a libel claim, CBS asked for summary judgment, or a dismissal without trial. Because Barbara Goldstein was then CBS's only identified source, the network's entire argument for dismissal rested on her. But with her history of mental instability, the years elapsed since her Greenberg visits, and the apparent conflict between her memory and written records, she lacked credibility. In fact, CBS had built its story with information from several sources, but they insisted upon remaining anonymous and would not come forward to help in the defense against the libel charges.

The court treated the case as if CBS's only source was Goldstein. To the court, it seemed that CBS had ignored the obvious need to verify the rather farfetched claims of an unreliable source. The court denied CBS's summary judgment motion and ordered a trial. The judge conceded that at trial no one could force disclosure of the secret sources, but, he said, unless CBS chose to unveil its investigation, it would be precluded from any use of those unidentified sources and any information they had provided as proof of verification or carefulness. In other words, if Barbara Goldstein was the only source identified by the time of the trial, CBS would be treated as if it had no other source, just as it had been treated on the summary judgment issue. Given Goldstein's lack of credibility, the judge suggested, CBS might be regarded as having acted with gross irresponsibility.

The main question at trial, the judge said, would be whether CBS had acted with "gross irresponsibility." CBS had unsuccessfully urged the stiffer actual malice standard, pointing to Greenberg's obesity practice and his scientific articles as proof that he had thrust himself into the public controversy over amphetamine therapy.

The judge saw Greenberg as a private figure, but he recognized that the subject of "Over the Speed Limit" was of "public concern" and applied New York's unique standard between negligence and actual malice—gross irresponsibility—that is reserved for private people's libel complaints about public issue stories. Greenberg would have to prove that CBS had acted in a grossly irresponsible manner without due consideration for reasonable newsgathering standards.

The issue of irresponsibility was never decided. Four weeks into trial, Greenberg withdrew his suit. He got a jury that the CBS lawyer, Eugene L. Girden, said he'd "packed with CBS fans, '60 Minutes' fans, and Mike Wallace fans." Greenberg apparently felt that CBS was on the way to convincing them that he had suffered no damages. "Greenberg hadn't lost a dime, so he wasn't going to collect compensatory damages or punitive damages, and he was going to keep on making his $750,000 a year," Girden said. "He folded his tent, figuring that even if he won he wouldn't win any money and if he lost, his reputation would be a lot worse off and he might lose his practice. Why go on? The '60 Minutes' show was over. Who remembered?"

Girden said that Barbara Goldstein remained the only identified source. He said the producer had paid too little attention to her, probably because Greenberg was not the main target of the documentary, but just an incidental figure. Still, he said, no irresponsibility or even negligence was proved and the posttrial poll showed that "the jury was a hundred percent for CBS."

This case spotlights the classic confidential source dilemma. The plaintiff needs to examine sources' knowledge and credibility to prove that the report had no solid basis and was, indeed, a libel. Private plaintiffs feel this need in negligence cases, but public officials and public figures who must meet the malice standard and those governed by a gross irresponsibility standard feel it even more urgently. Weak sourcing is evidence of irresponsible or reckless journalistic behavior, in short, libel. The journalists also need to be able to show reliance on a worthy source or conscientious verification of statements offered by a source of doubtful credibility. If both sides' proofs are frustrated by faceless, nameless informants, it is the news organization that suffers.

When the only source is a confidential one, some courts have offered the journalist the choice of disclosing the source or taking an automatic loss. A few judges will allow the defendant to prove truth by other means, but others use the *Greenberg* solution: In arguing that the journalists acted responsibly, there can be no reference to the number of sources used or their believability, indeed not even to their existence, unless they are identified.

Because this limitation can maim or kill a defense, many respected editors and publishers will not run potentially libelous information based entirely on confidential informants, and except in rare instances will insist on having credible on-the-record sources or at least a guarantee that the confidential sources will come forward in a suit. As the *Greenberg* case illustrates, it is tricky to defend a libel case while shielding crucial sources.

SOURCING, VERIFYING, GETTING COMMENT, AND LOOKING GOOD

In attempting to establish actual malice, plaintiffs look for flaws in the journalistic process. Much depends upon their proving actual malice: at stake is the entire case of a public official or public figure and any punitive award—whether to a public plaintiff or to a private plaintiff suing over a story about a public issue. The stakes are too high for some people's liking, and that sentiment may account for the emasculation of the public figure category by some courts and the disregard of actual malice requirements by some juries.

The journalist should concentrate on getting facts from people who appear reliable and are willing to be identified, at least in the event of a libel suit. A confidential tip may start you on the reporting trail, but the final story should include corroborating facts from people you can name and from documents you have read, and whatever other evidence has enforced your belief in the story. Be prepared to tell what you did to verify the story and how you tried to reach the subject for comment before deadline. Whether or not to make a practice of saving notes is discussed in the next chapter, but recognize that whatever you save probably can be used by the other side—including *bon mots* and cackles that you may have scribbled about your poor victim.

Crepe hangers say that the actual malice protections are largely imaginary today, handily defeated by charming plaintiffs, hostile judges, and guileless jurors. I believe that if defense lawyers improve their actual malice sales pitch and journalists do more to shore up the reporting steps, the actual malice standard will give them protection strong as garlic.

3

Due Care:
Careful Reporting
and Editing

THE actual malice standard imposed on public official and public figure libel plaintiffs stands in sharp contrast to the standard of care in private figure cases. As General Ariel Sharon and other public plaintiffs have learned, not even shoddy work and gaping holes in investigations are proof of actual malice, and since actual malice is rare, public officials and public figures usually lose.

The law is intent upon giving journalists considerable leeway in reporting on officials and celebrities, but it is equally intent upon protecting private citizens. For private individuals to sustain a claim of libel, they need only to show that a journalist was careless.

"Negligence," the standard for private figure libel cases in the vast majority of states, amounts to showing that a reporter or editor made a mistake that a careful person would not have made or would have corrected.

Journalists can protect themselves by taking good notes, diligently corroborating and checking facts, and relying on official records whenever possible. Most reporters find that getting comment from a person who is the subject of a damaging report adds to the story journalistically and also lends an appearance of fairness, which helps legally. When reviewing stories for accuracy and completeness before publication, take stock of all the elements—headlines, pictures, and captions included.

Pay close attention to minor characters who are not the focus of a story but who are mentioned in some unflattering way. If the reporting on them is not complete, either devote the necessary time to verifying the information or consider omitting it. And be a stickler for accuracy in the area of police and court reporting, a treacherous minefield where almost any misstep may result in libel. Typical mishaps occur with a mistaken identification of a criminal—right name but wrong address, or wrong name—or a misunderstanding of legal terms.

When a slip-up has occurred, a quick, coherent correction can do a lot to assuage hurt and, in some states, preclude punitive damages.

CAREFUL REPORTING AND EDITING

A Shooting Party

Ruth Ann Nichols, a Memphis housewife, told the jury, "The article in the paper has tore up my home and has tore up my children. We had to move. It's tore up my reputation. My friends has turned down on me. People has talked about me. They've talked about my husband. They've talked about my children."

Four times, Nichols said, she had been forced to change her telephone number because of harassing calls. "They would call me and say, 'Oh, you finally got caught.' " Some of them even laughed at the retraction and asked, " 'How much did they charge; how much did it cost your husband to get the rewrite in the paper or get the retraction wrote up?' "

At the factory where Nichols's husband, Bobby Lee, worked, a fellow worker testified, people had begun whispering about her. Nichols's lawyer asked what was being said. "They said she was a whore," the factory worker replied.

The newspaper article that the Nicholses said had brought them to this sorry pass had been only five paragraphs long, about a hundred words, published on a page filled with death notices and classified advertisements, deep inside the *Memphis Press-Scimitar:*

WOMAN HURT BY GUNSHOT

Mrs. Ruth A. Nichols, 164 Eastview, was treated at St. Joseph Hospital for a bullet wound in her arm after a shooting at her home, police said.

A 40-year-old woman was held by police in connection with the shooting with a .22 rifle. Police said a shot was also fired at the suspect's husband.

Officers said the incident took place Thursday night after the suspect arrived at the Nichols home and found her husband there with Mrs. Nichols.

Witnesses said the suspect first fired a shot at her husband and then at Mrs. Nichols, striking her in the arm, police reported.

No charges have been placed.

Nichols complained that the article implied that she had been committing adultery with the unnamed suspect's husband and that the jealous woman had walked in on them and started shooting. Nichols pointed out that the article had misstated the time of the incident—it had happened at three o'clock in the afternoon rather than at night—and had failed to mention the presence of three others, including Bobby Lee Nichols, and that Mr. Nichols had tried to stop the shooting.

Nearly a month later, the *Press-Scimitar* responded with a corrective article almost twice as long as the first, prominently displayed on the front page under the headline "Assault Charge Is Dismissed."

The article, which began by saying that the charges had been dropped in exchange for an agreement to receive psychiatric treatment, recounted the incident in greater detail, making clear that Ruth Nichols and the suspect's husband had not been alone. It made no reference to the time of the shooting, but ended with an apology, saying that an earlier news story about the incident had "failed to state" that Bobby Lee Nichols "was present and tried to prevent the shooting. . . . The Press-Scimitar regrets this error."

Nevertheless, Nichols sued. The case was tried twice and finally decided in favor of the newspaper.

Leo Bearman, Jr., the lawyer who represented the *Press-Scimitar*, said later that while there were indications that the jury that reached the final verdict had believed the newspaper's reporting had been careless, it apparently felt the newspaper had intended no harm.

He also said it appeared that the jury felt the Nicholses had exaggerated the damages they had suffered, and this had undermined their credibility. "Nichols had a good lawsuit," Bearman said. "It was a technical libel and there were inaccuracies. But the bottom line was that the jury was more offended by the exaggerated claims of injury and loss."

The case, one of the legion of libel suits from routine crime reports, demonstrates the extraordinary attention to detail demanded from the reporter on the police beat. Because the Supreme Court has held that involvement in a criminal incident is not the sort of "voluntary activity" that is capable of converting an ordinary citizen into a public figure, often the plaintiff is a private figure. Therefore, the complaint is often decided on the basis of negligence, leaving the journalist to argue that he or she prepared the report carefully and, preferably, while working directly from police records. If discrepancies between the story and the police record have been challenged as libelous, as in the Nichols suit, the journalist must try to convince the jury that, even if there were mistakes, they were not the result of carelessness.

This kind of case is a challenge for the defense because juries automatically sympathize with a victim of inaccurate reporting, probably do not appreciate the rigors of police reporting, and may not even fully understand why police incidents are considered to be news. At the *Press-Scimitar* trial, for example, Nichols's lawyer questioned why the newspaper published police reports at all, to which an editor explained that the paper felt an obligation to inform people about violent and unusual crimes in their neighborhoods. They got criticized either way, he said—for publishing and for not publishing.

In the first trial, the judge ruled summarily, in what is known as a directed verdict, that the evidence presented by Nichols's lawyer was insufficient for a finding of libel against the newspaper. On appeal, the Supreme Court of Tennessee thought otherwise and reversed the decision. Its reversal was prompted in part by the United States Supreme Court decision in *Gertz* v. *Robert Welch, Inc.*, which had just been announced. In line with *Gertz*, the Tennessee court declared that negligence would be the state standard for private libel cases and sent the *Nichols* case back to be certain that her complaint was judged according to that standard.

Menno Duerksen, the *Press-Scimitar* police reporter who wrote the article, testified at the trial that he had gotten his information from a police arrest report that he had read at a Memphis police station where he went every morning at 4:30. Duerksen, who had been a reporter for more than twenty years, including service as a correspondent during World War II, and had a reputation for accuracy, said the arrest report had not referred to others at the scene of the shooting and that there was no way he could have known about their presence. He said the implication of adultery had never occurred to him.

Duerksen said that after he had filed his report, which he described as a "routine filler," the police issued a supplemental "offense report," mentioning the others at the shooting. The police contended that both reports had been available at the same time, but Duerksen testified that he was certain they had not been. Both police reports, introduced by Nichols's lawyer, indicated that the shooting had taken place in midafternoon.

The newspaper might have lost the case, since the jury might have considered Duerksen's report premature and faulted him for not using the supplemental police record. Or the newspaper might have won, with the jury concluding that Duerksen, whose regular and methodical culling of police reports had proved reliable in the past, had exercised care with the Nichols report, had been substantially accurate, and had not negligently omitted the information Nichols claimed had resulted in a scandal.

The newspaper won not on the merits of its carefulness, but because the plaintiff apparently alienated the jury by marching in dozens of friends, who all said they had dropped the Nicholses and had talked about them behind their backs after the story appeared. Investigation destroyed even the claim that they had had to move to get away from the neighbors. The newspaper's lawyer learned that the Nicholses' new house across town was right next door to the new house of their closest friend and neighbor from the old place. The jury was back in five minutes with a verdict for the newspaper.

The newspaper had done just about everything right in the Nichols report. The reporter had an established, regular routine of visits to police headquarters to see official records and had followed the routine in preparing the report of the shooting. Such a pattern—of visiting or telephoning regularly for information from the records—is helpful as evidence of the carefulness with which the newspaper routinely prepares police reports. The reporter's reputation for accuracy proved that the routine he had devised generally produced reliable police news. And the *Press-Scimitar* report of the shooting in this case was a substantially accurate statement of the official record, except the seemingly inconsequential characterization of the time of day. Since neither the reporter nor any editor had considered the implication of adultery, it is uncertain that the reporter would have included any mention of the witnesses, even if he had learned of them from the supplemental report. Then, when the newspaper learned of the Nicholses' objection, it ran a corrective article. The strength of the newspaper's case here, as with negligence libel suits generally, lay in showing that a responsible journalist carefully prepared a report based on a reliable source without an inkling that it was incorrect.

HUMANIZING THE BIG PICTURE

In a five-part series in the New York *Daily News*, one sentence, which was not the focus of the story, became a nemesis. After New York State transferred 50,000 mental patients out of hospitals and into nursing homes where the sane, elderly residents didn't want them and the custodians didn't care for them, the *Daily News* investigated and published "Homing In on Institutions Where the Care Is Careless."

The fourth article in the series began:

> When he was 41, George Nies, a Queens construction worker, suffered a nervous breakdown that psychiatrists said was precipitated by a messy divorce and the fact that his son killed himself because his mother dated other men.
>
> George was institutionalized, first in a Veteran's Administration hospital and then in Creedmoor State Hospital for the mentally ill in Queens Village. After two years there, he appeared to be making progress.
>
> Then, without his family's knowledge, state mental health officials discharged him and sent him to the Elmhurst Manor Home for Adults, 100–30 Ditmars Boulevard, Flushing. Approximately half the residents of Elmhurst Manor are sane elderly men and women, the rest are discharged mental patients like George Nies.

The journalistic device of using an individual case to attract and hold readers and to enliven the story attracted the attention of George Nies's former wife, Catherine Gaeta, and she sued.

Gaeta (pronounced GAY-tah) said everything in the lead was false and libelous. The fifty-year-old waitress said that her former husband suffered brain damage from years of drinking, not a "nervous breakdown." Only sporadically working as a day laborer digging ditches, Nies had spent much of their twenty-year marriage wracked by alcoholism while she worked to support them and their three sons. Their divorce wasn't "messy," she stated. They legally separated and she got an uncontested Mexican divorce, according to her lawyer.

Their eldest, George, Jr., was not a suicide. He had been a twenty-five-year-old heroin addict who overdosed on methadone while in a Queens methadone maintenance and rehabilitation program.

The handsome, dark-eyed brunette said she wasn't dating at the time of her son's death; she had remarried five years before he died. Before that she was working too hard and too late to have a social life. Her son, George, Jr., had lived with her, and her second husband, Sal Gaeta, had gotten the young man a maintenance job at Aqueduct Racetrack and had tried to help him kick his drug habit.

As with all libel cases where factual errors have been made, the lawyer for Gaeta argued that the journalists' sourcing and verification attempts had been insufficient. But Gaeta lost the case because the New York courts found that the reporter had adequately investigated and reasonably believed the source—Gaeta's sister-in-law. The case is an illustration of the scrupulous reporting required even for material that is not the focus of the story.

Two months' investigation for the series on deinstitutionalization of mental patients had led prize-winning reporter Marcia Kramer to the Office of Nursing Homes Special Prosecutor, among many other sources. An unnamed person in that office had told her about the Elmhurst Home in Queens, New York, and said that the sister of one of the patients there had been a reliable source for the prosecutor's investigation and might be helpful to her. The source was Dorothy Sorrentino, sister of George Nies.

Kramer spoke with Nies's sister two or three times on the telephone. Dorothy Sorrentino described poor conditions at the Elmhurst Home and her brother's history of mental illness, which she said his psychiatrists linked to his messy divorce and his son's committing suicide over his mother's dating.

Kramer confirmed the sister's report on conditions at the Queens Home by visiting it undercover, saying that she was scouting for a residence for her old mother. George Nies was there at the time, but she did not speak to him.

Kramer twice contacted psychiatrists at the hospital Nies had left, Creedmoor State Hospital, but they said the doctor-patient privilege forbade them from talking about his condition and suggested that she contact his family or guardian. Kramer said later that she thought Nies's sister was his guardian. The libel lawyer for Catherine Gaeta said this was incorrect. Nies's mother had been designated to receive his checks but technically no guardian had been named.

Kramer had no reason to doubt Sorrentino's word. She did not try to interview Nies's other relatives or his former wife. Although Catherine Gaeta was using her new married name, she would have been easy to find at the Airport City Restaurant in Ozone Park, Queens, near John F. Kennedy Airport, where she had waitressed since 1960.

While "Homing In on Institutions" won awards for exposing tragic injustices to the state's mentally ill, the series hurt a private citizen whose personal tragedy was summarized incorrectly in one devastating sentence. Because that sentence was not the center of the investigation, it may have received less scrutiny from the reporter and editors. In most states, with negligence governing private figure libel, Gaeta might have won because failure to check records of hospitalization, divorce, and death or to interview other family members could have been ruled careless. But New York did not employ the negligence standard. Even though Gaeta was a private person, New York recognized her former husband's medical history as legitimately of public interest in the context of the broader story about mental patient care. Accordingly, the court applied New York's unique "gross irresponsibility" standard for public interest reporting—a standard midway between actual malice and negligence. It held that the journalist's reliance on a family source, who had seemed knowledgeable and credible and who had demonstrated no animosity toward Gaeta, coupled with an attempt to verify with psychiatrists, could not be deemed grossly irresponsible reporting.

Catherine Gaeta believes that the system failed her. According to her lawyer, Frank C. McDermott of Brooklyn, the court was wrong in considering Nies's mental picture as "related" to the public concern over institutional care. The life of Nies's former wife "had nothing at all to do with the story," he said. He also criticized the finding that the paper had acted responsibly because the editors should have seen a "red flag" in the expression "psychiatrists said," and should have demanded details.

McDermott said his client had telephoned the *Daily News* to ask for a correction but that whoever answered had hung up. The lead lawyer on the case for the *Daily News*, Michael B. Mukasey, said the paper had never received a demand for a correction.

Catherine Gaeta's is one of a host of libel cases involving an anecdote in a big investigative report that is the culmination of months of digging and interviewing. *Gaeta* is a reminder that in many stories, a peripheral fact may require as much reporting as some facts more central to the theme. When thinking about vignettes that particularize and humanize the big picture, especially if they are unflattering or painful, reporters should consider making the subjects unidentifiable unless the facts are verified, or substituting information about people whose experiences can be confirmed.

CHECKING AND CONFIRMING

A great number of libel suits are cases of mistaken identity. A paper publishes the name of someone caught doing something wrong, but mistakenly gives the address of a different person—always, it seems, a law-abiding, stand-up kind of guy who happens to be unlucky enough to have the same name as a criminal. Or the person whom the newspaper calls the "suspect" turns out to be the victim or the complaining witness or a hapless bystander.

The ubiquitous, regularly appearing "Police Blotter," sometimes called "On the Record," a popular and avidly read staple of community papers, is libel-prone. If less experienced reporters draw this assignment, they should receive training and help from veteran reporters and editors in reading police incident reports and working with the police, understanding terminology and learning their way around the court and public offices and record rooms.

The detail work of getting information from the public record and getting it right demands skill and concentration. There probably is no other beat on the paper with stories so sensitive and of such legal consequence and where virtually any small error may be libelous. The following two cases are illustrative.

Right Name, Wrong Address

A court record indicated that "Anthony Liquori of Agawam (Mass.)" had changed his plea to "not guilty" on an indictment that charged him and six other men with conspiring, in 1968, to break into both a bank and a supermarket in Pittsfield, Massachusetts. Liquori had pleaded guilty when the indictment was issued in 1973.

Liquori's new plea, in 1974, was to be written up as a small item for the *Springfield Union*. The reporter took down the name from the official record, but since no address was shown there, he took it from the telephone book: Anthony P. Liquori, 658 Cooper Street, Agawam.

Liquori was on vacation when the item ran on Friday, but his brother immediately called the night city editor and told him there had been a mistake. The editor and reporter discovered that the Liquori who was indicted had since moved from Agawam, and they found his address in another town.

Unfortunately, the *Springfield Union*'s affiliate publication, the *Springfield Daily News*, picked up the same "filler," uncorrected, and ran it Monday. Both newspapers retracted—five weeks later.

Just as he returned from vacation, Liquori said at the libel trial, he ran into his bank loan officer who asked when he had been released from jail. A private figure, Liquori won $60,000 compensatory damages, partly on a showing that his construction company had lost its financing and had suffered two bad years after the false reports. The Massachusetts Appeals Court considered the reporter negligent for taking the address from the telephone book, rather than from court records, court personnel, or the attorneys on the case. In addition, the failure of the *Union* to warn its sister paper away from the mistake and the delay in retracting were taken by the court as further evidence of carelessness.

Father or Son?

The reporter had been on the job four months. When he was hired, he'd had "several hours" of training. And now, for the first time, he was covering the court. One of the first cases he covered concerned a young man on trial for possession of narcotics and for being present, with two other defendants, where narcotics were being kept.

There was a press table set up near the witness stand, but the reporter didn't know that, so he took a seat in the back. Some of the witnesses didn't speak up, and it was hard to hear them.

Back at the office, the reporter wrote up the conviction of John J. Stone. When he turned it in, the editor was "surprised"; he had known Stone for twenty years and had considered him an "excellent citizen." Stone owned a catering business that served food at the local schools and was serving on the Newburyport Redevelopment Authority. Nobody checked.

The item ended up being "crowded out" that day, but it ran the next day—followed by a prompt retraction. The person on trial had been Stone's twenty-year-old son, Jeffrey C. Stone. Both father and son had been present at the trial. The mix-up occurred when the reporter thought he had heard a police official testify that "Mr. Stone" had been identified as the owner of the drug by the other two defendants. The reporter inferred that the "Mister" was meant to distinguish the father, who he knew was in the courtroom, from the son. When he wrote up the story, he translated his note on "Mr. Stone" to "John J. Stone."

At the first trial Stone won $7,500, but the newspaper appealed. The Massachusetts Supreme Judicial Court canceled the verdict and sent the case back for retrial to determine whether Stone was a public official and could prove actual malice. If not, the appeals court said, he should be considered a private figure and required to prove negligence, this in line with the United States Supreme Court decision just announced, in *Gertz* v. *Robert Welch, Inc.* In addition to adopting negligence as the state standard for private libel cases, the court also stated that Massachusetts would not permit punitive damages in libel cases.

Before sending the Stone case back to trial, the appeals court remarked that, although there ordinarily is no cause to check a report from official records or proceedings, in this case a jury could find actual malice in the failure of the newspaper to double-check damaging information about a long-respected citizen when the editor admittedly had considered it "surprising" and knew it had been prepared by an untrained cub.

Stone lost in the second trial. Declared a public official because of his position on the Redevelopment Authority, he apparently did not convince the jury that the newspaper had acted with actual malice.

GOOD, CONTEMPORANEOUS NOTES

Advice on whether to keep reporters' notes after the publication of stories varies from lawyer to lawyer. A few newspapers and broadcasters have formal policies on the destruction or retention of notes, and these policies are to be followed consistently, by everybody on every story. But most publishers apparently have no policy and leave the choice to the individual.

Of course, the choice evaporates as soon as a suit is threatened or filed. If that happens, no relevant files can be removed or altered because that would look sneaky. In a suit, files connected to the challenged story and files of the people who worked on the story may have to be turned over to lawyers for the plaintiff. Lawyers will argue over what's relevant and skirmish over source protection, but in general, not much of the material gathered in preparation for a story can legally be withheld in a suit.

Some press lawyers believe in saving everything. They say the jury just never will believe you'd have thrown stuff away unless you had something to hide. And they think it makes a good impression on the jury to show the volume of research material the reporter collected and studied before writing the piece.

Other lawyers say to throw everything out! They prefer to defend just the published story, if you don't mind. "I bet you can't name me a case that was lost because the reporter didn't have notes. There aren't any," one of them noted. The notes can be big trouble. Either nobody can read them, or when you can read them, they just lead to lots of questions from the plaintiff's lawyer that may have no answers: "What's this name, over here in the margin? Uh-huh. Well, did you interview him? No? Why not? Isn't it true that you didn't interview him because he might have said something nice about the plaintiff, something that would blow your story out of the water? And you didn't want that to happen, did you? Huh?"

The in-between school advises throwing away all drafts of the story but keeping backup documentation (such as copies of public records and reports gathered during the reporting) and creating a memorandum summarizing the reporting steps. The memorandum would list nonconfidential sources, interviews conducted, attempts to reach the subject of the story, and other significant facts. With this as a record, the handwritten notebooks and internal reporter-editor memoranda can be thrown out. This isn't as time-consuming as it may sound, but still it may take more time than many reporters can spare. What's good about it is that it leaves the reporter with some aids to memory yet cuts back on materials that normally are of no future use to the reporter and can be burdensome in litigation. What's bad about the practice is that it must be followed consistently, not used with some stories and ignored with others.

Staffs with formal policies on retention of notes should make every effort to conform. Consistency is extremely important. Journalists left to individual choice might consider whether they can bear to part with notebooks or not and how they personally would prefer to face a libel challenge. The lawyer who represents the news organization in libel matters should be consulted.

An Accurate Quote?

In one libel suit, where a reporter's notes did not help his defense, the main issue was the accuracy of a quote. The gas station attendant denied ever having said what the *Boston Globe* printed as his words. They were false and their effect, he said, was to libel him by making him look like a racist. *Globe* columnist Michael Barnicle had written:

> Eddie Schrottman stood looking out the window of his gas station on Blue Hill Avenue and talked about how his neighborhood and his business have changed over the eleven years that he's been pumping gas and fixing cars in what was once this city's great Jewish ghetto:
> "Business is o.k. It's just changed color."

Other things have changed too.

Eleven years ago, Eddie used to carry his change and maybe a cigarette lighter in his right pants pocket. Now he carries a small Smith and Wesson revolver . . . all day . . . every day. Eddie says "there are too many nuts in the world." Four years ago, Eddie moved his family to the suburbs so his wife could shop and his kids could go to school without getting mugged.

According to Eddie, life on Blue Hill Avenue in 1972 . . . "is o.k., if you're a nigger." What used to be an area of fine homes and busy specialty shops is now a neighborhood of fear and suspicion; a place where the streets are Sunday night empty at noon on weekdays; a place where the few white merchants who remain are caged and locked like prisoners in their own stores; where the graffiti scarred, boarded up, abandoned fronts of places like Feldman's Pharmacy and the G & C Delicatessen stand as mute testimony to an earlier, easier time.

Barnicle had set out to gather information for a series of columns on "regular working people in the neighborhoods who are not usually covered by newspapers." A free-lancer who occasionally wrote for the *Globe* (he later joined the staff) and had written speeches for Robert F. Kennedy, Barnicle walked around Blue Hill Avenue's deteriorating houses and failed businesses in Dorchester, the largest and southernmost pocket of Boston, and stopped to conduct an interview at the gas station.

Schrottman said Barnicle didn't identify himself or say he was writing a column; he just struck up a conversation without any warning that it might be published. They talked, but Schrottman said he never made the "nigger" remark or the statement about moving his family to the suburbs for fear of muggings. No wonder Barnicle had got it wrong, Schrottman said. The reporter hadn't even taken any notes in his presence.

Barnicle said he had taken notes and produced them—they covered seven interviews. The phrase "o.k. if you're a nigger" appeared on the third page of the notes but was not set off by quotation marks. Schrottman's name appeared in between the lines just above the phrase, but it also appeared again several lines below. The rest of the notes between Schrottman's name and the next subject in Barnicle's interviews included some but not all of the statements and information attributed to Schrottman.

Barnicle testified that after interviewing a number of proprietors on Blue Hill Avenue, he had returned to his office to write, relying on a combination of notes and memory. However, with the notes and the conflicting testimony about them, the judge decided he believed Schrottman. He concluded that Barnicle had not taken notes in Schrottman's presence. With a finding of negligence, the *Globe* was ordered to pay Schrottman $25,000.

Many cases like Barnicle's come down to whether the judge or jury believes the reporter. Notes, if they are to be helpful, need to be thorough. Those taken in the presence of the person being interviewed are likely to be more reliable and may obviate a swearing match later over whether there was consent for the interview. The plaintiff's lawyer will exploit gaps, omissions, and discrepancies between the notes and the story, so if you plan to save your notes, make them as legible and complete as possible.

The Crucial Fact?

For New York free-lance writer Martha Hume, pit-training in her own libel trial drove home one of the fundamentals of good journalism: Accuracy is all important. "Being sued for libel made me hypersensitive about every little fact," she said.

Hume and *New York Magazine* had just won a libel suit brought by the director of a Manhattan exercise center because of Hume's article, "Warning: It has been determined that a stress test can be dangerous to your health."

The angry man in this case, Chris Chilvers, had abruptly closed his exercise center, the 21st Century Fitness and Testing Center, after *New York Magazine* criticized his practices as shoddy and dangerous. Like most libel suits, his action came as a shock to a writer whose work had never brought her a lick of trouble. The suit took money and great chunks of time to defend, but the magazine's lawyers prevailed.

Hume, who had been an editor for *Texas Medicine* magazine and had written for *Texas Monthly*, said she had always felt she was meticulous with facts, but the suits had taught her the importance of defensive note-taking and documentation of facts. She said that being sued and having every jot and comma scrutinized had led her to "double-check and triple-check every last detail." Another basic lesson she learned is that it's a mistake to depend on editors to catch mistakes. Two editors, one researcher, and a lawyer reviewed her article, and yet everyone missed minor slips that ended up causing major trouble.

In countering the suit, Hume offered her notes to back up the article she had written. However, one disputed fact was missing from her notebook.

Hume reported that the electronic readout of her heart rate had reached 178, a dangerous high, while she was taking a test on a jogging mat. She wrote that it was risky to push the heart rate to 178 without a doctor or even an emergency kit on the premises. Chilvers denied that Hume's test had taken her heart rate anywhere near 178. How could she prove it?

"I didn't write down the pulse rate," Hume said. Having the number in her notes would not have been conclusive proof, but it would have added to her credibility. She had a lot of other facts in her notes, but not the critical number. The slender, dark-haired writer recalled that she had been running in shorts, hooked up to a monitor, and didn't have pad and pencil handy. "Next time, I'd run with a note pad," she said.

The omission of "178" from Hume's notes prolonged her deposition—the oral examination before trial in which an opposing lawyer often tries to trip, confuse, anger, and intimidate a witness into equivocating or making damaging admissions. It could also have proven to be the turning point in the trial with the jury trying to decide, in the absence of any documentation, whether to believe the word of the writer or the director of the exercise center. Because of a tactical error on the part of the lawyer representing the owner of the exercise center, the jury was never asked to decide. In an attempt to underscore the damage caused by the article, Chilvers's lawyer told the court that his client had been one of New York's most prominent personalities in the fitness field, that he had received so much publicity in the past that he had become a virtual "media extravaganza."

This claim led at once to a ruling that Chilvers was a public figure, dramatically raising the standard he was required to meet to prove libel. As a private citizen, Chilvers would have had an easier fight against the magazine. As a public figure, he had to show actual malice on the part of the journalists—that is, that they had either known their information was wrong or had had grave doubts but published anyway.

After Chilvers's lawyer had presented his case in court, the judge ruled that, on the basis of what he had heard, it would be impossible for a jury to find actual malice. He dismissed the jury and directed a verdict in favor of Hume and *New York Magazine*.

However, this was not the end of the story. The same article led to a second suit that the magazine settled out of court. In that case, the head of another exercise center claimed Hume had libeled him by reporting that he had not received his Ph.D. degree. Hume had reported that the man referred to himself as "doctor" when she had interviewed him. But when she had telephoned an official at Springfield College where he said he had studied, she was told that there was only a record of his master's degree in physical education. Under a full-page portrait of the man, the caption, not written by Hume, said: "The poseur: 'Dr.' Maxim Asa has neither an M.D. nor the Ph.D. he claims. Still, it's useful to be called 'doctor' when you're director of the Stress Control Lab and several clinics at the New York Stress & Research Center."

It turned out that Asa had a doctoral degree, an Ed.D., and the college official simply had been wrong.

The lawyers for the magazine foresaw an expensive trial. As in most out-of-court settlements, the magazine would not say how much it paid the plaintiff to resolve the case on the theory that such information encourages suits.

Hume might have avoided the mistake on the degree had she gone back to the head of the exercise center and confronted him with the university's information. His response might well have led her to someone at the university who could have confirmed the graduation. If the man had not proved helpful, she would at least have made an effort to reconcile the conflicting information, and that would have been in her favor in a suit.

Even on the tightest of daily deadlines, a reporter facing a conflict like this should try to get back to the subject and give him or her a chance to refute the damaging information. Not doing so looks sneaky or unfair to jurors. Case histories show that most people don't hold newspaper deadlines in the same high regard as journalists do. They often ask, "Why couldn't that story have waited until they checked it out? What difference would a day have made?"

Daily newspapers often find it impossible to resolve such conflicts by deadline time and will take the calculated risk of publishing. The standard practice, for the sake of fairness and the appearance of fairness, is to publish at least the essence of what has been learned on both sides of the issue. Deadline pressures are often regarded as a mitigating factor in libel suits. Magazines, which generally have more leisurely deadlines, are not given much leeway in this area.

With stories such as the one involving Maxim Asa, in which the writer has days or even weeks before deadline, it is wise to get the damaging information in writing. A letter from the registrar's office would have been useful in this case. It would have demonstrated a degree of thoroughness and would have documented the information provided by the university, thereby eliminating questions about whether the reporter got the university's answer straight.

The libel problems were personally expensive for Hume, whose living depends entirely on her free-lance work. She spent three days in preparation and seven days in depositions as the suits began. Five years later, she took off a whole month to prepare and go through with the Chilvers trial, which was dismissed after six days in court. *New York Magazine* paid for lawyer Slade R. Metcalf's defense work, but for Hume, all those days of zero income were "pretty hard."

The emotional toll was also high. The only other trial Hume had seen was a murder trial in East Kentucky when she was a young girl, and she found herself "scared to death" awaiting her own libel trial in Manhattan's civil court. She was struck that the process was filled with subjectivity and that all the variables—the judge, the jury, the lawyer for the other side—made it "so much luck." Luck dealt her a judge with libel trial expertise and an adversary without it.

USING PUBLIC RECORDS AND OFFICIAL PROCEEDINGS

Fair and Accurate Report

Many states grant a privilege for the publication of information based on official records and official proceedings. The privilege enables official charges, findings, recommendations, and official debate to be passed on to readers, free from the usual obligation that the journalist verify the truth before publishing and refrain from publishing unless it is confirmed. Reducing the burden and risk of libel suits on stories drawn from official records and proceedings is intended to further the press's vital function of keeping people informed of government and public issues.

Official charges against a person are often lodged well before any proof of their validity is publicly available. Public reports of investigations may draw conclusions that are not otherwise substantiated or formalized with legal proofs. Private citizens' litigation against one another may go on for years before there is any resolution. And inflamed opponents' debates over public projects and problems can extend over a series of public meetings before coming to a head.

Even while the accusations and criticisms remain unproved, the privilege to use certain records and proceedings as the basis for a report attaches as soon as they are classified "official." Generally, the privilege covers fair reports based on open records filed in connection with a public proceeding, such as papers filed in judicial proceedings, including motions and exhibits presented with the motions, affidavits, and deposition transcripts that are signed and filed. The privilege also covers public audits; individual and business filings for regulatory, real estate, and tax purposes; and coroner's reports. It covers press releases of governmental authorities and their public reports, police records, and public minutes of proceedings of government boards and agencies. Specifically, what is and is not an "official" record or proceeding for the purposes of the privilege is best left to local lawyers, as definitions and experience vary widely. But in every town, city, and state, the principle of the privilege applies: Publication of information from public records or public proceedings is protected. That is, it can be fairly reported from the record or proceeding without any obligation on the part of the journalist to investigate and determine whether it is true.

Four Cautions

1. *Eyes-On, Hands-On.* Wherever possible, actually see and read the entire official record, attend the official proceeding, or review the entire transcript. Some jurisdictions have refused the record privilege where reporters relied on what somebody else said was in the record. Even police reports are best seen by the reporter, where police allow it. If they don't, the next most defensible practice on the police beat is to establish a routine of regularly telephoning the desk officer in charge of reading the incident reports to the police reporter. A pattern of regular inquiries is extremely helpful because it allows the reporter to testify later that a careful practice, which had been established and habitually followed, had proved reliable over time. This strengthens the argument that, even if an error did occur, it could not be said to have been caused by carelessness, since the routine had resulted in accurate reporting over the long run. Surprising as it may seem, quoting a cop on the scene is riskier under the law than quoting from the official police record. The information obtained from the police officer may not qualify for the privilege, because, according to the thinking of some courts, the officer has not formalized his or her thoughts and made them part of the official record. To the journalist, this means that if "police say" they nabbed the "suspect" but mistakenly give the name of the victim (and then deny ever laying eyes on the reporter), it can be a lonely lawsuit. On the other hand, libelous errors copied from the official record make for an open and shut case in favor of the reporter, or no case at all.

2. *Privilege May Be Conditional.* Abuse may void the privilege. Publishing public record material with knowledge that it is false, for example, may be an abuse. Some town clerks are authorized to include in the public record whatever is offered for filing, and sometimes feuding locals insert some rather nasty prose. The record privilege may not be adequate protection if the reporter knows the charges are malicious. Sometimes the wild or extreme nature of the remarks is enough to tip off even a stranger to the community. Also, town meetings or official proceedings may feature some scurrilous name-calling, which is unrelated to the main business and unprotected by the privilege. The privilege is intended to protect newsworthy reports from the public forum but doesn't guarantee impunity for every drop of poison and every provocative epithet that spill into a proceeding. Whether it's news or not is a judgment call based in part on its connection to the official business being conducted and on the prominence of the speaker. The journalist should make an independent judgment of the newsworthiness of the material regardless of whether it is privileged, and seek a lawyer's advice on whether it is protectible.

3. *Parochial Definitions of "Official."* Official records are those that are made or maintained in the course of business of government and its agents, such as police, courts, corrections, tax and public finance offices, and health and welfare agencies. Various personal papers become official by virtue of being publicly filed—frequently having to do with business, money and property interests (such as reports filed in compliance with government regulations, wills in probate, liens and loans, deeds and mortgages), and life events (birth and adoption, citizenship, marriage and divorce, and death). Some records that one would expect to qualify for the privilege, however, may not. A civil complaint is recognized in some jurisdictions as "official" upon filing, but not in others, and a lawyer's advice on the local practice is necessary. A sealed or secret record, even if it is filed in connection with a public proceeding, may or may not be an official record for privilege purposes. Affidavits, deposition transcripts, and other papers prepared for court proceedings may become "official" only after they are signed and filed with the court. State press associations and press lawyers practicing in the jurisdiction have expertise in defining "official" for purposes of reporting on records and proceedings and should be consulted. Local definitions usually depend upon how resistant officials have been and how pushy the press has been.

4. *Fair and Accurate.* A fair report places charges or accusations in context and gives a balanced rendition of both sides of an issue if both sides are represented in the record or proceeding that forms the

basis for the report. When reporting on a record or proceeding in which only one side of a dispute is presented, the journalist should place the information in context for the readers by summarizing the official opposing positions or at least referring to the existence of an opposing position. For example, in reporting on one session of a trial in which only the plaintiff's arguments were heard, the journalist should state that the defendant has denied the accusation (or whatever the defendant officially has pleaded) or should note that the defendant will be heard next at trial. In reporting on a filed civil complaint, the summary should note when an answer is due. In addition to fairness, there is the requirement that the report be accurate. Accuracy may be stringently, even hypertechnically, construed. A report that is a "substantially accurate" account of the record or proceeding should suffice, but courts have been known to nit-pick, finding particular fault with lay misinterpretations of judicial proceedings. The privilege may be withheld if the report rendered by the journalist is judged to be unfair or incorrect, as demonstrated by the following decisions on pet parrots and office wolves. If the privilege is withheld it does not mean the newspaper automatically loses, just that normal libel rules apply without the shield of privilege.

Rescuing the Parrot

Based on a filed civil complaint in a $400,000 negligence suit, the *Chicago Daily News* reported on the death of a twenty-year-old woman who had been trapped by flames in an upstairs bedroom of a suburban house as her host carried a pet parrot to safety. The information about the suit, the newspaper had argued, was protected by the public records privilege. However, the newspaper lost its protection under the privilege because the Illinois Appellate Court ruled that its handling of the information had been unfair. The result was a reversal of a summary judgment in favor of the newspaper and an order that the case be tried. The six-year libel fight was settled without a trial for what a lawyer for the *Daily News* called "nuisance value."

This is another example of an unexpected eruption over a tiny item, regarded as nothing more than "filler" and treated as routine court news. Another court might have protected the item as a "fair and accurate" report of an official record, but the appeals court found as it did because of a seven-word headline and a few words in the lead.

In the legal battle, George O. Newell, a thirty-two-year-old salesman, testified that after lighting an oil lamp in a ground-floor family room, he had fallen asleep on a nearby couch. The young woman he had been dating, Joan Marie Dini, had earlier gone upstairs to sleep. Newell said he bolted awake at the sound of the "screaming" parrot and saw fire climbing the curtains of the family room.

Compare the "wrongful death" complaint by Dini's family against Newell and his estranged wife, as co-owners of the house, with the *Daily News's* description of the complaint. The day after the complaint was filed, the *Daily News* ran its report under the headline "Saved Parrot, Let Woman Die, Suit Says."

COMPLAINT (Excerpt)

Defendant George O. Newell, upon discovering the fire, made efforts to save his pet parrot from the fire by tearing down the curtains which were in flames.

Defendant George O. Newell made no immediate attempt to reach decedent [Joan Marie Dini], to wake her directly or to help her escape from the fire, despite the fact that the bedroom in which decedent was asleep at the time was above the location of the fire visible to defendant George O. Newell.

Defendant George O. Newell removed his pet parrot from the family room to another room in the home, went outside the home to get fresh air and escape the heat and smoke then filling the home, returned to a separate part of the home to telephone the fire department, and removed the parrot to outside the home, but did not reach or assist the decedent in any way.

Defendant then attempted, from outside the home, to break a window in the upstairs master bedroom by throwing snowballs in order to attract decedent's attention to the windows because defendant knew that the windows were entirely draped on the inside and obscured from decedent's view from within the bedroom.

As a direct and proximate result of the aforesaid negligence of defendants, decedent then and there sustained severe injuries from the fire and resulting heat and smoke, of which she died.

ITEM

A Glenview man has been accused in a damage suit of saving his parrot from his burning home while making no effort to rescue a young woman who was staying there.

The charge was included in a $400,000 negligence suit filed in Circuit Court Wednesday against George and Kathleen Newell, who lived at 1043 Queens Lane at the time of the fire.

The suit was filed on behalf of the estate of Miss Joan Marie Dini, 20, of 619 Gunderson, Carol Stream, who died as the result of injuries from the fire.

The couple is charged with having "gun powder and other flammables" in their home which contributed to the fire.

The suit alleges that before the fire on January 17, Newell had filled an oil-burning lamp in the home and left it burning. The lamp was near some curtains in the family room of the home, the suit says.

When the fire broke out, Newell rescued his parrot, but did not attempt to rescue Miss Dini from an upstairs bedroom in the home, the suit charges.

In Newell's libel suit, the court denied the *Daily News's* claim of privilege for a "fair and accurate" report of a public record because it had implied, in the court's view, that Newell had made no effort to help the victim and, "to his greater shame," had chosen a parrot over her. In contrast, the court said, the complaint had described his tearing down the curtains, telephoning the fire department, and, finally, throwing snowballs at her window. "While these acts may not constitute bravery of the highest order, they are definite efforts to combat the fire and to aid or warn Joan Marie Dini," the court said.

After the case was closed, Ronald G. Zamarin, the Chicago lawyer for the *Daily News*, said he thought the court had gone off on a "nonissue," a "red herring" that had technically provided a basis for a libel. But he said he was convinced a jury would not have sustained the claim.

"The *News*'s report was basically faithful to the complaint," Zamarin said, adding that it was the headline that had "killed us," or had opened the way for the lawsuit.

"The truth was," the newspaper's lawyer continued, "Newell moved that parrot around that house several times before he even tried to call to Joan Marie Dini. A long time went by. By the time he and the parrot were out on the lawn and he had started with the snowballs, the house was an inferno."

In a significant decision for journalists in Illinois, the state appellate court ruled in this case that a civil complaint is an official judicial record as of the time of filing, and thus is privileged. This is probably the majority position today, according to New York libel lawyer Robert D. Sack. But in a minority of states, civil complaints are regarded as official records for the purpose of the privilege only after they have been answered or some judicial action has been taken on them. This is to prevent the publicizing of malicious suits that may have been filed solely for publicity, rather than for legitimate aims.

The decision set a useful precedent, but it did not help the *Daily News* in this instance because the court went on to say that the report on the Dinis' suit against Newell had not been fair and accurate and therefore did not qualify for the privilege. With the privilege eliminated, the court held that Newell was entitled to have a jury determine whether the *News* had libeled him with a negligent false report.

Instead of going to trial, the *News*'s lawyers continued discovery. They took depositions of people who Newell said had ostracized him—friends and customers of the Newells' family company, which represented manufacturers of industrial engines and parts. Those people said that, to the contrary, they thought he was a wonderful guy and that nothing had changed their opinion. Eventually Newell agreed to settle the case out of court. Newell also reached a settlement of the negligence suit by paying the Dini family between $5,000 and $6,000.

Trapping Office Wolves

To "fairly" report on a pending complaint, give at least enough of both sides to alert the reader that the accusations are in dispute and to maintain neutrality. In legal contests, people can, and do, say just about anything about their adversaries; so to rely on the record privilege, reporting must not give the impression of endorsing or crediting accusations that have not yet been formally decided by a court.

Where a general, broad story about a problem needs specific examples, it may be safer to cite finished cases and final judgments than to cite pending cases. The reason for this is that until a complaint is disposed of, it is just an unverified accusation that cannot be assumed to exemplify any problem. A report on it while it remains unresolved must be neutral and uncommitted in order to earn the privilege for a fair and accurate report of a judicial record. A story from the Bergen (New Jersey) *Record* about sexual harassment, "Trapping Office Wolves with Lawsuits," is a case in point:

> It started as an office flirtation but when the secretary lost her job, it became a federal case.
>
> Last February, a year after Jereline Short was fired from the secretarial job she had held at Western Electric Corp. for 13 years, she sued, claiming that she was dismissed because she rejected the advances of her supervisor, Larry J. Holt, manager of the company's benefit administration office.

The *Record* reported that Short's federal civil rights complaint about sexual harassment on her job was one of hundreds brought by women across the country. Although many women had won sizable judgments, the *Record* said, the cases often were hard to prove because they boiled down to the woman's word against the man's. The *Record* quoted Manhattan discrimination attorney Judith Vladeck, as saying, "Women are widely held to be culpable. It's the old 'She must have done something to encourage it.' Especially in an environment where women are second-class citizens, the employer is always going to side with the male supervisor against the female underling."

Short's environment at Western Electric had been one of "pervasive misogyny," the *Record* said, according to employees' testimony in a recent successful sex discrimination suit. Short, a thirty-five-year-old married black secretary, had stated in her harassment complaint that she was fired because she "rebuffed the advances of her supervisor." The *Record* said that after the rebuff, according to Short's complaint, Holt's criticisms of her work escalated until Holt, who is white, fired her. The company denied the accusations, the *Record* said, stating that it had fired her for "sloppy" typing and showing "disloyalty" by spreading a rumor about an employee's romance with Holt, who was married.

"Most victims of sexual harassment have no evidence," the *Record* said, and "Mrs. Short is no different." Western Electric, however, kept memos to the personnel department on Short's attitude and time-wasting and samples of typing errors, the *Record* said.

Short's harassment action was dismissed as insufficient, but Holt's libel action against the *Record* held on for years. He argued that the newspaper had not remained neutral and "fair," and that it should be denied the privilege for a report on an official complaint. The headline and story, he said, "convicted" him. The *Record*'s insurer settled out of court because it appeared to the company that Holt's case, a private figure negligence suit, might result in a jury verdict against the newspaper and substantial legal fees. The suit points up the danger of discussing an undecided legal complaint as if it were an example of a proven offense or injustice. The privilege to recite the terms of a complaint fairly and accurately may be denied if the reporter's analysis of the complaint implies, in a court's view, that it is true. The better journalistic practice when trying to particularize a general discussion of a widespread problem with real cases, is to cite closed cases as exemplifying the principles on which they were finally decided.

A Loss of the Privilege

The California Court of Appeal upheld a $4.56 million verdict against the *San Francisco Examiner* and two reporters, one of the biggest newspaper libel losses ever, after rejecting the official records privilege as one of the journalists' main lines of defense.

The court, in a case that was appealed further by the newspaper and the reporters, said the reporters had helped create deceptive legal documents that were entered into the official record and then used to buttress an article they wrote.

The intent of the official records privilege is to insulate reporters from errors in official documents that they would have no reasonable way of recognizing or guarding against. The records privilege, the court said, does not apply to reporters "who create and file false charges to legitimize their publication."

The reporters denied that they had done anything of the sort. Lawyers continuing the appeal on behalf of the reporters said evidence showing that their clients had good professional reputations and had done a thorough investigation had been wrongly kept from the jury by the trial judge. At the same time, the appeal lawyers said, the judge permitted references in court about another libel suit pending against one of the reporters and testimony that he had fathered children out of wedlock. Meanwhile, the appeal lawyers said, the judge permitted testimony showing that the law enforcement officials had been respected public servants with blossoming careers placed in jeopardy by the *Examiner*'s article.

In a lengthy, prominently displayed, four-part series, the *Examiner* had reported that a Chinatown gang member serving a life sentence for murder had been convicted on the basis of false testimony by an inmate with a long criminal history. It said a new trial was being sought.

The third article in the series, carrying the byline of Raul Ramirez of the *Examiner* staff and a note acknowledging the collaboration of Lowell Bergman, a free-lance, quoted the key witness in the murder trial as saying that law enforcement officials had beaten and threatened him and promised they would reduce his time in jail in exchange for his testimony against the gang member.

"Chinatown Murder—How witness was coerced" brought an immediate demand for a retraction from the two policemen and a deputy district attorney named in the article. The newspaper ignored their demand for a retraction and a few days later published an editorial recommending a new murder trial.

The centerpiece of the article was a sworn statement by the key witness, Thomas Henry Porter, Jr., recanting his earlier testimony at the murder trial. Lowell Bergman had located Porter at the federal penitentiary in Terre Haute, Indiana, where he was serving a sentence for auto theft and facing terms for armed robbery, kidnapping, and escape. After talking with the free-lance reporter, the twenty-two-year-old black inmate agreed to give an Indiana lawyer a sworn statement recanting the murder testimony.

Back in San Francisco, a lawyer friend of Bergman used the sworn statement of the inmate as part of the supporting documentation to request a new murder trial.

The petition for the new trial and supporting documents were made available to *Examiner* reporters, and they prepared and published their article a few days before the documents were actually filed in court.

Generally the official records privilege takes effect after documents have been formally filed, but in some states the privilege has sometimes been extended to reports on documents published in advance of their formal filing.

In the *Examiner* case, the Court of Appeal said it might have been prepared to grant the privilege the newspaper had requested even though its report was based on documents not yet filed with the court. But the appeals court said timing was not the issue in this case. The court said it was denying the privilege because it believed the free-lance reporter had knowingly created a faulty document after persuading the inmate to change his story with a promise to help arrange for California to drop charges against him.

During pretrial questioning that was read to the jury in the libel trial, the inmate said that, before the sworn statement was prepared, he told the free-lance reporter that his recantation had been a lie; that he stood by the original murder trial testimony and also disavowed being subjected to beatings or threats. The inmate said the reporter told him that unless he affirmed the recantation in a formal statement, the reporter would not intervene for him with the authorities in California. He also said the reporter suggested the wording of the sworn statement.

Bergman disputed the inmate's claim, but the inmate produced several letters from the reporter, including one in which Bergman had written that he had a friend "right smack in the middle of the governor's office." To the court, this was an implied promise that the friend would help the inmate once the sworn statement was signed.

Without the official records privilege, the newspaper and the reporters were left to defend themselves on the issue of actual malice—that is, whether they had doubts about the veracity of their story or published it knowing it to be false. The jury and later the Court of Appeal said there was clear evidence of actual malice. They found Bergman had made up the allegations against the police and prosecutor and Ramirez had gone along with the story despite doubts about its accuracy.

In the libel trial, Charles O. Morgan, Jr., a lawyer for the law enforcement officers, introduced a deposition from the Indiana lawyer in which he said he had advised the free-lance reporter that he had been unable to clarify certain details with the inmate and that he believed the inmate "would say or do anything to improve his position behind bars." Morgan told the jury that going ahead with the story despite the expressed disbelief of the principal go-between amounted to actual malice.

In a later interview, Margaret C. Crosby, an American Civil Liberties Union lawyer who was working on the appeal, contended the Indiana lawyer had not meant that he disbelieved the inmate but that he thought the word of a veteran criminal might not be given serious consideration by a court deliberating the question of convening a new murder trial. But she said the trial judge disallowed explanatory testimony by the Indiana lawyer, and the exclusion of this and other evidence might have turned the jury against the paper and the reporters. During the trial, Ramirez testified that, although the law enforcement officials declined to be interviewed, he was able to confirm some of what the inmate had asserted in his sworn statement, and this led him to believe he was reliable. But the law enforcement officials brought subpoenaed newsroom files into the court which included a memo from Ramirez to an editor indicating that the inmate's statement should be viewed with skepticism.

While the conclusion of this case remains unclear, it nevertheless underscores that the privilege to report on an official record or proceeding is just that: a privilege. It can be lost if it is abused. The privilege is designed to protect fair and true accounts of the official business of government by exempting them from the reach of libel judgments. Accurate and impartial reports of court records and proceedings, police news, and other official statements and actions generally qualify for the privilege. Some courts, like the California court in this case, even go so far as to extend the privilege to reports that are published before documents have been officially filed in the official record as well as statements about official proceedings made both in and out of court.

The official records privilege has limits and cannot be counted on to protect absolutely every report based on an official record under all circumstances. For example, the courts do not say reporters may not be justified in encouraging the filing of legal documents, but the courts may be unwilling to extend an exemption from liability to the journalist who authors both an official record and a story relying on the record. The spirit of the privilege is to protect journalist from libelous statements lurking in documents that on their face raise no hint of suspicion.

Understanding the Record

Lawyers are fond of saying "The record speaks for itself," but nothing could be further from the truth. The public record, much of it lawyer-written, is no exception. Consulting an expert on the meaning of an official document in an accusatory story is a good idea. Judicial records in particular may be incomprehensible because of jargon or misleading organization. And the disarray of public files may be such that important pieces to the puzzle are missing or separately logged or superseded or confusingly incomplete.

A misunderstanding of mortgages and financing caused a New Jersey newspaper to lose a $1.05 million libel case to a horse breeder who claimed that the articles cost him hundreds of thousands of dollars in stud fees and ruined his reputation.

In its opinion, the court said the breeder, who had recently retired as chairman of a local bank, was a private figure and announced that the state's standard of liability in private figure libel cases was simple negligence. The case was on appeal to the New Jersey Supreme Court as this book went to press.

The Bridgewater, New Jersey, newspaper, the daily *Courier-News*, mistakenly reported that the bank lent its former officer $2 million for his horse farm, secured only by a mortgage on an already heavily mortgaged two-story office building. That turned out to be just part of the security for a consolidation of previous loans for the farm. There was no new $2 million loan. A three-judge appeals court said the newspaper reporter had misread a mortgage filed in one county and failed to find records filed in the county where the horse farm was located. Those records, the judges said, made it clear that there had been no financial irregularities. Before the story ran, the bank president warned the paper that the facts were wrong.

After a one-month trial, a jury awarded horse breeder Mayo S. Sisler more than $1 million in compensatory damages for injury to his reputation and lost profits from the farm—an extraordinarily high award for compensation of losses. Usually, big libel verdicts come from punitive damages, designed to punish.

The breeder said an owner of champion racehorses canceled an agreement to place stallions on the farm because the story made him question the breeder's financial health and honesty.

The lead lawyer for the *Courier-News*, John B. McCrory, said he expected the state supreme court to overturn the $850,000 award for lost stud fees because an individual cannot properly collect corporate damages. In addition, he said, the $200,000 verdict for injury to reputation was not proved. He disagreed with the finding that the newspaper was negligent in basing a story on what the court called a "complete misunderstanding of the use of 'side collateral' or 'additional collateral.' "

The negligence standard for private plaintiffs applied, despite Sisler's longtime prominence as a banker and businessman. The court did not consider him a public figure even for the limited purpose of reporting on bank business, a position urged by lawyer Thomas J. Cafferty, who represented the New Jersey Press Association and appeared as a "friend of the court."

The newspaper investigation began with a tip from an unidentified law enforcement official that the FBI was investigating a report that a local car dealer had obtained more than $2 million in consumer loans from Franklin State Bank by falsifying customers' credit statements. The car lot was on land bought and leased from a company owned by Sisler and other bank officers. Sisler said he had dealt only with the dealer's landlord and had had nothing to do with the car loans. The *Courier-News* ran a story that said the investigation of the dealership was linked to the bank officers.

The next day a second article appeared, headlined "Bank's Ex-Chief Used Low Collateral in Loan." The source was a mortgage, filed in the Somerset County clerk's office.

A reporter concluded from the mortgage that Sisler had received from his bank a $2 million loan on nothing more than his pledge of an already-mortgaged office in Somerset County. The mortgage referred to separate bank agreements with the horse farm, but the county clerk said those were not public. The reporter confirmed his reading of the mortgage with the clerk and an unnamed lawyer friend whom he met by chance on the street.

Another reporter on the way to the beach for the weekend was asked to search Monmouth County records, where Sisler owned a house and the farm. The clerk's office closed before the reporter could check the filings on the farm, but no one was assigned to finish the search. The court said that that search would have cleared up financing arrangements for the horse farm, including the use of the office building mortgage as additional collateral.

Lawyer Robert C. Bernius, who helped McCrory defend the *Courier-News*, disagreed with the court. He said that even the most complete search of public documents would not have solved the puzzle because the record was "totally misleading" and out of date: Monmouth's filings would actually have reinforced the impression that Sisler had more loans than collateral because they gave no indication of which mortgages were paid off.

The reporter confronted Sisler, who denied getting the $2 million loan and said he owed only the balance of $200,000 on the office building. Sisler warned that the facts were wrong and threatened to sue if they were published.

Bank president Kenneth Bott also told the paper that the facts were wrong and testified that he tried to explain that the office building mortgage had served only as "additional collateral" for other loans. He said no new money had been given to Sisler but declined to be more specific. Bott said there had been no wrongdoing.

When the story ran, it caused a furor at the bank, and after bank officials explained Sisler's financing, the *Courier-News* ran two retractions.

"If you look at what happened here, the newspaper relied on public records, which were incomplete, and Sisler and the bank had all the information but wouldn't talk," Cafferty said. "Mortgages are confusing if you're not a lawyer," he said. In case of doubt about the meaning of financial or technical data, it is useful to ask an expert for translation and interpretation.

New York City libel lawyer Slade R. Metcalf agrees that interpreting official terms and legalese can require a specialist and advises journalists to ask a lawyer for help in understanding the meaning and function of legal documents.

Equally important, Metcalf says, is taking the time and care to read the entire document. "Deadline pressure," he says, "can put reporters in a difficult position. With an editor putting the lumber to them to get the work out, there may be a temptation to quickly scan a file or a transcript to see if there's anything there that's usable. I know it's not easy, but you just hope the reporters have enough moxy to say to their editors, 'No, I don't have a story because I have to read this whole transcript.' "

A danger of a quick scan, Metcalf says, is that information may be misunderstood or placed in an incorrect context. Deposition transcripts, for example, which can be multivolume works, may contain accusations and misstatements that are tempered or even contradicted by passages elsewhere in the transcript. So it is necessary to read the whole deposition in order to be sure of giving a fair and accurate reflection of the total picture.

CORRECTIONS

"City Police Sergeant Lodged in Jail On Bad Check Charges"

Raleigh (West Virginia) *Register*, June 13, 1968

"City Police Sergeant's Son Jailed On Bad Check Charges"

Raleigh Register, a while later, June 13, 1968

Many prospective libel plaintiffs contact the news organization before deciding to sue. Frequently the news organization misses that early warning signal and mishandles the disgruntled person. Shabby or discourteous treatment propels the person to court. "Overwhelmingly, the plaintiffs told us that their post-publication experiences with the press influenced them to bring suit," reported a group of researchers from the University of Iowa.

Professors Randall P. Bezanson, Gilbert Cranberg, and John Soloski of the Iowa Research Project concluded that news organizations are ill-prepared to deal with and diffuse complaints, and recommended paying more attention to postpublication practices. Their survey of libel and privacy cases from 1974 to 1984, including interviews with numerous lawyers on both sides, was presented May 15, 1985, at the University of Minnesota's Silha Center for the Study of Media Ethics and Law.

> ## CORRECTION
> The China Seafood Restaurant
> ad that ran in last Saturday's
> Green Section was incorrect. It
> read 和國史:揆娜乳 . It should
> have read 店飯鮮海國中 . We
> regret any inconvenience this
> may have caused.
> ### CHINA SEAFOOD RESTAURANT
> **6400 HORSEPEN RD.   282-7055**

Richmond (Virginia) *News Leader*, October 23, 1982

[In other words, "China Seafood Restaurant" was upside-down and backwards.—BD]

Every news organization should have a smooth and efficient procedure for handling requests for corrections. At a minimum, the complainer should meet with a courteous and prompt reaction and follow-through. On the rare occasion when legal action is threatened or is a distinct possibility, it may be advisable to involve a lawyer in deliberations on whether and how to handle a correction. This is especially true in states with retraction statutes, because of technical requirements on placement and timing.

Most mistakes are not libelous, and only occasionally do corrections take on legal overtones. Of these examples, only some look "lawyered."

Well, what is there to retract? The *Times* does not now and never did claim that Mayor Sam Yorty was or is insane, and Paul Conrad does not now and never did claim that Mayor Yorty was or is insane. Upon reflection, on the contrary, it does seem possible that the *Times* itself was a little insane when it endorsed Yorty the last time he ran for mayor. . . .

But again, upon reflection, the notion to appoint him secretary of defense might not be such an insane notion after all, for what the nation might lose by it Los Angeles would certainly gain by it.

Los Angeles Times, December 11, 1968

[This soothing "correction" followed the Conrad cartoon shown on page 120, and is not one that averted a threatened suit.—BD]

An item in this column on March 2 erroneously reported that Carol Burnett had an argument with Henry Kissinger at a Washington restaurant and became boisterous, disturbing other guests. We understand these events did not occur and we are sorry for any embarrassment our report may have caused Miss Burnett.   *The National Enquirer*, April 6, 1976

[The court considered this correction "half-hearted," disliked its display—"buried" at the bottom of a gossip column—and rejected its "equivocating" language: "We understand." Neither did the correction satisfy Burnett, who sued and won a $1.6 million verdict, later reduced to $200,000.—BD]

A caption on Page A-2 of yesterday's *Press-Enterprise* was misleading. Most of the birds in the foreground of a picture taken at a West German Zoo were flamingoes, not swans.

The Press-Enterprise, Riverside, California, January 18, 1985

A Washington dispatch yesterday about President Reagan's welcome for President Li Xiannian of China incorrectly described Grace Bumbry. Though she has occasionally sung soprano roles, she is a mezzo-soprano.

The New York Times, Thursday, July 25, 1985

A correction in this space on Thursday, referring to Grace Bumbry as a mezzo-soprano, was itself erroneous. As described in a Washington dispatch Wednesday about the state dinner for President Li Xiannian of China, Miss Bumbry is a soprano. She once sang mostly mezzo-soprano parts, but in recent years has taken predominantly soprano roles and now regards herself as a soprano.   *The New York Times*, Saturday, July 27, 1985

[Ah, yes! So she does! Bumbry says her voice "wanted" to be a soprano all along. But opera buffs say the potentially great mezzo forced her voice to become an undistinguished soprano.—BD]

The *Herald* erroneously reported Friday that Miami City Commission candidate Manolo Reyes is delinquent in his Dade County personal property taxes. The delinquent taxpayer is another Manolo Reyes, whose office is near the commission candidate's.   *The Miami Herald*, April 27, 1985

An article in The Living Section on Wednesday about decorative cooking incorrectly described a presentation of Muscovy duck by Michel Fitoussi,

Policy Caucus, I can attest to his hard work as chairman of the Population and Development Task Force. His work is all the more impressive given the time constraints imposed by his chairmanship of the board of directors of the Global Committee of Parliamentarians on Population and Development. The Global Committee is the first association to bring together world parliamentary leaders, former heads of government, and experts from international organizations to provide parliamentarians with program knowledge and organizational resources to enhance their participation in population and development policymaking.

His international success in the eighties should come as no surprise to those of us familiar with his pioneering work on population in the sixties and seventies.
(continued on page 60)

> **Correction:**
> In our September issue, we published a story that included allegations that Rep. Tom Luken of Ohio had thrown a telephone at one of his assistants and accidentally locked himself into his office. We published these allegations believing them to be true, but now retract them as untrue. The article also falsely implied that Luken made extensive use of interns to contact PACs. We apologize for this error.

return old address label. New subscriptions only: 1-800-341-1522. Postmaster: Send form 3579 to The Washington Monthly, 1711 Connecticut Ave. N.W., Washington, D.C. 20009.

The Washington Monthly is indexed in the Book Review Index, Political Science Abstracts, Public Affairs Information Service, the Readers' Guide to Periodical Literature, the Social Science Index, and Ulrich's International Periodicals Directory, and may be obtained on microfilm from University Microfilms International, Ann Arbor, Michigan, 48106.

Unsolicited manuscripts must be accompanied by a stamped, self-addressed envelope.

Second class postage paid at Washington, D.C.

A JOB

We soon will have an opening for a reporter-editor. Desirable qualifications include practical experience working in or writing about politics and government. More important are intelligence, humor, and the willingness to work long hours for low pay. Applications should be accompanied by a list of at least three references, and by writing samples, not necessarily published but designed to demonstrate fact-gathering and analytical ability.

The Washington Monthly

4

The Washington Monthly, November 1984

a New York chef. In preparing it, Mr. Fitoussi uses a duck that has been killed.   *The New York Times*, April 25, 1981

In an article on May 20, The *Herald* incorrectly referred to an incident outside of a Coconut Grove nightclub as "a drunken brawl." Two people were arrested and one suffered minor injuries outside of Biscayne Baby, but police said it was not a brawl.   *The Miami Herald*, May 30, 1985

TOWN CLERK ACCUSED OF SEXUAL HARASSMENT

Correction—A headline Friday incorrectly identified a complaint filed with the Equal Employment Opportunity Commission against Brunswick County Clerk of Court Greg Bellamy. The headline also incorrectly identified Bellamy's position. Bellamy is accused of harassment and discrimination against a black employee.

Wilmington (North Carolina) *Morning Star*, March 21, 1981

As the result of an editing error, the description of last week's Buy of the Week, zucchini, was incorrect. The best zucchini is small and firm.

The New York Times, August 11, 1982

ST. KITTS OFFICIAL JAILED FOR ARSON

CORRECTION—OFFICIAL ARRESTED FOR INCITING VIOLENCE

St. Thomas (Virgin Islands) *Daily News*, September 8, 1984

In a May 23 Broward News story, a Fort Lauderdale police officer quoted Florida Mission Pastor Gary 'Tree' Aluisy as stating that he had served four years in prison. Records show Aluisy never served time in prison.

The Miami Herald, July 18, 1985

SUMMARY: THE EXACTING NEGLIGENCE STANDARD

When a private plaintiff complains of libel, negligence governs the case in most states. Unlike the public official or public figure plaintiffs who need to prove that ruinous, reckless lies were published about them, private people need simply to show reputations hurt by a little sloppiness. Careful reporting and fact-checking of sensitive statements may avert some costly errors. Stories about businesses or business people in financial trouble, accusations of wrongdoing (with or without judicial records as foundation), and personal criticisms deserve all the reporting and editing attention they can get. Anecdotes used to particularize a big-issue story can backfire unless they are accurate in every detail or are de-fanged by the removal of references to identifiable people.

Where official records or official proceedings exist, be sure to actually see them. Furthermore, to qualify for the privilege for reporting on them, journalists must convey their substance and context fairly and accurately. To maintain the neutral tone, watch all the prominent elements—headline, lead, and cutlines—to be sure nothing throws the report off-balance. Another valuable privilege, discussed in the next chapter, protects opinion statements in news, editorial, and feature writing.

Finally, an acceptable correction has been known to save the day. Obviously no news organization can offer a correction unless it is warranted. Some people undoubtedly have their hearts set on suing and their hopes anchored to big winnings. Still, many experts say they feel certain that some libel suits would not have been brought if attempts to seek redress had not been rebuffed, sometimes abusively. In addition to formal corrections, op-ed columns and letters to the editor may provide a place in the sun for people who aren't absolutely fixed on having their day—or days—in court.

4

How to Use
the Opinion Privilege

A STATEMENT of opinion is never libelous.

The night Barbara Walters moderated the first presidential television debate between Ronald Reagan and Walter Mondale in the 1984 campaign, I was visiting an old friend who practices law in Dallas, and we watched the show together.

To me, Walters looked terrible. Her make-up seemed harsh. Her shoulder-length bleached hair was done in the latest windswept style, but I thought it looked brittle and flyaway. I felt the dress she had chosen would have been inappropriate for a woman half her age.

Curled up on my friend's couch, I kept my thoughts to myself. But he came right out with his: "Barbara Walters looks better every year, don't you think?"

Two people could hardly have had more radically opposed reactions. Yet neither was any more right or wrong than the other. This is the essence of the opinion privilege. It recognizes opinions as personal and subjective and, whether damning or cruel or even wrong, exempts them from claims of libel in the belief that a free society benefits from exposure to diverse ideas, opposing views, debate, and discussion, particularly about matters of public concern. Under the law, a statement of opinion cannot be found libelous. Another name for the opinion privilege is the right of "fair comment."

Having been told that "opinion" should be kept out of the news columns, many journalists mistakenly believe that opinion is properly found only in editorials and in reviews and criticism. But in fact, news stories frequently quote the opinions of people, and the writers themselves are free to express opinions in characterizations of people, events, and remarks.

Strikingly, most libel suits over opinion have arisen from news stories. There have been many fewer such suits from editorials and cartoons and still fewer from reviews and criticism. One reason is that readers and viewers, as well as courts, tend to give more leeway to the expression of opinion on the editorial page and in reviews, and they often fail to realize that a statement they have found offensive in a news story is actually a legally protected opinion and not a fact.

The opinion privilege is valuable because it permits journalists to go beyond the mere recitation of facts to interpret and draw conclusions with some degree of legal protection. But the privilege is tricky and far from foolproof.

As the courts usually see it, there are two broad categories of opinion. One is called mixed opinion; the other is called pure opinion.

Mixed opinion implies undisclosed facts, while pure opinion is based on stated or on known facts. Hyperbole and epithets are usually regarded as pure opinion, as is speculation, within certain limits. If mixed opinions turn out to be based on falsehoods, the privilege then becomes moot because the libel suit proceeds against the false statements.

An underlying theme of the courts has been that journalists have an obligation to make clear to readers when they are presenting opinions rather than facts.

The courts assume that facts are indisputable, but they have indicated that they believe if people realize they are confronting an opinion, they can decide independently whether they agree or not. In theory, mixed opinions are less obvious than pure opinions and, partly so that readers can more readily draw their own conclusions, the courts prefer opinions to be accompanied by supporting facts.

The courts have indicated that they believe the expression of opinion in the news columns, as well as in editorials and reviews, tends to stimulate thought and provoke ideas and is therefore socially useful.

When people sue for libel, they complain about damaging information, and contend that it is all presented as fact. If the statements complained about actually are opinion statements, then it is up to the press lawyers to argue for the privilege. The clearer the journalist has been in indicating that he or she was publishing opinion, the more likely the privilege will prevail. If the expressions that the reporter perceived as opinion are ruled to be statements of fact, the opinion privilege is lost and the information becomes subject to the libel test for facts.

One way to help flag a statement of opinion for readers and the courts is to preface the statement with a phrase such as, "Jones said that in his opinion . . . ," or "The inspector said that he believed that. . . ."

Newspapers often prefer to stack up facts and either elicit opinions from officials or let readers draw their own conclusions. For example: "A broken machine sat leaking a dark green fluid. It was surrounded by dirty pots. 'I think this shows . . . ,' Inspector Jones said. . . . " Journalists must remember that they are responsible for checking the truth of the underlying facts.

The application of the opinion privilege has been as subjective as opinion itself. So for writers and editors it is a somewhat unpredictable and unreliable protection. The main problem is that courts find it hard to separate opinion from libelous fact, and that is because language is imprecise and its interpretation often debatable. Local mores, tastes, and politics affect the opinion privilege. What is protected opinion in one permissive jurisdiction may be tried as libel in a conservative court.

The key for the writer is to recognize a statement of opinion and to determine whether it is mixed or pure opinion. With mixed opinion, the writer should fully and accurately supply the underlying facts. With both types of opinion—mixed and pure—the writer must couch the opinions in subjective terms which clearly tell the reader that opinions are being presented. For the sake of fairness, and the appearance of fairness, in these and all other reporting situations, the journalist should make every effort to include rebuttal and opposing views.

Since a libel suit cannot be based on a statement of opinion, courts are often asked to distinguish between fact and opinion. Judges typically cite as evidence for their decisions what they take to be indications of opinion. The more opinion indicators they find, the more likely they are to rule that a statement is opinion and not fact.

For that reason it is useful for a journalist to know what the indicators are and to use them liberally when stating opinion.

Following are eleven opinion indicators that I have compiled from a study of numerous cases:

1. *Appraising.* The subjective evaluation must be accompanied in an article by the facts upon which it is based. Example:"The Bar Association rated her 'unqualified' for the bench because she graduated

in the lower third of her law class, has practiced law only two years, and lacks criminal and ordinary commercial law experience." The judgment "unqualified" is followed by the facts upon which it was made. The privilege is meaningless if these facts prove to be false and damaging. In that case, the plaintiff just concentrates on trying to win the libel case on the misstatements of fact.

2. *Theoretical.* Speculation should be phrased as sheer conjecture so readers instantly are aware that the speaker concedes to being without factual support. Example: "I suspect the known injuries from multipiece tire rims are just the tip of the iceberg." At least one court found that the iceberg allusion indicated there was no factual basis for the statement and that the speaker was speculating.

3. *Not Dishonest.* The criticism does not charge anyone with a crime or illegal act or dishonesty, not even tentatively or obliquely. Example: "The judge is suspiciously lenient toward organized crime and probably is corrupt." This is a potential libel (if it is false) and not opinion, even with its expressed uncertainty. Questioning whether somebody is a criminal is also libel, and not opinion. Metaphors about criminality and illegality, such as "he's a bandit" or "he's an extortionist," even though not meant literally or seriously, are risky and should not be tossed off lightly. Skip them unless they are vital to the story. Examples: "The Question Is, Who Is Stealing From Whom?" asks an editorial, criticizing a shopkeeper who had a child prosecuted for stealing one pack of gum and fined $100. Similarly, a letter to the editor about three juveniles charged with seventy counts of burglary and robbery stated, "Many people must wonder how the parents remained ignorant of their children's crimes, or were they sharing the loot?" Both of these statements were ruled opinion, but more conservative courts could have cried, "Libel!"

4. *Unverifiable.* This refers to a statement that cannot be proved and is open to wide interpretation. At most, people would agree or disagree with the statement. Example: "He's gone a long way on a pretty face and old-boy connections." By contrast, "The general conspired to underreport the enemy" is a statement that could be proved or disproved, theoretically, at least, and is not opinion.

5. *Not Insinuating.* This means not based upon undisclosed facts, either express or implied, which would be libelous if false. In this example, the statement does not seem to imply any unstated facts: "With that mustache, he looks like a walrus." By contrast, "Wilson is a racist" implies knowledge that would lead to such a conclusion: that Wilson systematically gives undeserved low grades to black students

and uses racial epithets. Without the substantiating facts, the courts tend to take the charge "racist" as a fact, denying the opinion privilege and applying the appropriate libel tests. Such terms as "coward" and "deserter" have generally been treated similarly and should not be used without buttressing evidence.

6. *Exaggerated.*   This means that a statement is so whimsical or obviously fanciful as to be an unmistakable expression of opinion rather than of fact. Many an unflattering metaphor and dastardly allusion have passed as opinions because judges considered them to be "hyperbole." Examples: "The professor's course is a giggle of a gut." And, from an interview with "Colonel" Harland Sanders after his sale of the Kentucky Fried Chicken business to Heublein Corporation: "That new 'Crispy' recipe is nothing but a damned fried doughball stuck on a chicken leg. Their gravy is wallpaper paste and sludge." Paradoxically, the most outrageous opinions are the most protectible. The difference between them and statements of fact is so sharp that neither readers nor judges are likely to see them as anything other than opinion.

7. *Mudslinging.*   These are words or phrases that characterize people in a disparaging way. Examples: "Rude and vulgar pigs," "bastard," "idiot," "jerk," and "dunderhead" are all examples of epithets, and judges have generally regarded them as being protected against libel judgments under the opinion privilege. The reason is that the courts presume that readers instantly recognize name-calling and distinguish it from factual accusation. Nevertheless, "insulting words," as they were called in old criminal libel statutes still provoke an accursed stream of libel suits, and although the complaints almost invariably have failed, it takes time and money to beat them. In this area, restraint is strongly suggested.

8. *Funny.*   The statement is humor. There is no formal dispensation for humor, but it enjoys a bit of extra freedom, perhaps because courts believe readers know better than to mistake jokes or cartoons for serious fact statements. For example, a court thought the intention—if not the result—was humorous and not libelous when a food reviewer for a West Virginia college newspaper said of a particular restaurant, "If you plan to eat here, paint your neck red; it looks like a truck stop." A court up north in New York gave comparable treatment to *Newsday*'s critique of highway dining on Long Island: "On the whole, it was mostly all fake food, ground-up *schmutz.*" The opinion privilege often stretches to political satire, caricature, and benign humor. But sex and race jokes aimed at an individual are taboo, and instead of receiving

protection as opinion, they may be treated as libel, an invasion of privacy, or even an infliction of emotional distress.

9. *Billboarding.* To preface a statement with "In my opinion," or "He said that he believed," indicates to the reader that opinion, and not fact, is being expressed. However, if the statement following the preface is a damaging fact, the preface will not automatically convert it to protectible opinion. So, "In my opinion, George is an embezzler" is still potentially libelous.

10. *Cue from Context.* Statements that appear in places traditionally devoted to opinion, such as the editorials, the letters to the editor column, the op-ed page, and signed columns and reviews draw some measure of protection from their setting. Some courts have said they presume readers of the editorial page normally expect to see opinion statements there, rather than factual reporting. One team of nationally syndicated columnists attacked a university professor, a self-proclaimed Marxist, saying that he was "widely viewed in his profession as a political activist" and quoting an unnamed source as saying he had "no status within the profession, but is a pure and simple activist." The columnists were taken to court but successfully argued that they were entitled to the opinion privilege, partly on the ground that readers would have expected to find opinion rather than fact in the column and would have recognized the remarks about the professor as such.

11. *Cue from Backdrop.* Electioneering, public debate, political controversy—certain combustible situations are known to spark off acrimonious exchanges. In a scrap on rezoning, for example, an opponent asked, "Can a land options speculator posing as a developer override the land use planning process?" Readers, and courts, are likely to recognize that the speaker is expressing an opinion, not stating a fact.

OPINIONS IN THE NEWS

The opinion privilege applies to objective reporting, because it protects the opinions of those being quoted, and to conclusions and interpretations by reporters reached on the basis of accompanying facts. Three news situations in which the reporter often needs to present opinion statements are in reporting on a public debate or controversy, covering candidates and elections, and investigating the quality of public servants and institutions in such fields as education, health, and justice.

REPORTING ON PUBLIC DEBATES
AND CONTROVERSIES

When people square off against one another to fight for or against some community project or governmental proposal or private plan, a reporter risks being caught in the middle and getting hit with a libel suit for publishing the caustic remarks of one adversary about another. Yet zoning battles, resistance to the closing of a school or hospital, opposition to highways, rehabilitation centers, shopping malls, and virtually every other sort of neighborhood change are the subjects about which readers want to be informed. They are fundamental to local news coverage.

Neighbors Oppose Home for Retarded

As a hypothetical assignment, try reporting on a neighborhood struggle over a proposal to open a group home for the retarded. The plan is to convert a big, old, five-bedroom house to a residence for thirteen retarded adults. The other houses on the street are one- and two-family dwellings. A spokesperson for those trying to block the home says that it will cause traffic jams and unduly burden water, sewage, and garbage systems.

The planner of the group home calls those objections "a sham." She says that traffic and parking would be unaffected because the retarded adults don't drive, and according to the water and sanitation departments, any added burden on municipal systems would be negligible. "The problem is esthetic," she says. "The neighbors don't like seeing retarded people and figure other people feel the same way. They really have no doubt that there's room on their street for thirteen more people. They're liars, in my opinion, who are only worried about property values." Which of these remarks is opinion? Is it safe to quote the planner?

Calling the neighbors "liars" and their objections "a sham" libels them by impugning their integrity and implying that resale values mean more to them than human values. Opinion protection probably is out, even though the statement appears against a social backdrop—a housing controversy—that is notorious for riling the public (Indicator 11, *Cue from Backdrop*). Two cardinal opinion indicators are violated: The planner is accusing her opponents of deceitfulness (Indicator 3, *Not Dishonest*), and the words express and insinuate base motives (In-

dicator 5, *Not Insinuating*). Because her words are a fact statement—
that opponents deliberately say one thing and believe another—they
can't be helped or saved by the preface "in my opinion" (Indicator 9,
Billboarding).

How can this story be reported? One way is to select nonlibelous
quotes, dropping the planner's views of her opponents altogether or, at
most, paraphrasing her view that "some people may not want retarded
neighbors." Phrased as conjecture without implying any knowledge of
the facts (Indicators 2, *Theoretical*, and 5, *Not Insinuating*), her suspicion concerns "some" people and does not focus on any particular individual or accuse anyone of dishonesty (Indicator 3, *Not Dishonest*).
Now the story is one that a nervous lawyer could admire, but it is di-
luted, and it doesn't have to be.

A better approach is to interview the neighbors and quote their
reasons for endorsing or opposing the home. Most likely, somebody
will voice a general concern over property values. Such a quote will
make a stronger story and will obviate the libel dangers of publishing a
personal attack by one individual upon another. The writer must do
the homework on gathering and verifying the facts on the issue: how
many residents are expected, what are their conditions, where are they
now, what permits are necessary and which have been secured, how
will the home be staffed and run, and why was the site chosen? Then,
based on those facts, the gamut of opinions on the plan can be reported, with as many indicators as possible, skipping the personal vitu-
perative.

A third, less enterprising and perhaps less interesting way to cover
this debate is to report it from a town meeting or some other official
proceeding. A fair and accurate report of the proceedings is protected
without any need to resort to the opinion shield. Since it is unclear
whether the official proceedings privilege encompasses every vicious
attack made in an official forum, edit with some caution and a sense of
newsworthiness and limit the quotes to comments on the issues. In a
public meeting a speech by the mayor, or a political leader's verbal assault, will probably be more newsworthy and unquestionably safer to
publish than a private citizen's curses and slurs because of the protection provided for reporting on public officials.

In writing the story, give the readers the background on the situation, at least briefly, and include reactions from those criticized. If they
were not present, or for some other reason did not reply during the
meeting, interview them, if possible. Do not, however, publish critical
remarks without either including a response or explaining why the re-

sponse is not included. The story achieves some balance even from the explanation, "Peters could not be reached despite repeated telephone calls to his office and home."

Doctor's Equipment Called "Obsolete"

In Louisiana bayou country a public official's quoted opinion about a private doctor's medical equipment led to a lawsuit against a newspaper and the official. The newspaper reported that the Department of Health and Human Resources was proposing a cancer facility with the latest diagnostic and treatment equipment, including an X-ray machine called a linear accelerator, which beams high-energy radiation at specific points of the body to destroy cancerous tissue. An administrator of a public health facility said he wanted to spare the county's cancer patients the long trip to New Orleans for treatment.

After that story ran, a private doctor in the community told the newspaper the equipment would be redundant, that his clinic had been treating cancer patients for years with a linear accelerator.

The reporter asked the official for comment. "Oh, the equipment we're requesting is the very latest," he said. "That doctor's linear accelerator is obsolete."

The reporter ran this exchange in a second story without getting any factual comparison of the two X-ray machines and without getting back to the doctor for rebuttal. Publishing the official's naked opinion ("obsolete") without facts and without comment from the other side was a mistake.

Including a response from the doctor in the story might have averted the libel suit. Often, people are unhappy about being criticized in public but do not sue because they feel they have been given a fair chance to state their case. Furthermore, a balancing statement of opinion gives extra protection to a journalist under the opinion privilege because it shows that the issue is a matter of debate. In addition, publishing statements from both sides is generally taken as a sign of fairness.

The newspaper won summary judgment. Had the case gone to trial, one defense might have been the opinion privilege. The view that the equipment was obsolete could be considered a privileged opinion, based on the true facts, which would have been offered by the newspaper's lawyer, that it was old and had been superseded by other models

(Indicator 1, *Appraising*). Even if remarking on "obsolete" equipment implies criticism of the doctor—and it needn't be construed that way—it certainly does not charge him with any wrongdoing (Indicator 3, *Not Dishonest*). And depending upon one's definition of "obsolete," the characterization might be unverifiable, but rather one of those debatable propositions on which people may differ (Indicator 4, *Unverifiable*).

The court dispensed with the case without reaching the opinion issue by adopting a nondefamatory definition of "obsolete": simply, "superseded." Still another argument was that the remark was about the equipment and not about the doctor—that is, not technically "of and concerning the plaintiff," as required in a libel action.

The X-ray machine case presents four reminders for treating opinion in news coverage. First, recognize the danger of remarks that denigrate the way in which somebody makes a living—in this case the quality of a doctor's services. Reputation may be a professional's chief asset.

Second, two important people are having a fight. One effect is that their rival empires are threatened. The reporter caught in the middle of the fight needs to develop an accurate, carefully balanced story. Take time to do all the homework.

Third, don't just deliver an attack; instead, serve up some balanced facts so readers can understand the context of the criticism and can judge for themselves (Indicator 1, *Appraising*). By itself, a jab is not informative and serves only to bruise. Does the doctor actually have an older model? Is it still being sold or has it been discontinued? Does the official know the relative advantages of his linear accelerator over the doctor's model? What would make the new one superior? Is, it faster? More exacting? Does it require less maintenance? Is there anything wrong with the older model, and who says so? Is it unreliable? Hard to operate? The official and the doctor are both sources to tap for such information. The equipment manufacturers should also have verifiable facts about the supposed improvements of one model over another.

Finally, including reactions to charges in the same story is critical to fairness and to staying out of court. Too often, on deadline stories, there is no attempt to contact the subject of criticism, as may have been the case in the X-ray machine story, or there is a last-minute stab instead of a sustained attempt to interview an important source. The interview can only enhance protection and it often sheds needed light on interpretive questions.

CAMPAIGNS AND CANDIDATES

Stories about politicians sometimes rank the best and worst of them, bemoan or ridicule their behavior. An article in *Rolling Stone* magazine, written by William Greider and entitled "The Fools on the Hill," urged voters, "For America's sake, don't reelect these losers." That example whistles up the opinion privilege, starting, but not ending, with the headline. "First, the sleazebags," Greider wrote: "Among Washington insiders, regardless of political persuasion there is general agreement that Representative Dan Rostenkowski, a Democrat from Chicago's Thirty-second Ward, is a standout in this category. . . . "

Would you expect this to be covered by the opinion privilege? Well, it is. First, journalists have been given more latitude for criticizing politicians than private citizens. Besides facing the difficult actual malice standard in libel, public officials and candidates for office are often disinclined to sue. With access to reporters and press conferences at will, they sometimes consider themselves better served by settling scores out of court by publicly rebutting the criticism.

Next, a number of indicators earmark "sleazebag" as opinion. It is the sort of appraisal (Indicator 1, *Appraising*) that stops short of charging dishonesty (Indicator 3, *Not Dishonest*) and seems to be debatable—a judgment with which people might disagree (Indicator 4, *Unverifiable*). It's mudslinging (Indicator 7), complete with a billboard citing "general agreement" (Indicator 9) against the backdrop of electoral politics (Indicator 11).

The opinion that Rostenkowski, chairman of the Ways and Means Committee, is a "standout" in the sleazebag category is attributed to "Washington insiders" and is followed by facts that supply the basis for the opinion: After a quarter-century in the safest seat in the House, Rostenkowski, fifty-eight, has accumulated a campaign war chest of $595,000 from special interest groups; has flown at their expense to golf resorts in Doral Beach, Boca Raton, Palm Springs, and Hawaii, and in six months earned $10,000 in speaking fees. Note that the facts must be verified before they can be safely published. A reader might agree that this conduct is sleazy or might just think it goes with the territory.

"Sleaze is bipartisan, however," Greider continues, congratulating Republicans for harboring the only indicted and convicted felon serving in the United States Congress, George Hansen of Idaho. This statement of opinion, that Hansen is "sleaze," is Greider's own view. His basis is the fact that Hansen was convicted of violating financial disclosure laws by concealing loans from Texas billionaire Nelson Bunker Hunt and profits of $87,000 in silver contracts purchased with Hunt's help. Hunt had a huge financial interest in legislation that Hansen was sponsoring.

Even if Greider had been quoting someone else's opinion concerning Hansen, the opinion privilege would apply. The privilege protects the words, regardless of source, if the words convey an opinion.

Heading "everyone's meanness list," Greider wrote, is North Carolina Republican senator Jesse Helms, known for "blatant racism" and "plain nastiness." Greider pointed to Helms's voting record on race and his old statement that blacks may have preferred segregation to being forced to compete beyond their capabilities in racially mixed schools. "Racism" is regarded by the courts as a statement of fact, not opinion; the term insinuates that facts are known which "prove" racism (violating Indicators 4 and 5, *Unverifiable* and *Not Insinuating*). Therefore, the characterization must be amplified with true facts about specific actions or incidents that demonstrate racism. The facts need to be verified by the writer because they become libelous if they are false.

In treating copy that contains negative views about politicians, either epithets volleyed among candidates or criticisms of them by a source or by the writer, recite accurate facts and earmark the opinions with as many strong indicators as possible. The more major the public official or candidate, the more reliable is the press's protection for criticizing him or her.

When criticizing a minor bureaucrat or a minor official or an essentially private citizen who has assumed some role in a public controversy, a reporter has to be especially careful. But if the facts are solid, there is no reason not to go with the story. Provocative, harsh comment should be avoided, and all criticism should directly and unequivocally relate to suitability and qualifications for office rather than any charges of shortcomings that are arguably irrelevant to public responsibility. Have the critic or critics, through direct and indirect quotes, articulate in the story itself how the qualities being criticized impair the subject's official conduct or suitability.

Don't hesitate to tell the reader that opinion is what is being delivered, even if it means paraphrasing, as in "Jones said that in his opinion . . . " (Indicator 9, *Billboarding*). Carefully consider the meaning of the words used. Does the term go beyond the opinion privilege to insinuate some dishonest or base conduct, such as "fast-buck boy" (Indicators 3, and 5, *Not Dishonest* and *Not Insinuating*)? Or is it only mudslinging, such as "jerk" or "idiot" (Indicator 7)?

Whenever possible, get to the person who is being criticized and include his or her comment. Balancing remarks undoubtedly avert many suits by defusing some of the anger and giving the appearance of fairness.

INVESTIGATING PUBLIC SERVANTS AND INSTITUTIONS

Maligning anyone's professional abilities or job-related qualifications calls for extreme caution; proof of ineptness or mismanagement or unsuitability is crucial. Even criticism of a public official's performance is risky and should be previewed by libel counsel to make sure that the charges are well grounded.

When reporters play watchdog over public institutions, they serve the most vital function of a free press. But they also run the risk of libel suits. The actual malice standard gives some protection, at least where the official being criticized holds a major office. Recently, however, lower-level officials bringing libel complaints sometimes have been ruled private figures. This makes it easier for them to win because they have only to prove that a careless mistake was made; and in most states there will be no special allowance for the reporter's having acted in the public interest. The opinion privilege enhances libel protection for reports about what is wrong with public institutions where a writer carefully verifies the facts that form the basis for a critical opinion and reports the facts, along with the response from the other side.

Quality of Educators

Of all public servants, teachers hold one of the most delicate positions of trust and responsibility. Throughout the country, the quality of schools and teachers is a topic of high interest and concern. The story is also high-risk and hard to get.

"Our High School Principals—How Good are They?," an article by Bob Woodward and Bill Bancroft, is a case in point. When the *Montgomery County Sentinel* ran that story, the principal who received the lowest ranking, "unsuited," sued for libel. The principal acknowledged having had scraps with teachers, the Parent-Teachers Association, and the yearbook staff, and that the student government had voted, 48–2, to have him transferred. The article said that he had banned some speakers from the school and was a rigid disciplinarian with no innovative programs. But it incorrectly reported that the principal had censored the school paper.

The jury awarded the principal a staggering $356,000 in damages, which included $250,000 in compensatory damages that the trial judge reduced to $175,000.

The appeals court threw out the verdict. It ruled that the opinion privilege protected the subjective ranking based on disclosed facts, which were substantially accurate. Even opinions based in part on misstatements are privileged where a public person is criticized without actual malice, the court stated. The appeals court rebuked the trial judge for sending the case to the jury in the first place, stating that he should have recognized that the statement was opinion and disposed of the case himself.

How can a journalist research and write a story about teaching performance and minimize the risk of suit? The main problem is to find reliable sources. In the unlikely event that the teacher has been the subject of a public hearing, a fair and accurate report of testimony would be privileged. But most "personnel" matters are exempted from open meetings and open records laws. A writer may find that the only people who are familiar with the teacher's work and willing to criticize it are those with axes to grind.

Take this example: Two fifth graders say their teacher taunts minority students with racist remarks in class. Both students had failed her course. One says she hit him a month earlier for talking back. The child's mother says she complained at the time, but the teacher accused the student of lying. The mother insists her son had never before been a discipline problem and that the teacher is "unstable and lacks the temperament" for the job.

Another parent says the teacher is "incapable," an opinion based on the teacher's ungrammatical critiques of homework and notes sent home. That parent's fifth grader received D's from the teacher and, at the parent's insistence, was finally placed in another class.

Though the sources may be truthful, the motives are suspect. This story must be corroborated by unbiased sources because in a libel suit the reporter could be considered careless for having proceeded with information solely from the teacher's enemies. Such a story must be put together painstakingly. If the most ominous charges are true—assaults and racist remarks in class—there should be several witnesses. Students, parents, and school supervisors must be questioned. The reporter must look into the teacher's background and credentials: Where was she last employed and how was she regarded? Have any formal complaints been lodged and how have they been decided?

Assume the reporter has found some students who fared poorly in the teacher's class but otherwise seem credible. They are willing to speak on the record, but there is no corroboration from neutral sources. Other faculty members either don't know anything or don't wish to be involved. The principal acknowledges receiving a few complaints but says only that they are being investigated. He won't say what the complaints allege or identify the sources of the complaints, calling the matter a confidential personnel issue. The teacher denies all the accusations.

Is there enough to run a story safely if only a few disappointed parents and children attack a teacher's reputation? No. In this case, verifiable facts turn out to be few, and as always, unproved rumor is no basis for impugning professionalism and competency. The opinions "unstable and lacks temperament" and "incapable" would be protected by the opinion privilege if their factual basis were solid, but the reporter is shy on supporting evidence.

This is an example of an important investigative story that needs to be held until proof is indisputable or until an official proceeding makes it safe to report unproved accusations. As it is, even if this story were balanced by the teacher's statements, she would be able to sue for libel and present a sympathetic case. The truth of the fact statements, as a basis for the pejorative opinions, would be at issue. The outcome of the case would depend upon the teacher's believability, compared with other witnesses', and the proof of the charges she says are false.

The teacher might win if she were classified as a private figure and were able to persuade the judge or jury that the reporting had been careless and irresponsible. Even if she were classified a public figure, she could conceivably persuade the court that the reporter had been reckless in publishing the accusations of biased sources in the face of her denials and without supporting evidence.

A Virginia teacher's libel victory is on appeal at this writing. A jury found actual malice in a story which reported that certain parents considered her "unfit to teach" and thought she "should be barred from the classroom." These are opinions, but the jury apparently concluded the underlying facts were false—that the teacher was frequently late or absent and gave some students undeservedly low grades and humiliating treatment.

One problem was that the newspaper had relied upon disgruntled children and parents as sources. Another problem was that without any formal disciplinary action against the teacher, which might safely have been reported had it occurred in an open official proceeding, the report was strictly enterprise journalism, which apparently is unpopular with jurors who may pity the target and disapprove of reporters' taking the initiative to stir up trouble. In the absence of official records, the libel proofs in investigative stories may simply be one person's word against another's. And this means that at a showdown in a libel trial, much will depend upon whether the jury likes the newspaper, its reporter, the sources, and the lawyer enough to temper its natural sympathy for the victim of a damaging report.

So to protect against a libel suit, what value is there to the opinion privilege in such stories as the one about the teacher? Thorough reporting of facts does provide the basis for passing on negative opinions about a teacher (Indicator 1, *Appraising*). Proving the accusations may be hard, but if the facts can be documented, then going a step further to presenting the subjective criticism can be justified. The tone should be elevated and the criticism should remain narrowly focused on skills and performance. For fairness and the appearance of fairness, the opinion of someone not obviously out gunning for a teacher is preferable to the views of enemies. Use as many indicators as possible to set off the opinion as the source's personal view, such as the preface "in my opinion," coupled with terms of appraisal, such as "unqualified" or "unsuited." Words that connote a ranking or rating, such as "the worst" or "the harshest," are typically unverifiable and are obvious expressions of opinion (Indicator 4, *Unverifiable*). Words that accuse the teacher of dishonesty or imply damaging facts, such as "racist," are not opinions and are potentially libelous, so all the proof needs to be laid out (Indicators 3 and 5, *Not Dishonest* and *Not Insinuating*). Don't assume that a teacher, or anyone on the public payroll, will automatically be ruled a public figure for libel purposes. A uniformed police officer always should be judged as a public official, but teachers have been considered public plaintiffs in some jurisdictions and private figures in others.

A libel lawyer may shed light on local precedent for that question and may perform a prepublication review to help the writer and editors assess the risk and make certain the copy is well grounded on all points. Along with confirmed facts about the teacher's conduct and credentials, critical opinions delineated with as many indicators as possible should be balanced with the teacher's own rebuttal and statements from supporters.

Lawyers Sue for Libel

What has been said about criticizing teacher performance applies to stories about the conduct of any professional, in the public or private sphere. Lawyers, in a class by themselves, are the most prolific libel plaintiffs in America, and they bear special mention. Attorneys so permeate society that they are often in the news as primary subjects or tangential figures, as practicing attorneys, heads of government agencies, professors, theatrical agents, contractors, developers, judges, legislators, politicians, and oil company presidents. Lawyers know their way to the courthouse and are ready to sue for libel at the drop of a slight. They take themselves seriously. Flag any negative reference to a lawyer for prodigious and paranoid nit-picking.

When a newspaper quoted bankers ridiculing Melvin Belli, he sued both his critics and the paper for libel. Belli had called a press conference to announce his $85-million class action against certain savings and loan institutions. Bankers who considered the suit misguided claimed that Belli didn't know a federal savings and loan association from a state bank, that he was "not known for his research," and that he was "in a time warp."

Belli's libel suit failed. The court scolded him, "If you can't stand the heat, stay out of the kitchen." As a public figure who had advertised his own opinions in a public controversy, he was expected to bear up under opposing viewpoints. But the libel suit, over a few little quips, might have been more onerous to the paper if Belli had not been so famous. As a rule, with both prominent and low-profile lawyers, criticize competency only when the charges can be meticulously documented in print.

ON THE EDITORIAL PAGE

There are several misconceptions about the opinion privilege and how far its protection extends. One misconception is that the privilege covers all copy clearly designated as opinion, such as an essay marked "Editorial" or a column called "As I See It."

A related misconception is that everything on the editorial page qualifies for the privilege. Although the label and context are opinion indicators, the privilege is not automatic. The shield works only for statements of opinion on the editorial page. Statements of fact in editorials, cartoons, and letters to the editor are covered by the principles of libel.

Editorial Blames Prison Doctor for Inmate's Death

A twenty-three-year-old Alaska pipeline worker was jailed for disorderly conduct and began behaving violently in his cell. The prison doctor, concerned that the young man might hurt himself, applied to have him hospitalized. Days passed with no action taken, and the prisoner visibly deteriorated. Nine days after being arrested, the young man died in his cell.

The *Anchorage Daily News* investigated the death of David Paul Selberg and published a series of articles showing how individual failures of initiative in a sluggish bureaucracy had deprived a desperately sick person of care that might have saved his life.

According to the newspaper articles, the day Selberg entered the jail, a prison doctor saw that he was "hallucinating wildly" and "physically agitated," running around his cell naked. Following procedure, the paper said, the doctor asked a court to order a psychiatric examination for Selberg "as soon as possible," meanwhile leaving him in an unpadded cell without blanket or mattress.

According to the newspaper story, the doctor, Thomas F. Green, doing prison rounds one week later, was surprised that Selberg had not yet been moved to the Psychiatric Institute. Observing him through the window in his cell door, without going inside, the doctor saw that Selberg's condition had not improved. Later, he received a report that Selberg had refused to eat or shower, sometimes had smeared his naked body with food and excrement, and had constantly thrown himself against the metal slab that was his bunk and beat his head and body against the walls. The guards said they had all noticed that the young man had steadily lost weight.

Noting that the psychiatric appointment was scheduled for just two days away, the paper reported, Green left the jail. Twenty-eight hours later, Selberg was dead.

The newspaper said the judge who acted on Green's written request to transfer Selberg claimed he had not understood that there was any emergency, and no one in the jail or court system had taken the initiative to get psychiatric help for Selberg, who apparently had been suffering from a reaction to drugs. No lawyer had been appointed.

The Health and Social Services commissioner later summed up the tragedy this way: "It looks like a total foul-up. . . . There was a major breakdown in just about every element of the system. If anyone along the way had made another decision, Selberg would still be alive."

The *Anchorage Daily News* investigation inspired the Health and

Social Services agency to conduct its own official investigation, cul-minating in the commissioner's firing of Dr. Green. The *Daily News* reacted with this editorial:

> Finally, the state has recognized its responsibility for the death of David Paul Selberg.
>
> The 23-year-old pipeline worker died in an Anchorage jail Jan. 7. In February a coroner's jury ruled that death was from natural causes. Then everyone involved chose to drop the sordid matter—to forget that a very sick man who had committed no crime had been locked in a 8 ½ by 7 ½ foot concrete cell for nine days and left to die.
>
> Earlier this month The Daily News published an exclusive series on Selberg's death after an extensive investigation. Soon after, the state Department of Health and Social Services (HSS) began to look into the case. . . .
>
> Since then, HSS Commissioner Frank Williamson has taken steps to assure that such a tragedy does not happen again.
>
> First, he abruptly cancelled the $125,000 a year contract of Dr. Thomas F. Green, the physician serving Anchorage jails for the past six years.
>
> Second, [he met with corrections personnel and third, appointed a committee to set procedures for police and court handling of disturbed citizens.] . . . The actions he has taken so far have been constructive, if overdue. . . .

Dr. Green sued for libel, saying that the editorial falsely implied that contrary to the coroner's decision, he was to blame for Selberg's death. The coroner had ruled that the death was due to "natural causes," both lungs collapsing "spontaneously" for unknown reasons. He found no criminal negligence and said he did not believe Selberg's mental disturbance contributed to his death.

Does the editorial blame Green? And if so, is that a protected opinion? Or a libelous fact statement?

Yes, the editorial approving of Green's dismissal does imply that Green was negligent. But this fault-finding should be protected as opinion.

Opinion indicators argue that the statement is judgmental, in the sense that it is neither right nor wrong but an assessment with which people might agree or disagree (Indicator 4, *Unverifiable*). In personal injury trials, for example, the jury votes on whether there seems to be evidence of negligence and whether an award of damages should be made in the end. In the *Green* case, the statement implying that Green was at fault is an assessment based on the facts of the prisoner's handling (Indicator 1, *Appraising*) that were reported in the news series. It is a position taken in an editorial (Indicator 10 *Cue from Context*), which does not purport to rest on undisclosed facts (Indicator 5, *Not Insinuating*). Although some people might, based on the facts, see Green as someone who went "by the book" and was turned into a scapegoat, the editorial writer saw him as negligent.

Green and the coroner both firmly shared the opposite view—that Green was not responsible—and their view was given ample coverage. The reporting of opposing viewpoints in news coverage, in itself, adds a measure of protection to an editorial position because the object of criticism may decide against suing if he or she feels that, on the whole, the treatment was fair. Also, the balancing remarks indirectly function as another opinion indicator, informing the reader—and the court—that more than one view exists.

The coroner's jurors had views, too, that were reported with the results of the inquest, which was limited to a ruling on whether to charge criminal negligence. The jurors answered "no," but in addition to the formal ruling, individual jurors amplified the public record with their own statements. One juror wrote, "I do strongly feel there was negligence" and that Green or his medical assistants should have followed up on his order for an examination. Another saw negligence in the "cursory medical examination" and the delay before Selberg's psychiatric appointment. A third felt the medical care had been "minimal" and couldn't understand why a physician would allow such delay when he had ordered treatment "as soon as possible."

Green responded that he had followed procedures governing inmate transfers and that reexamining Selberg in his cell the second week probably would have made no difference. "This is how I've rationalized it to myself," he told the newspaper. Green did concede that Selberg's lungs could have been weak and could have developed leaks from his falling, stumbling, and hitting the bunk in his cell.

The newspaper's initial summary judgment, based on the opinion privilege, was reversed by the Alaska Supreme Court.

The majority of the court which ordered the case to trial regarded the implication that Green caused Selberg's death as a fact statement, not an opinion. And as a fact statement, it must be false, the court stated, because it was directly contradicted by the public record, the coroner's report.

The editorial writers, the court said, "knew of substantial evidence that Dr. Green was not responsible for Selberg's death," or must have entertained serious doubts about whether he was actually at fault. It concluded that a libel trial would have to determine whether the newspaper had been reckless in endorsing the commissioner's view that

Green was negligent despite the coroner's exoneration of him. After all, the court noted, the commissioner was not a medical doctor. The actual malice standard would apply, the court agreed, because Green, as supervisor of medical care for all five Anchorage prisons, was ruled a public official.

There are two flaws in the court's thinking. First, the coroner's report was, of course, not a fact statement but merely an opinion, formally finding no criminal negligence in a death from "natural causes," supposedly unaffected by Selberg's mental condition. The coroner had one view, the editorial expressed another. Both were simply opinions.

The second error by the court was that it focused too technically on the specific cause of Selberg's death, which was unknown, and thus missed the point. The editorial writer placed responsibility for the death on Green for not expediting the transfer of the young man to a hospital or providing care and protection for Selberg in jail. The court's logic seemed to be that the "natural causes" verdict relieved Green of any responsibility. The commissioner of Health and Social Services and the newspaper disagreed with the court.

The newspaper did exactly what newspapers are supposed to do in reporting and taking a position on an important public issue. It should win the libel case, either with the court recognizing the editorial as protected opinion based on true facts, or excusing it as statements about a public official made without actual malice. The reversal of summary judgment is a disappointment in such a clear case of privileged reporting about a matter of public concern and protected criticism of the conduct of government, but I think it is only a temporary setback.

As the two dissenters on the Alaska Supreme Court lamented the reversal of summary judgment, the *Daily News* series on Selberg's death won commendations from the American Bar Association and the American Trial Lawyers Association for exposing shortcomings in the state's care of disturbed people and generating pressure for reform.

What lesson emerges from the *Green* editorial? Full reporting of true facts is the basis for a statement of opinion. The paper unfortunately was sued for commenting on an important public issue, but placed itself in a strong defensive position by reporting information from all the actors and observers including police and prison guards, the doctor and the judge empowered to transfer inmates, the coroner and his jurors, and the Health and Social Services commissioner. Drawing from the facts, the editorial writer took a position and, I'm sure, will ultimately be vindicated.

CARTOONS

Although there is no automatic dispensation for humor, editorial cartoons usually carry a number of clear indicators that they are intended as expressions of opinion. Several libel courts have stated that readers naturally expect opinion on public issues from the cartoonist (Indicators 9, 10, and 11: *Billboarding, Cue from Context,* and *Cue from Backdrop*) and further recognize it from the tone (Indicators 6, 7, and 8: *Exaggerated, Mudslinging,* and *Funny*). Some incidents that involved cartoons are discussed on pages 120–124.

The courts protected as privileged opinion Paul Conrad's comment about Los Angeles mayor Samuel W. Yorty in a *Los Angeles Times* cartoon. Yorty believed President Richard M. Nixon was considering him for the post of secretary of defense. The *Times* thought Yorty so unqualified for the appointment, only delusions of grandeur could have led him to expect it.

To be sure nobody mistook the cartoon for an insinuation of insanity, the paper ran a clarification, sort of (see p. 94). Yorty went ahead and sued, but he lost.

I've got to go now ... I've been appointed Secretary of Defense
and the Secret Service men are here!"

The *Boston Globe* picked on William Loeb, publisher of the *Manchester* (New Hampshire) *Union Leader.* He objected to a cartoon by Paul Szep and to a syndicated column by Robert Strout that called Loeb's newspaper a "daily drip of venom" and said he edited it "like a nineteenth-century yellow journal." The courts held that the cartoon and column were privileged statements of opinion.

THE THOUGHTS OF CHAIRMAN LOEB

The New York *Daily News* criticized two policemen for their handling of an arrest of a teacher. Acting on a parent's complaint about the teacher's manhandling of a boy in a scuffle, the police arrested the teacher at school, searched him, handcuffed him, and led him away. The *Daily News* considered the police action overly dramatic and unnecessarily humiliating. Alongside Frank Evers's cartoon, an editorial said of the police, "THEY FLUNK," because "maybe the book says

NOT TOO SMART

that's how you do it . . . but we give the police a big fat 'F' for dunder-headedness.'' Both cartoon and editorial were ruled privileged comment about the conduct of public officials.

To a Florida nursing home that was closed because of substandard conditions, *The Miami Herald* bid a wry farewell, first with Jim Morin's cartoon, later in court. The nursing home lost its suit over this privileged expression of opinion.

'DON'T WORRY, BOSS. WE CAN ALWAYS REOPEN IT AS A HAUNTED HOUSE FOR THE KIDDIES...'

Killington Ski Resort proposed a new use for treated sewage effluent: turn it into snow on the slopes. The resort greeted Timothy Newcomb's cartoon with a libel suit against the *Times Argus* of Barre-Montpelier, Vermont, that was pending as this book went to press. The court surely will protect the paper's comment on a public issue as privileged opinion.

"UH-OH — LOOKS LIKE THE SNOW-MAKING MACHINES ARE CLOGGED AGAIN"

FEATURES

Judgments in consumer reports, reviews, and feature stories are among those covered by the opinion privilege. As in other areas of journalism, derogatory remarks about businesses or individuals require particular care regardless of whether the comments come from the writer or a source who is being quoted.

Readers are conditioned to expect statements of opinion in consumer reports and reviews, and material in these categories therefore enjoys a bit more latitude than straight news articles. However, it is not automatically safe from claims of libel. Likewise, feature stories about people and how they live can also raise the specter of libel, so the interviewer should be on the alert.

The feature writer needs to meticulously report the facts, and then deliver conclusions based on those facts as delineated by opinion indicators. Balancing remarks from the person or organization being criticized should be included in consumer reports. Watch CBS's "60 Minutes" tackle a story on product safety. The key ingredients are that the subject is of legitimate public interest and researchers do thorough fact-gathering. Wherever possible they rely on public records and facts established in court proceedings. They are careful to include balancing comments from "the other side," not legally mandatory, but good journalistic practice. It is the fair thing to do and it tends to make a good impression on viewers and the courts.

Consumer Reports

In a "60 Minutes" segment entitled "Killer Wheels," CBS told viewers about the dangers of a kind of tire rim, used on most trucks and buses, that consists of two or three separate pieces which, in some cases, have become lethal spears when the tires have suddenly exploded.

After the segment was broadcast, CBS was sued by a firm called Redco Corporation; it had not been mentioned in the "60 Minutes" segment but it was a manufacturer of the so-called multipiece rims and it charged that its sales had suffered. Redco was entitled to sue, the court said, because viewers could reasonably conclude that the information referred to the company's multipiece rims, as well as those manufactured by the four companies that had been named. The other manufacturers did not sue.

Redco objected to the term "killer wheels," and the statement that "multipiece rims have killed more people than the Ford Pinto or the Firestone 500 Tire." It claimed that there had been fewer deaths per product from multipiece rims than from Pintos or Firestone 500 tires.

CBS had quoted several truck drivers who referred to the product as "killer wheels." Narrator Mike Wallace said the federal government knew of a hundred deaths and 400 injuries involving the multipiece rims, compared with twenty-seven dead in Pinto rear-end collisions and forty-one killed as a result of Firestone 500 tire malfunctions.

The court said that as long as CBS's statistics were accurate, the network could not be required to make a particular interpretation that Redco—or anyone else—might find more acceptable.

Statistics are facts from which conclusions ordinarily are drawn. In reporting statistics and their negative implications, write opinion indicators into the copy. For example, "The statistics indicate . . .," or "the numbers suggest . . .," makes clear that an interpretation based on the data is being offered (Indicators 1 and 9).

Redco also objected to a film segment showing a tire exploding and parts of a multipiece rim flying through the air and to the remarks of Ben Kelley of the Insurance Institute for Highway Safety and those of a lawyer who recently had won a big judgment for a client injured in a multipiece rim explosion.

The court found that the film represented a true event and the implication that the product was dangerous was an opinion based on demonstrated evidence. At one point in the "60 Minutes" segment, Kelley said, "The known deaths and injuries are just the tip of the iceberg." He said accidents often involve innocent bystanders and, "These 'freak accidents' aren't so freak."

Lawyer Gary Gardner, who had won a $250,000 judgment against Firestone, had argued to the jury that the companies had refused to stamp warnings on the rims for fear of having to undertake an expensive product recall and of prejudicing their position in the many pending suits against them. (Firestone actually had at one point considered stamping a warning on its rims.)

Redco said that Kelley was all wet about the known victims being "just the tip of the iceberg"; accidents were extremely rare. The court said it didn't know who was right, but felt Kelley was entitled to his opinion. By the use of the phrase "tip of the iceberg," Kelley had made clear that he was expressing an opinion not based on undisclosed facts, the court said; it was just a theory (Indicator 2). The court reasoned that no one had the facts because no one had seen more than the tip; the rest was unverifiable (Indicator 4).

Redco claimed Gardner was unmistakably implying that the manufacturers were unethical in putting profits before safety. The court said it was true that the manufacturers had refused to stamp warnings on the multipiece rims, adding that they had been asked to do so and two companies had even drafted proposed warnings, but there was no law requiring them to do so. The court found that this formed the factual basis for the lawyer's opinion, that they had refrained because of the costs. The court also found that the lawyer was speculating from no basis other than what had been disclosed (Indicator 2, *Theoretical*), and that while some might disagree with the industry's motives (Indicator 4, *Unverifiable*), Gardner was entitled to his opinion. In addition, the court interpreted Gardner's generalization as nondefamatory, saying it is widely understood that businesses always assess both risks and costs in arriving at product decisions.

Consumer reports perform a service but carry the risk of libel where negative assessments of products and services are published. Readers expect opinions in consumer reports, and so critical statements draw some protection simply from the context. Additional steps, such as reporting the facts that form the basis for opinions as well as using precise terms and occasionally raising flags to highlight interpretative remarks, such as "He says that in his opinion . . .," or "I believe . . .," also provide protection from libel suits. Out of fairness and a desire for a fuller picture, give the object of the criticism a chance to reply or comment.

Reviews: "An Apology Does Not Make a Hard Pear Soft"

The review is a classic example of the protected expression of opinion. Readers and the courts understand that reviews of food, music, drama, books, and films consist substantially of opinion, and therefore they are given a bit more elbowroom than straight news articles. Even so, they are not automatically safe from claims of libel. The risk of negative reviews, even the most lighthearted, is that an attack upon professional skills and reputation may bring a counterattack in court. Some subjects of negative reviews, such as restaurants, lose money after a bad review. But even with such a powerful incentive, few restaurants and public performers take reviewers to court.

The usual rules of libel apply to damaging statements of fact. If they are false and the plaintiff is ruled a public figure, the plaintiff would have to show actual malice—knowing or reckless falsity. If the plaintiff is ruled a private figure—and in some states either a restaurant owner or the restaurant itself might be ruled a private figure—then the negligence standard would govern, with the plaintiff having to show only a careless mistake of fact.

But most reviews are notoriously light on facts, and it is understood by the courts that reviews often do not include the objective facts that form the basis for the critic's conclusions because it is impossible to fully depict a meal or concert or film. Nevertheless, reviewers should try to show the readers some of the basis for their opinions and should state their opinions clearly as subjective views, highlighting their personal reactions and conclusions with as many opinion indicators as possible.

In one hallmark case at the turn of the century, three Iowa sisters who performed a vaudeville song and dance routine complained that they had been libeled by the *Des Moines Leader*. The reviewer had depicted the youngest of the sisters, Addie, as "the flower of the family, a capering monstrosity of 35," and he wrote that when Addie and her sisters Effie and Jessie sang a eulogy to themselves, "The mouths of their rancid features opened like caverns, and sounds like the wailing of damned souls issued therefrom."

In the Cherry Sisters' libel case the judge seconded the opinion of the reviewer, after demanding to see a bit of the performance himself right in the courtroom. "If ever there was a case justifying ridicule and sarcasm, this is it," the judge wrote. The Cherry Sisters' show, the judge found, was "not only childish, but ridiculous in the extreme."

Getting a judge to agree with the opinion of the reviewer in every case is not vital for gaining the protection of the opinion privilege. But it is important for the court to recognize the review as legitimately of public interest, as did the judge in the Cherry Sisters' suit, who wrote that the public nature of their show made it fair game for criticism because "the public should be informed about the character of the entertainment." And it is crucial that the court is able to distinguish the reviewer's expressions of opinion and not mistake them for potentially libelous fact.

Where possible, the reviewer's opinion should be couched as a conclusion based on fact. This hypothetical review condemns slow and inept service in a restaurant: "If you expect service here, you're likely to be disappointed with everything but the salad bar, where you serve yourself."

The review might explain that the party waited twenty-five minutes before anyone came to the table to offer menus and take drink orders. A prime rib arrived cold, with a baked potato instead of the promised "curlicue" potatoes. It took ten minutes to flag down the waiter. The young man cheerfully agreed to have the meat heated and the potato replaced, but when he returned with the plate, he had managed only the curlicues. The meat was colder than before. By now, the fork was gone, and so was the waiter, who did not come again until check time.

A review shored up with detailed facts may avert a libel suit. Even though the restaurant owner may threaten, his or her legal advisors are likely to urge restraint. They should perceive the case as unwinnable if true facts are recited as the basis for criticism (Indicator 1, *Appraising*) and may warn the client that suing may draw more attention to a critical review.

"Nothing to go cross-country for" was the verdict on the Aspen Inn of Columbus, Ohio, a restaurant organized around a ski motif. The reviewer and the publisher, the *Columbus Monthly,* won the resulting libel suit thanks to thorough factual reporting and the opinion privilege.

When the writer said that her fish "tasted like old ski boots," the judge felt sure that reasonable readers would understand she meant the fish was tough, not that the place was actually serving ski boots. The fanciful, exaggerated tone would earmark the expression as opinion (Indicator 6).

The Aspen Inn claimed it was libeled when the *Columbus Monthly* called it "a fast-food joint masquerading as a restaurant." That characterization was found to be a privileged opinion based on stated specifics. High entree prices were on a par with those of fine restaurants, the critic wrote, but many dishes relied on convenience ingredients more common to "fast food," such as bottled salad dressing, canned croutons, and Lawry's seasoned salt. Making matters worse, the manager of the restaurant said in response to a question from the food critic, "We downplay the desserts because we want the tables to turn. If you have a reputation for good desserts, people stay longer."

The Aspen Inn, with its plastic ski-swizzles for the drinks and a real chair lift chair in the lobby, failed, and so did its libel suit. The specificity and accuracy of the facts proved to be the key to protecting the opinion statements.

Judges rarely have trouble identifying reviewers' hyperbole as protected opinion and hypothesizing that "reasonable readers" will instantly do likewise. In one architectural review, "kitsch," "schlock," and "drek" were regarded by a court as merely an exaggerated expression of disapproval. In another protected architectural critique, a planned 150-story tower was called "an atrocious, ugly monstrosity" and "one of the silliest things anyone could inflict on New York or any other city." A court held that in a review of a how-to book on casino winning, it was the critic's privilege to denounce the "publication and sale of this book as the #1 fraud ever perpetrated upon the gambling reader." Still another privileged opinion concerned the talent of a television sports announcer in Boston, said to be "the only newscaster in town who is enrolled in a course for remedial speaking."

"Yellow death on duck" and "trout à la green plague" were the names that "Underground Gourmet" Richard H. Collin invented for dishes he tried at a restaurant near New Orleans, La Maison de Mashburn, which closed soon after his review. "Hyberbole" was how the judge dismissed the Maison de Mashburn's libel suit, relying on the opinion privilege.

As in the Aspen Inn review, facts, such as heavy use of paprika and sauces, were the true basis for the protected opinion, "t'ain't Creole, t'ain't Cajun, t'ain't French, t'ain't Country American, t'ain't good."

In a harsh review of a fashionable Chinese restaurant in New York, a critic wrote that he had found "more dough than meat" in one dish, green peppers "still frozen," fried rice "soaking" in oil, and pancakes "the thickness of a finger." Furthermore, Peking duck came in one dish instead of the traditional three. The review was published in an English translation of a French *Gault/Millau Guide to New York.*

Ruling that the review amounted to fair comment and was not libelous, an appeals court said that readers would readily understand all of these statements as hyperbole (Indicator 6, *Exaggerated*), except for the single fact statement about the one-dish presentation of Peking duck. The opinions were privileged and the fact statement, even if it were regarded as defamatory, was made without actual malice, the court said. Reversing the jury's $20,000 verdict, the court saw the review's "natural function" as conveying the critic's opinion. The appeals court said the trial judge should not have allowed the jury to decide in the first place, but should have recognized the review as protected opinion and dismissed the libel case himself.

Review cases make good law not only for food writers and theater critics, but for all the press. In deciding that reviews are protected opinions, the courts firmly reiterate the need for constitutional protection for statements of opinion and continually try to articulate ways of distinguishing opinion from fact. The court's decisions in review cases never fail to explain that critical comment based on truth is not libelous (Indicator 1, *Appraising*). They say that colorful figures of speech in and of themselves give notice to the audience that the writer is expressing opinion and not fact (Indicator 6, *Exaggerated*). They say people expect to find opinion in reviews (Indicator 10, *Cue from Context*) and they should be credited with understanding tone and usage beyond literal meaning. The courts' decisions remind people that there is value to society in allowing a free flow of opinion, even if some opinions are bizarre, unkind, unfair, or unpopular.

Interviews

Profiles and other features based on interviews need to be screened for unflattering remarks about a person or a business. Whether the remarks are negative opinions of sources or are characterizations by the writer, they should be included in the story if they add something journalistically, are solidly grounded in fact, and are presented with fairness.

An exploding car bomb shattered the right arm and left hand of a bomb squad sergeant trying to dismantle it and left him blind and partly deaf. The story of his adjustment to life as a disabled man was the focus of a feature entitled "Dangerous Occupations," broadcast on Denver's KMGH-TV (Channel 7) five o'clock evening news.

Sergeant Jack O. Burns's accident and its aftermath had changed his life, said reporter Marion Brewer on camera. In addition to his injuries, she said, "his wife and five children have deserted him since the accident." Brewer later said that she had adopted the term "deserted" from Burns, who had said that the breakup of his family was more traumatic than his injuries.

Yvonne C. Burns said that her nineteen-year marriage to Jack Burns had been "stormy" from the beginning, that she had contemplated divorce numerous times during the marriage, and that she had filed for divorce and had her husband move out of the family home two years before the explosion. Several months before the accident, the couple had reconciled and Burns had returned home. Afterward, she had tried to nurse him, she said, but the reconciliation failed. She testified that "living with a man with no sense of sight, no sense of hearing, no sense of feeling" had put a "strain" on their relationship. She said that Burns, always difficult to get along with, had plunged into a deep "depression" over his disabilities and had become impossible to live with. She eventually left and was granted an uncontested divorce. Desertion had not been the ground for the divorce.

The word *deserted* might have been intended as opinion in the sense that it was the husband's characterization of his former wife's motivation. During the one-week jury trial, Burns testified that he had confided to the reporter, "I know what it feels like to be deserted." The sergeant said that he was not critical of his family for acting as they did and that to him "deserted" meant "left alone." Brewer, a reporter with more than eight years of experience, testified that she had been aware of the couple's long-standing marital problems and had chosen to use the word *deserted* because she considered it to be a descriptive term without bad connotations, meaning simply "left."

The jury determined that Mrs. Burns and the four children who had joined her in the suit had been libeled and awarded them $175,-000. The presiding judge lowered the award to $45,000.

An appeals court gave station KMGH a brief reprieve when it reversed on the ground that "deserted" was protected opinion. However, the highest court, the Colorado Supreme Court, refused to hold that "deserted" was opinion, as the television station had argued, and ruled instead that it was a libelous statement of fact.

The court faulted the television reporter for failing to investigate Mrs. Burns's reasons for leaving—Brewer said she had not been able to contact Mrs. Burns—and for using the word *deserted,* which the court regarded not as an opinion, but as a libelous statement that implied undisclosed facts. It was, in the court's view, a term of derision that meant "to leave in the lurch." Failure to investigate amounted to reckless disregard of the truth, the court said, especially considering the story was one part of a feature series with long lead time that allowed the reporter plenty of time to gather the facts and contact Mrs. Burns.

Reckless disregard of the truth was the standard in the *Burns* case because under Colorado law the court recognized that the story concerned a matter of public interest and must be judged by the actual malice principle even though it involved private plaintiffs. In most other states, the *Burns* case would have been governed by a simple negligence standard, as a suit by private plaintiffs.

Three months after the televised interview with Burns, the *Denver Post* interviewed him for a news story about an impending eye operation and quoted another of his remarks about his former wife. Mrs. Burns sued the newspaper, but this time she lost.

The *Post* story by Sandra Dillard did not use the word *deserted,* but it conveyed the impression that Burns believed his wife had left him because of his injuries.

Dillard had been assigned to write a story for the next day's paper about Burns's proposed surgery. She read the clip file and telephoned Burns at St. Louis's Barnes Hospital. They discussed the operation, scheduled for the next morning, and his general condition. Burns told the reporter that he had "a new insight and perspective" on life since the explosion. "I'm not bitter about the accident," he was quoted as saying, "but the thing that tore me up was my wife divorcing me. She just couldn't live with a blind man." The newspaper also quoted Burns as saying he had "learned to tell the good and worthwhile people from people who just give you lip service."

The *Denver Post* won summary judgment on the ground that the remarks were protected statements of opinion. No jury considered the case. The summary judgment was upheld by the appeals court and was not reviewed by the Colorado Supreme Court. The appeals court said that Burns's assertions could not be proved or disproved (Indicator 4, *Unverifiable*) and were just expressions of his personal view. Dillard, the reporter, submitted an affidavit in the case in which she said she had not questioned Burns's credibility and had not been conscious of any possibility of injury to Mrs. Burns. The appeals court said it did not regard the remarks as insinuating (Indicator 5) or implying the existence of damaging unstated facts.

Several factors account for the diametrically opposed verdicts in the two suits. The television station lost its case partly because the court believed the reporter had accepted as apparent fact the police sergeant's conclusion that he had been deserted without obtaining sufficient detail from him or comment from others, including his former wife, to indicate that a controversy existed and that this interpretation was one of several possible viewpoints. The court found that nothing in the broadcast allowed the viewer to evaluate "deserted," and the way in which it was presented could have led the audience to suppose that the reporter had "inside knowledge" to support the charge.

The courts that considered the newspaper case believed the *Post* reporter, in quoting Burns directly, at some length, had provided the perspective that suggested opinion, even though she, too, had failed to interview Mrs. Burns. The results should not be taken to imply that the television reporter with much less space in which to tell her story was facing an impossible task. Flags announcing controversy and indicating opinion could have been hoisted in a sentence or two, or perhaps even in a few phrases. The problem, most likely, was that no one considered the damaging implication of the remarks.

The opposing results in these cases involving essentially the same issue, as it was handled by two reporters, underscore just how fragile the opinion privilege is, resting ultimately on subjective calls from the bench. One lawyer who was involved with the suits sees the KMGH-TV decision as "a pimple on the otherwise fair complexion of Colorado libel law," a sore that still "rankles" him.

Both the television story and the newspaper story could have been further girded against claims of libel and both pieces would have benefited journalistically. An interview with Mrs. Burns, her lawyer, or some other spokesperson would have been enlightening and would have probably signaled a controversy. Even the information that Mrs. Burns refused to comment might have provided insight, particularly if the reporter could have said why Mrs. Burns refused to comment. Looking into the records of the Burns's divorce would have at least provided the official ground for divorce and might have yielded other helpful clues.

Stories involving family disputes and wrecked marriages are libel-prone, but journalists can hardly avoid them any more than they should avoid any story. The solution is to recognize that a story is particularly sensitive and to handle it with utmost caution, striving as always to tell it in the most lively fashion.

REVIEWING THE OPINION PRIVILEGE

The opinion privilege, weak and flawed as it is, exempts negative expressions of opinion from the reach of libel judgments, and that makes it valuable. To qualify for the privilege, choose terms carefully, paying strict attention to their precise meaning and pejorative connotations. To play it safe, tone down provocative epithets.

Report opposing views whenever possible to give the subject of an attack a chance to defend himself or herself in the same story. Label opinion statements to show that they are intended as opinion. Don't be reluctant to add a preface to a source's quoted opinion to emphasize its subjectivity. The opinion issue, in all its subtle complexity, is one about which it may be useful and helpful to ask a lawyer's advice.

How the courts react to suits over critical comments about quality, personal ethics, or job performance varies from place to place. Judges are individuals; jurisdictions are liberal or conservative. No libel ruling springs from a vacuum, and opinion cases are no exception.

5

Privacy Law:
Embarrassment

P RIVACY law encompasses four different types of complaints. The
first and best known are called embarrassment complaints. They
arise from objections to publicity of embarrassing private information. Three other types of "privacy" complaints actually have nothing much to do with privacy: False light resembles libel in that the
plaintiff is complaining about some false aspect of publicity about him
or her; misappropriation is the use of names or portraits in advertising
without consent; intrusion is trespassing or taping without consent.

Embarrassment suits pit the right to publish the truth against the
individual's right to be left alone, and every embarrassment suit poses
the same question: Was this newsworthy?

CONFLICT BETWEEN RIGHT OF PRIVACY
AND PUBLIC INTEREST

Probably no two people have identical news judgment. For newspeople, the basic question is usually, "Is this interesting?" But when the
issue of a person's privacy is at stake, the legal question becomes, "Is
the publication of this material in the public interest and does the
public interest in the material outweigh the private person's right to

remain out of the public eye?" Privacy complaints about embarrassing true publicity involve weighing private versus public rights to information.

In the film *Absence of Malice*, publishing the name of a young woman with an unwanted pregnancy in a crime story in which she was a minor figure was probably an instance where public interest did not outweigh private interest. On the other hand, it was in the public interest to publish the fact that Thomas F. Eagleton, the Missouri senator being considered for the vice presidency in 1972, had previously undergone shock therapy. The information was intimate but related to the public's appraisal of his fitness for office.

Even though news may at times be embarrassing to figures in the public eye, legitimate news coverage is protected as an exercise of free speech even when it offends some readers. Those who claim that their privacy was invaded by the publication of true but private facts about them without their consent must prove that there was no legitimate public interest in the information. That is an uphill fight because "newsworthiness" is such a broad concept in the law and there is such a strong presumption in favor of the truthful publication of information. For that reason, successful "embarrassment" cases are rare and extreme. The ones described in this chapter are typical—they're not the exception, but the rule. Their common denominator is vulgarity or callousness toward a subject whose activities are only marginally in the public interest.

In the dominant view of the courts, the public interest is served by all sorts of information. "Newsworthy" facts include not just descriptions of events and information related to politics, economics, and social policy, but also facts that show how people live and work and think. Entertaining vignettes, interesting profiles of ordinary as well as extraordinary people, and true-life pictures of spectators and passersby as well as of those at the center of a main event—all are "newsworthy." It is not the role of courts to sit as censors or to impose their own views about what should interest the public. So they give rather wide berth to the concept of a free press serving diverse audiences with a range of tastes and styles.

Information about public figures—whether voluntary or involuntary public figures—is newsworthy in the eyes of the courts when it relates to particular events in which they have assumed a role and even, within reason, when it extends beyond those events to details about their daily habits and past experiences. Private people's lives are less open for scrutiny, but even their secrets may be newsworthy and reportable by virtue of their close connection to a significant public issue.

Community mores define the limits of what is permissible and draw the line where publicity stops being informational and starts being just sensational, and where newsgathering turns into indecent prying for its own sake. This means that newspapers in a conservative locale might be found guilty of indecency in their news reporting, although the same reporting would be tolerated or even expected in a liberal community. Nevertheless, even in conservative regions, true reporting will not be judged to violate privacy rights unless it is unredeemably offensive and not even remotely in the public interest.

The weights that affect the balance of public and private information are cast from two ingredients: the nature of the information that was published and the justification for publishing. There are four key questions posed by all "embarrassment" complaints:

1. Is the information private?
2. Is it intimate?
3. Is it newsworthy?
4. Is it highly offensive?

The following cases show how all four principles are weighed when the interest of personal privacy clashes with journalists' judgments of what makes news.

IS THE INFORMATION PRIVATE?

Hero's Sexual Preference Publicized

A man who became a national celebrity overnight by preventing the shooting of President Gerald R. Ford lost his privacy claim against a newspaper that reported he was gay.

After Oliver "Bill" Sipple, a husky former marine, lunged at Sara Jane Moore to deflect her revolver from the presidential party as it trooped past a crowd in downtown San Francisco on September 22, 1975, Sipple's name was mentioned in radio, television, and newspaper reports around the country. Two days later, Herb Caen strongly implied in his column in the *San Francisco Chronicle* that the unemployed veteran was gay. Caen wrote that on the evening of the attempted assassination, Sipple "was the center of midnight attention at the Red Lantern, a Golden Gate Avenue bar he favors [in a well-known gay section]. The Rev. Ray Broshears, head of Helping Hand, and Gay Politico, Harvey Milk, who claim to be among Sipple's close friends, describe themselves as 'proud—maybe this will help break the stereotype.' Sipple is one of the workers in Milk's campaign for Supervisor."

After Caen's column appeared, news reports throughout the United States referred to Sipple as gay. And when the White House still had not telephoned to thank Sipple three days after the attempted assassination, the *Los Angeles Times* quoted Harvey Milk, the leading spokesman for the city's large gay population, as saying that it was more than an oversight; Ford was shunning Sipple because he was gay. Milk, later elected to the board of supervisors (the equivalent of city council), was murdered in city hall July 15, 1979, by former supervisor Daniel James White, who said he had committed the killing while "high on junk food." White committed suicide in 1985.

Sipple sued the *Chronicle* for giving unwarranted publicity to what he said was a private, embarrassing fact. The California courts, however, ruled that Sipple's sexual orientation was not a private fact since he had done nothing to hide it, and that the publicity was legitimate news.

A vital element of a privacy claim was missing. Sipple's sexual preference had not been "private information," the court said, but was "already in the public domain." Sipple testified that he had made no secret of his sexual orientation. He acknowledged that he frequented San Francisco's gay Tenderloin and Castro neighborhoods, and he said his friendship with Harvey Milk had been publicized in such gay magazines as *Data Boy, Pacific Coast Times,* and *Male Express.* He also admitted that he had been a member of the Court of the Crowned Emperor of gay San Francisco, and that he had marched in gay parades before hundreds of people in New York, Dallas, Houston, San Diego, Los Angeles, and San Francisco long before he made news by foiling President Ford's would-be assassin.

Besides finding that Sipple's gay preference was a public fact rather than a private one, the court recognized that the disclosure also was protected by the "broad privilege for truthful publication of newsworthy matters." It said the reporting was legitimate coverage of an important public incident, and not so offensive as to shock the community's notions of decency.

A Campus Leader Sues

Toni Ann Diaz was the first woman ever elected student body president of the College of Alameda, a two-year California state community college in the Bay area. But she was not what she appeared to be. About six months into her presidency, somebody told the *Oakland Tribune* that she was a transsexual, a man who had undergone a surgical sex change.

Diaz had gone to great lengths to keep her secret, she said later, and when she read about it in the *Tribune's* education column, she was "devastated." In her privacy suit, she told the court that the publicity had caused her to withdraw from people, lose sleep, suffer memory lapses and nightmares, and eventually to need psychotherapy. Previously, she testified, only her family had known about her sex change. Before enrolling at Alameda she had changed her name on her high school records and on her driver's license from Antonio to Toni Ann, and had even tried to change her birth records in Puerto Rico.

Diaz had recently been in the news because of a dispute in which she accused officials of the college of improperly withdrawing money from a student fund by affixing her signature to checks with a rubber stamp. The *Oakland Tribune* and the campus paper covered the dispute.

Sidney Jones, who wrote the *Tribune's* education column, got a tip that for most of her life, Toni Ann Diaz had been a man.

Jones testified later that he thought this had the makings of a story, but he wasn't going to go with it until he could check it out. His city editor at the *Tribune,* Richard Paoli, turned up some Oakland Police Department records showing that a man named Antonio Diaz had been arrested a few years earlier for soliciting an undercover policeman, a misdemeanor charge. Jones said his source told him that Toni Ann and Antonio were the same person. That cinched it for him and he broke the news in his column:

> The students at the College of Alameda will be surprised to learn their student body president, Toni Diaz, is no lady, but is in fact a man whose real name is Antonio.
>
> Now I realize that in these times such a matter is no big deal, but I suspect his female classmates in P.E. 97 may wish to make other showering arrangements.

Diaz acknowledged in a California state court that she had undergone an operation to change her gender several years earlier at the

Stanford University Gender Dysphoria Clinic. And she detailed the steps she had taken to keep her sex change secret.

A jury found that Diaz's privacy had indeed been invaded and awarded her $775,000, which included $250,000 to compensate for her injury and $525,000 punitive damages ($25,000 of which was assessed against the writer personally) to punish the *Tribune* for humiliating her.

Jones and the *Tribune* appealed.

The California Court of Appeal agreed that the sex change had been private information and it buttressed its finding partly on the state's constitutional provision ensuring the right to live without unwarranted publicity. The appeals court also cited the steps Diaz had taken to conceal her past life and the fact that the information on the sex change was not contained in any public records. Her medical history, the court said, was a confidential, nonpublic record. The court accepted the *Tribune*'s contention that the police record was public. But it pointed out that there was nothing in the public record to link Antonio Diaz with Toni Ann Diaz.

Considering the extent to which Diaz voluntarily had put herself in a position of notoriety, the court concluded that while the student body presidency made her a public figure for limited purposes in a "concededly small arena," inquiry into her sexual identity was not justified. Her sexual identity was not integral to her leadership position. The court rejected the argument that the arrest record reflected on her fitness for office or honesty and ridiculed what it called the *Tribune*'s hollow "pretense" of trying to defend the column as an attempt to enlighten readers about "the changing roles of women in society." Jones himself had conceded in court that he had not intended the column as sweeping social commentary but had directed the article at the college students and their president.

The court condemned the column's treatment of Diaz as "highly offensive" and said it gave unwarranted publicity to true but intimate facts. The court recognized that news judgment involves a "sliding scale of competing interests"—a person's right to privacy against the public's right to know. But, it said, embarrassing details had been revealed, resulting in psychological damage without any compensating social value.

The court found evidence of reckless disregard in the writer's "flip" style, and said he must have known Diaz would suffer. Jones had not tried to get comment from Diaz, and the court said this failing demonstrated further insensitivity toward her and indifference to her injury. The appeals court found the jury's $775,000 verdict steep, but "not excessive." Still, it overturned the judgment and ordered another trial because it said the judge's instructions to the jury were flawed and should have assigned Diaz the burden of proving that the story was not newsworthy.

Five years after bringing the suit, Diaz accepted a sum "in the low six figures, under $200,000" to drop the case, according to a director of the insurance company that negotiated the settlement.

The Sipple and Diaz stories both concerned the sensitive subject of sex. Yet only the Diaz publicity was judged to be an invasion of privacy. Why: newsworthiness. Unlike Diaz, Sipple was a national news figure who was open about his sexual preference. Sipple really had already "consented" to being publicly identified as gay. His embarrassment suit may have surprised friends who had freely given interviews about him, since he had not indicated such shyness before and had even sought recognition as a gay activist.

Even if Sipple had been secretive, the magnitude of the event he was involved in would seem to ensure that the press would be protected in straightforwardly reporting personal details, including his sexual preference. Does his sexual preference have anything to do with the story of saving the president? No, it's no more "relevant" than if he were married or divorced or white or black, and not every journalist would choose to report it. Because of his sudden prominence, however, the law would support an editorial decision to report virtually any detail about him.

By contrast, I find it painfully difficult to argue the newsworthiness of the Diaz story as published. Diaz had no national prominence. She was only a student leader involved in a campus squabble. She had managed to hide her sex change before being unmasked by a cruel tipster and a crude columnist, and this made the infringement greater than with Sipple, who had not treated his sexual preference as a private matter. The newsworthiness justification seems weaker than with Sipple, and the tone of the Diaz column belied a belief in its social importance or relevance to the main story, displaying instead a naked intention of belittling Diaz.

When deciding whether or not to run a story with embarrassing personal details, make sure first that they're true. Then consider the relevance of the particular information to the core of the story and the amount of prominence the subject enjoys in the community. If you can't get the subject to discuss the information with you, you and your editors will want to discuss and clearly identify the legitimate social interest in disclosure—your newsworthiness judgment—before you publish.

IS THE INFORMATION INTIMATE?

Many years ago *Time* magazine ran the following item in a section labeled "Medicine":

STARVING GLUTTON

One night last week pretty Mrs. Dorothy Barber of Kansas City grabbed a candy bar, packed up some clothes, and walked to General Hospital. "I want to stay here," she said between bites. "I want to eat all the time. I can finish a normal meal and be back in the kitchen in ten minutes, eating again."

Dr. R. K. Simpson immediately packed her off to a ward, ordered a big meal from the hospital kitchen while he questioned Mrs. Barber. He found that although she had eaten enough in the last year to feed a family of ten, she had lost 25 pounds. After a preliminary examination Dr. Simpson thought that Mrs. Barber's pancreas might be functioning abnormally, that it might be burning up too much sugar in her blood and somehow causing an excessive flow of digestive juices, which sharpened her appetite.

While he made painstaking laboratory tests and discussed the advisability of a rare operation, Mrs. Barber lay in bed and ate.

A picture of the young, dark-eyed brunette sitting up in her hospital bed, a blanket pulled up to her chest, accompanied the brief report. The caption read, "Insatiable-eater Barber, She eats for ten." What *Time* magazine didn't know was that she had not given consent for either the interview or the photograph, obtained by a United Press reporter and photographer. Barber testified that she had tried to get the journalists to leave her alone, but that after barging into her hospital room, one of them had taken her picture while the other had tried to persuade her to answer questions.

Does the picture invade privacy? Yes. In a hospital room, as in one's own room at home, a patient is entitled to expect privacy, and a photograph cannot be published without permission. Oral permission may be sufficient, but written permission is strongly advised since that form of consent is the easiest to prove.

Does the story invade privacy? Yes. The pancreatic disorder arguably is of interest to the public, but Barber's identity was not news, the court ruled, and should not have been disclosed without her permission. Courts usually construe consent to an interview or a photograph as authorization to identify the person.

Medical records and, in general, medical information about private people should be treated as confidential. This is not to say that special circumstances mightn't militate to publishing a medical story about a private person without consent, but what may be needed later in court is a cogent explanation of why both the condition and the subject's identity were newsworthy. Whether the means of obtaining them were acceptable or boorish will probably count, too. Medical information taken from public records and published is more apt to be protected by the courts than secrets snatched or wormed out of unwitting victims. But in either case, medical histories of private people are so inherently confidential that even those personal medical facts that are taken from public records should not be published without a reasoned judgment about what makes them newsworthy.

Barber won on both counts. The court ruled that intrusive means had been used to obtain a story that had no news value, and that her privacy had been invaded. Unlike her disease, her name had no news value, in the court's mind, and the journalists' strong-arm tactics employed on a defenseless captive in a hospital bed were not a plus. She won compensatory damages but no punitive damages because the court found that *Time* had assumed she had consented and had had no intention of offending her.

Forced Sterilization of Teenager in County Home

Three teenage girls at a 144-bed Jasper County, Iowa, home for troubled youths and the mentally ill were coerced into submitting to sterilization operations; two residents were scalded to death in bathtub accidents; two others died and another was permanently injured in a highway accident on Interstate 80 as they were being driven to help round up stray cattle owned by a former state senator; some patients were overmedicated through "slipshod" and haphazard drug-dispensing; and the administrator and head nurse quit when the health department announced that it was going to revoke the home's custodial and nursing licenses, citing a long list of health, safety, and management violations. Against this backdrop, Margaret Engel, a reporter for the *Des Moines Register*, spent two weeks digging into the public records on the home, covering public hearings, and interviewing thirty-eight people. Here is part of what she wrote:

> Newton, Iowa.— . . . The Register also learned that an 18-year-old woman sterilized in 1970 was not retarded or mentally disabled, but an "impulsive, hair-triggered young girl," in the words of Dr. Roy C. Sloan, the home's psychiatrist.
>
> He said the decision to sterilize the resident, Robin Woody, was made by her parents and himself. He does not recall whether Woody agreed to the operation, but a woman who was a nurse at the home at the time said "she didn't want it at all."

> *FORCED STERILIZATION*
>
> "For two to three weeks when I came to work she was crying," said Collene Blakely of Newton. "She was told the only way she could be dismissed from the home is if she would agree to be sterilized."
>
> Dr. Sloan denied that, saying, "We don't think in terms of punishment. That child—she was a young girl—was a very explosive, impulsive young girl largely without controls over her aggressive and, at times, irrational behavior."
>
> He said she was sterilized because "she would be a very questionable risk as far as having and rearing a baby. The people who hold on that way are those who move on to child abuse."
>
> Robin's mother, Mrs. Gladys Woody of Newton, said she agreed with the decision then and now. She would not discuss the matter further. . . .

Robin Woody Howard sued Engel and the *Des Moines Register* charging that her privacy had been invaded. A jury disagreed, and so did the Iowa Supreme Court, which functions as the state's highest appeals court. The revelation of her deeply personal secret without her consent caused her anguish, she told the court. She said she was never contacted, even though she lived in Des Moines and her parents knew her address. The *Register* said it had not known how to find her and argued that the story did not invade her privacy because it was a newsworthy report based on a public record.

The public record in this case consisted of a file in the office of Governor Robert D. Ray concerning conditions at the Jasper County home. It included a letter from a columnist for a small daily newspaper with a statement from a former nurse at the home, which described Robin Woody Howard's treatment, and a county audit indicating that surgery of an unspecified type had been performed on Howard.

The file, which the newspaper had obtained through a request to the governor from a former press secretary who had joined the staff of the *Register*, also contained information on two other sterilizations that took place at about the same time as Howard's. But the *Register* did not report the two other names because the documentation in those cases was less definitive.

The Iowa Supreme Court agreed that the governor's file containing the Howard medical information was a public record, over a dissent that medical data are "personal and sensitive" information intended to remain private under the state records law that exempts "medical records" from disclosure. Despite the unusually sensitive nature of the information, the court declared it had become a public record because it had been gathered in the course of an official investigation of the public home and had been placed in a public file maintained in a government office.

Even if Howard's surgical history had been ruled a nonpublic record, the determinative question would still have been whether the story was newsworthy. Given that the *Register* could have run the story without identifying her, what newsworthy purpose was served by publishing her name?

Human interest and impact made her name newsworthy, the court said.

The use of her name "offered a personalized frame of reference to which the reader could relate, fostering perception and understanding." Moreover, said the court, it lent specificity and credibility to the report at a time when it was important to separate fact from rumor. Not a spreading of gossip for its own sake, the *Register's* reference to Woody pinpointed an actual instance of mistreatment of a resident in a home whose mismanagement and mistreatment of people were of legitimate public concern.

The United States Supreme Court has recognized a constitutional right of personal privacy and a right to be protected from unjustified invasions, the Iowa court said, but the public needs information to help it cope with public issues and the "exigencies of the period." Sometimes important information legitimately concerns the public even though it contains embarrassing personal facts. Here, the court found, investigative journalists had exposed a grave social problem in a pattern of abuses at a public institution. The chronicling of Howard's treatment as a concrete example of the problem was not for the purpose of "morbid and sensational prying," the court said, but to attract attention and deepen public understanding.

The case of Robin Woody Howard exemplifies a liberal and broad-reaching view of what is newsworthy. Everyone would agree that it is important to educate the public about mistreatment of people in institutions, but some people would differ on whether to give away Robin's medical secret without her permission. Some journalists would withhold Robin's name unless she were contacted and agreed to publication. Others would disguise her identity and include a note to the reader that the fiction was to protect her privacy. The *Des Moines Register* made an editorial judgment to name her, to add strength and impact, and the court endorsed that judgment.

The ruling in favor of the *Register* provides an excellent precedent for editorial freedom, but other courts might decide differently. When treating an important public interest story that entails embarrassing intimate facts about private people whose consent cannot be obtained, weigh the journalistic costs of omitting their names against the justification for naming them and the risk that they will sue. A lawyer's advice may help clarify the issues, but the answers—lawyers', journalists', and courts'—are necessarily subjective. They reflect our concept of the "essential dignity and worth of every human being," as the late Supreme Court Justice Potter Stewart wrote in *Rosenblatt* v. *Baer*, "a concept at the root of any decent system of ordered liberty."

IS THE INFORMATION NEWSWORTHY?

The front page photograph in the Friday, October 13, 1961, edition of the *Cullman* (Alabama) *Times Democrat* showing a chicken farmer's wife passing an air jet as she left the funhouse at the county fair was no fun for the newspaper. The woman brought a privacy suit and the newspaper lost. Years later, Robert Bryan, the editor and publisher of the paper, which is now called the *Cullman Times*, still argues that her face was turned away from the camera at such an angle that she was unidentifiable. However, the judge and jury found that her children's faces were clearly visible and through them she was identified.

Journalists should look critically at photographs that reveal more flesh than people ordinarily display in public and should decide, before publishing, what makes them newsworthy. Both hard news and feature photographs may be considered legitimately of public interest, but when a photograph that seems likely to be embarrassing is in every sense optional for the newspaper, like that of the woman with her skirt flying over her head, consider choosing another photograph or giving anonymity to the person with cropping or printing techniques that eliminate the identifying features.

Bryan said he printed the photograph in the spirit of fun. "I gave a

ALL'S FAIR IN FAIR FUN.

speed graphic camera to an editor and sent him to the county fair. I said, 'Get some pictures that show people having fun.' When he came back, it seemed like all he'd done was to sit down outside the funhouse and take pictures of ladies' dresses being blown by the air jet. I looked at his pictures, and I picked this one. I didn't have any evil in my heart. I didn't recognize the lady and I didn't imagine anybody else would, either."

Bryan said the woman telephoned the paper at least twice to complain, and he turned her call over to the man who took the picture, who didn't sympathize. "I think now that if I'd talked with her and apologized, that would have been the end of it. But she got no satisfaction and I guess her relatives teased her or something and made her mad. Just before the time ran out, she got a lawyer and sued."

This is another example of how a quick, courteous response to a complaint might well have headed off a lawsuit.

"Where Are They Now?" Profile Provokes a Failed Genius

The unfulfilled promise of a famous child genius, who became a failure, a boy star who grew to hate his accomplishments and to crave privacy: This was the subject of a *New Yorker* magazine profile some twenty years after William James Sidis had dropped out of the limelight. It was called, "Where Are They Now? April Fool!"

At the age of one, William James Sidis, who had been named for the philosopher and family friend, William James, could read and type English and French; at age five, he wrote a treatise on anatomy. At the age of eleven, wearing black velvet knickers and speaking so softly it was a strain to hear, Sidis amazed an audience of about a hundred professors and advanced students of mathematics at Harvard College with a lecture on four-dimensional bodies, in which he presented an original speculative theory of relationships. His performance made the front pages of newspapers across the country.

Sidis's father, a Kiev-born psychologist, had experimented with hypnotizing the boy to speed the learning process. His grasp of intellectual problems was astounding, but he never enjoyed childhood pastimes or had any concept of fun or play. He scorned girls and vowed never to marry. He tore through a seven-year course in Brookline, Massachusetts, public school in six months and quickly was bored. He enrolled in Tufts College in Medford at the age of ten. The next year he was working on the writing of his own Latin and Greek grammars and Harvard accepted him as a special student. He graduated from Harvard College at the age of sixteen.

The pressure and public attention during his college years had been unbearable. Sidis had suffered a breakdown and left school for a term to recuperate at his father's Brookline psychotherapeutic institute. He returned shyer, more withdrawn, and suspicious of people.

He went on to Harvard Law School, but after three years left to teach math at Rice Institute (now Rice University) in Houston. He did not stay long at Rice, and from there he drifted from city to city, taking clerical jobs where the work was routine and didn't require much thinking. Everywhere he went, his reputation as a whiz kid followed, and with it the pressures. He was a loner. A former landlord at 112

West 119th Street in New York City, once recalled, "He has a kind of chronic bitterness, like a lot of people you see living in furnished rooms."

At one point in the 3,650-word *New Yorker* profile of Sidis, Jared L. Manley wrote:

> William James Sidis lives today, at the age of 39, in a hall bedroom of Boston's shabby south end. For a picture of him and his activities, this record is indebted to a young woman who succeeded in interviewing him there. She found him in a small room papered with a design of huge, pinkish flowers, considerably discolored. There was a large, untidy bed and an enormous wardrobe trunk, standing half open. A map of the United States hung on the wall. On a table beside the door was a pack of streetcar transfers neatly held together with an elastic.

The *New Yorker* reported that Sidis had a clerical job which required no math prowess but did allow him to perfect his lightning-fast touch on the adding machine. "He said that he never stays in one office long because his employers or fellow-workers soon find out that he is the famous boy wonder and he can't tolerate a position after that," the *New Yorker* reported. " 'The very sight of a mathematical formula makes me ill,' he said. 'All I want to do is run an adding machine, but they won't let me alone.' "

The *New Yorker* described Sidis as fair-haired and blue-eyed with a reddish mustache, and said he nodded his head jerkily to emphasize his points. According to the magazine he seemed to have two hobbies. He had amassed and catalogued thousands of streetcar and bus transfers and had paid a "vanity press" in Philadelphia to publish his book, *Notes on the Collection of Transfers*, inexplicably using the pen-name "Frank Folupa."

His other hobby was the lore of the Okamakammessett Indians, a tribe about which nothing appears in the principal encyclopedias of American Indians and which, acquaintances say, he may have invented. Sidis had half a dozen students interested in the Okamakammessetts; they would meet in his bedroom every two weeks and sit on the floor listening to him recite their history and poetry and even sing their songs.

The *New Yorker* reported that Sidis's speech was punctuated by an intermittent little gasping laugh, and that he showed "a certain childlike charm," but very little sign of his former brilliance. When reminded of the mathematicians' predictions of his future greatness, the magazine said, Sidis replied with a grin, " 'It's strange, but, you know, I was born on April Fools' Day.' "

When the profile appeared in the *New Yorker*, Sidis sued, claiming his privacy had been invaded by the publication of true, embarrassing facts. He had not consented to an interview or known that a young woman who came to his house had been on a mission for the *New Yorker*. Sidis briefed his own case, according to *The New York Times*, carrying it all the way through the federal courts in New York. He lost.

Was his profile newsworthy? And was it newsworthy enough to outweigh his passion for privacy?

There were "great reader interest" and much "popular news interest" in the uncommon achievements and personality of this former celebrity who had slipped from the public eye, the court said. Community mores determine what is a legitimate subject for inquiry, and, said the federal appeals court in New York that reviewed Sidis's complaint, "Regrettably or not, the misfortunes and frailties of neighbors and 'public figures' are subjects of considerable interest and discussion to the rest of the population."

Conceding that Sidis could not be equated with a politician or statesman, the judge recognized that the person who as a boy had so fascinated newspaper readers remained just as intriguing to them years later as an adult.

The tone of the profile was not unsympathetic, but it made Sidis out to be a pathetic figure. Still, the court found the information was not so intimate as to be highly offensive and it had a legitimate purpose, to tell people what Sidis had become. "Everyone will agree that at some point the public interest in obtaining information becomes dominant over the individual's desire for privacy," the judge wrote, and for him the *New Yorker* profile had reached that point.

This case was tried nearly fifty years ago. Although the Supreme Court did not review it, it is frequently cited today as an example of how broadly the concept of newsworthiness has been interpreted. It remains important, too, for its emphasis on whether the subject matter serves a legitimate public curiosity and does so without deeply intruding into intimate facts. Still Sidis's efforts to shun publicity lend such poignancy to his complaint that another court in a similar situation might decide differently.

One of the lawyers who represented the *New Yorker*, Harriet F. Pilpel, said that while she "had no misgivings about the overwhelming policy considerations" in the case, she nevertheless had been touched by Sidis. "We felt strongly that the privacy issue posed a threat of censorship. But I felt sorry for Mr. Sidis. He had tried very hard not to become a public person. He came to my office once after the case. He was a nice, sort of shy man. I felt sorry for him."

One night not long after the case had been decided, William James Sidis was found in a coma in his room in a Brookline boarding house. After lying unconscious for four days in a hospital, he died on July 17, 1944. He was forty-six, unemployed, and apparently destitute.

IS THE INFORMATION HIGHLY OFFENSIVE?

Commemorative Edition Reports Old Conviction

"Page from Our Past" was a popular feature of the *Iberville South,* a 4,000-circulation weekly published in Plaquemine, Louisiana, in the bayou country fifteen miles south of Baton Rouge. Shortly after Gary J. Hebert (pronounced Eh-BEAR) had bought the newspaper, one of the oldest in the country, and had become its editor and publisher, he had begun randomly selecting front pages from the past and reproducing them in their original form inside the paper. Not a week went by without a "Page from Our Past."

"It was a tremendous hit with our readers," Hebert said. "I had all these original, bound volumes of a newspaper that went back a whole century into the life of our parish. I was excited."

Not everybody was as excited as Hebert of being reminded of the past. After about a year of "Page from Our Past," a man named E. R. Roshto complained, came right into the office and wanted to see the editor. Roshto and his brothers, Carlysle and Alfred, had been caught rustling a heifer twenty years back. Now the week's commemorative page was bringing it all up again, carrying the court report of their trial as the lead story, headlined "Cattle Stealing Case Goes Into Fifth Day In Court Here Today." The Roshtos—then aged eighteen, twenty, and thirty, had been accused of stealing, shooting, and butchering a heifer belonging to one Calvin Cook of Bayou Sorrel. The meat had been found in their homes, but they said they had bought it. The trial was a big event in Plaquemine, according to the *Iberville South:*

> A packed district courtroom watched the trial all week. Old timers say there is more public interest in the case than anything that has been tried here in many years.
>
> All available room was taken in the courtroom and in the balconies and there was no more standing room even in the outer hall. Judge C. Iris Dupont cleared the aisles of those standing because of the noise which interfered with the progress of the trial.
>
> At 8 a.m. this morning persons were streaming in to get a seat in the courtroom so they could witness the trial when court re-convened at 10

a.m. Some don't leave their seats for lunch but have a sandwich brought up to them.

The Roshto brothers were convicted and served a year in jail and a year on probation before being pardoned. But that was long past, now they lived respectably, and didn't want people to be reminded with a "Page from Our Past."

That's what Roshto told somebody in the newspaper office the day he went in to complain. He later told the court that he had driven thirty miles, all the way from Denham Springs, to speak with the editor, and that somebody who called himself the "editor" sat down and talked. To this day Hebert says he can't figure out who that person could have been; he's the only "editor" the newspaper's got, and he wasn't anywhere around the office that day. He says he can't remember where he'd gone, but his daughter-in-law says she believes he was on vacation.

Hebert testified that when he got back to the paper, nobody mentioned Roshto or his complaint. But whoever it was who visited with Roshto that day set things right, for the time being, the cattle farmer told the court. He said he had been assured that no future commemorative issues would mention the scrape the boys had had. He said the "editor" had apologized and had promised it wouldn't happen again.

When it did happen again four years later, the Roshtos sued. Again the story on the Roshtos was the lead of the quarter-century old front page. This time the headline read, "Brothers Facing Prison On Cattle Theft Charge, Are Denied New Trial." Hebert testified that while he was away at a newspaper convention in Houston, a staff member had chosen the page at random.

In their lawsuit, the Roshtos contended that their old criminal conviction was not newsworthy, and that the renewed publicity was an invasion of their privacy. The Louisiana Supreme Court found, however, that inadvertently publishing this public record information as incidental contents of an historic page, without any attempt to highlight it or intention of offending, was not an invasion of the brothers' privacy. Failing to take precautions against the Roshtos' embarrassment was "arguably insensitive or careless," the court said, but such a lapse was not enough to create a privacy case based on an embarrassing true report of public record. Besides, the court said, reckless disregard was utterly lacking, where no one had "deliberately pointed the finger of blame" at the Roshtos. Hebert contended that he had never met them, and there was no evidence that he had any malice toward them.

The fact that the convictions and sentence were public record was important, but the court made clear that it did not endorse blanket protection for all facts from public records without regard to their age, social value, or the publisher's motive. The privilege of publishing from public records can be lost through abuse where there is malice or reckless disregard for the offensiveness of the information, the court said.

The Roshto case ended as a victory for free speech in Louisiana's highest court six years after it began, but it had been a rocky road. The trial court first threw the case out because it regarded truth as an absolute defense. Then the tables turned and the brothers won on appeal. The appeal court pointed out that in privacy, as opposed to libel, publication of true but embarrassing information may be punishable if it's not newsworthy. It went on to say that the Roshto story had "absolutely no value as a newsworthy item," and set damages at $35,000 for each of the three brothers. The Heberts' paper had no libel insurance at the time.

The day of argument before the state supreme court, the chief justice opened with a question directed at the Roshtos' lawyer: "What do you suggest we do with our history?"

"I knew right then that we had it," Hebert said. He had spent "hours and hours" writing and calling publishers and press organizations asking for help and many Louisiana newspapers had filed supporting briefs.

Hebert's newspaper, which has since merged with another paper, creating a biweekly called the *Iberville Post/South*, is now insured against libel and no longer carries "Page from Our Past." Instead, Hebert's staff strings together items from yesteryear in a weekly column that he calls *"Dites Moi,"* French for "Tell Me." Sometimes the column is illustrated with old photographs from the newspaper's files.

"We had to give up on 'Page from Our Past,' " said Jeanetta Hebert, a daughter-in-law who coordinates advertising at the paper. "The problem was that no one had time to read a whole page before deadline to make sure that there was nothing dangerous on it. But 'Dites Moi' is very popular. People really like it."

Gary Hebert agrees, but says, "While most people were extremely disappointed when we discontinued 'Page from Our Past,' not everybody was sorry to see it go. There is a certain small number of people who live in fear that you'll let something out of their family closet."

Once, after *"Dites Moi"* replaced "Page from Our Past," Hebert left town for another newspaper convention and a summer interne was assigned to pick out some interesting old items for the historical column. She ran a report of a moonshiner being arraigned in Baton Rouge fifty years ago. The moonshiner, it turned out, had popped out of Hebert's own family closet. His relatives called up and said, "Please! Gary, that was fifty years ago. Can't you let it be?"

As "Page from Our Past" demonstrates, the law should protect the reporting of newsworthy true facts, at least where the journalist has not set out deliberately to hurt the person who claims to be embarrassed. Gary Hebert regarded local history as a matter of public interest— newsworthy. The old facts he republished happened to be about a criminal trial, and therefore a matter of judicial record, but true information from unofficial sources should merit equal protection. Otherwise, what will become of our history, as the Louisiana court demanded to know?

Courts are not entirely happy to see rehabilitated individuals suffer anew from dredged-up news of their past mistakes. The *Roshto* case itself had to go all the way to the state's highest court for victory. Some courts, notably California's, have sometimes reasoned that the state and the reformed miscreant are both better off letting bygones be bygones.

The Supreme Court has not yet addressed the question, but I believe when it does it will protect the right to report history accurately. Nevertheless, I also believe journalists have a responsibility to evaluate historical information about living people for newsworthiness before republishing it. Past misdeeds of today's leaders are surely inherently newsworthy. Old events that illuminate a trend or current development should be reportable, even if they involve people who are not now in public life, and true accounts of the roles people played in history should be protected as newsworthy.

Engagement Notice Recalls Old Scandal

Under the headline "Former City Atty. Werner to Wed Again," the *Los Angeles Times* published the following engagement notice:

[Los Angeles Times, Dec. 19, 1958] Former City Attorney Erwin P. (Pete) Werner, 65, a political storm center during the Mayor Shaw era of the 1930s, confirmed yesterday that he will be married for the third time sometime next year.

The bride-to-be is Marjorie Augusta Coburn, 46, of Glendale, Grand Royal Matron of the Order of the Amaranth, a State Masonic Order.

The couple obtained a marriage license at Santa Ana Wednesday.

Werner's first wife, Helen, won the sobriquet of Queen Helen in the Roaring 20s for her domination of Los Angeles politics.

She was regarded as the mastermind of Werner's rise to political prominence and managed his campaign for City Attorney after the marriage.

The Werners were rocked by a municipal scandal in the late 1930s, involving alleged bribery in connection with Los Angeles liquor licensing. Werner was vindicated after more than four years of litigation, but his wife served a 10-month sentence for grand theft. She died in 1947.

Werner ultimately was disbarred. He was reinstated four years ago after the State Supreme Court decided Werner had been rehabilitated and had regained the moral character necessary to practice law.

Werner sued and lost. The court said that while the engagement notice might not have been to everyone's taste, it was, all the same, not an actionable invasion of privacy. The court agreed that the information, drawn from the public record, was embarrassing, but it was not so highly offensive as to shock the conscience or offend notions of decency.

In the court's view, the historical note that caused Werner embarrassment met the test of newsworthiness. Not only had Werner been a public official, which made him legitimately a news subject even after he had left office, but he had been a prominent actor in events that remained a part of city history and a matter of public concern. Journalists attempting to judge the current newsworthiness of old records should examine the relative notoriety of the person, both at the time of the event and currently, and the interest of the public in having the information.

Identifying Victims of Sex Crimes and Juvenile Offenders

Many police officers and many journalists, too, seem to think that it is against the law to publish the names of rape victims and juveniles, even if they are found in public records. This is not so. Journalists may refrain from publishing such names out of special consideration for these subjects, but this is a decision based on ethical rather than legal grounds. Some publishers take a flexible approach and use the names only in special cases. For example, they may choose to publish a rape victim's name if it is revealed in open court during the prosecution of a suspect. They may choose to publish the names of juveniles charged with violent crimes or only those charged with serious crimes at an age bordering legal adulthood.

The United States Supreme Court has ruled that a state cannot constitutionally make laws prohibiting or punishing the publication of a rape victim's identity if it is learned from proceedings or records that are open to the public. If access to the records and proceedings is unrestricted, the state is powerless to bar publicity about them.

Neither can a state constitutionally forbid or punish a journalist for revealing a juvenile's name if the journalist has obtained it by legal means. States can, however, regulate and restrict public access to certain sensitive proceedings and records, such as those involving juveniles, and almost all of the fifty states have laws that provide for juvenile confidentiality in some way. The approach advocated by the National Council of Juvenile Court Judges is cooperation between court personnel and editors in the hope that they will exercise editorial discretion and will decline to publish without first consulting with a juvenile court judge.

The Supreme Court has stopped short of ruling that publishing true information from public records can never be the basis for a privacy suit, but its decisions, and those of lower courts, strongly suggest that if the press lawfully obtains true facts about a matter of public significance, the court will shield it from suits.

Portrait of a Daredevil

A daredevil body surfer who objected to the bizarre anecdotes that *Sports Illustrated* had published in a profile of him wiped out in court because the details of his mean competitiveness and lunacy were found to be newsworthy and not sufficiently offensive to sustain an action against the magazine.

Mike Virgil, the surfer, had willingly given *Sports Illustrated* an interview, but changed his mind about allowing his name to be used when he realized just before publication that the story was not going to be pure adulation. *Sports Illustrated* writer Curry Kirkpatrick had gone to Newport Beach's popular surfing spot, "the Wedge," intending to do a profile on surfers. He discovered that lots of young people on the beach idolized Virgil's recklessness and considered him the wild man of the Wedge, a spot where the conjunction of a 400-foot-long jetty and a stony beach create towering waves of raging water that had killed and crippled a number of surfers. The following summer, Kirkpatrick went back to the Wedge and interviewed half a dozen surfers for a 7,000-word story that focused on Virgil. He talked with Virgil and his pretty wife, Cherilee, several times, and Curt Gunther, a free-lance photographer, took pictures.

The quiet, shy, twenty-eight-year-old Virgil showed up on the beach only on the days of gargantuan waves, Kirkpatrick wrote. He specialized in a flat-out straight-down free fall, sometimes executed backwards, sometimes sideways. "I have a green room that I duck into where there's no turbulence. Only calm. I can reach out of the disaster and touch the calm. It's so damn great, I can't even believe it," he told Kirkpatrick.

The first time he tried to ride the Wedge, Virgil said, he did a backward over-the-falls flip that broke a leg into pieces and "destroyed" his knee. "I figured then the Wedge was a virility deal," he told Kirkpatrick. "At least it got me out of the army. I had to keep going back." He did go back, once to a broken collarbone and once to a collision in which he broke another surfer's jaw. But he couldn't stay away, the magazine said. Virgil told *Sports Illustrated* that he dreamed about the Wedge and got upset and nervous when he had to leave on vacation.

The character and personality of the fearless "Mr. Wipeout," as friends called him, came through in a few anecdotes that Virgil and his wife recounted. The handsome blond told how he once fought a bull in Mexico and another time had ridden a bull at a rodeo for six seconds, always looking for the sport in which he could be the best. He found it in body surfing at the Wedge.

"I'm not sure a lot of things I've done weren't pure lunacy," Virgil told the magazine, such as diving off billboards on his construction jobs as summer approached so he could collect unemployment and go surfing. The title of the *Sports Illustrated* piece told how Virgil felt about bodysurfing, "The Closest Thing to Being Born."

To impress women, Virgil once dove down a flight of stairs, the magazine said. "There were all these chicks around. I thought it would be groovy. Was I drunk? I think I might have been," he was quoted as saying.

Another time at a party, the magazine said, a woman asked if he'd seen an ashtray anywhere, and he said, "Why, my dear, right here," and extinguished her lighted cigarette in his mouth. Another cigarette trick was burning a hole in a $1 bill that was lying on the back of his hand. This allowed him to collect a small bet but left him with two burn holes in his wrist. Cherilee told the magazine, "Mike also eats spiders and other insects and things." The couple were vegetarians because, they said, meat burns too much energy and "isn't good for you."

Virgil's surfing feats were of public interest, the federal court in California decided. It found that the unflattering details about his other exploits seemed related as pieces to a puzzle about an exhibitionist and maverick who inspired admiration and curiosity. This was not a no-holds-barred rummaging through a private life, the court found, and the details were not inherently morbid and sensational. Rather, the court said, it was a legitimate journalistic attempt to explain the psychology of a reckless adventurer.

It wasn't until a *Sports Illustrated* fact checker called to verify information with Cherilee that Virgil said, "Stop the story!" and insisted his name be withheld. *Sports Illustrated* editors and lawyers were convinced that the story was newsworthy and not an invasion of privacy, so they published despite Virgil's revoking his consent. Virgil sued and the legal battle went on for more than five years.

In deciding against Virgil, California's federal courts ruled that a profile of a surfer was newsworthy and that the consent of the subject was not required for publication. It held that Virgil's withdrawal of his consent made no difference in this case because his consent was not needed anyway. The court did indicate, however, that there might be instances in which it would be a privacy violation to publish despite the withdrawal of consent by the subject: If a story about a private person includes intimate details that could be construed as offensive, but is of only marginal news or social value, it is risky to go ahead with publication if the subject withdraws consent while there is still time to physically stop the story. On stories of this type, where the news peg or public interest is not clear, it is good practice to ask a lawyer's advice.

REVIEW OF EMBARRASSMENT CASES:
NEWS VALUE OF PRIVATE FACTS

Newsworthiness is the strongest justification for identifying the subjects of true, embarrassing stories: Both the telling of the tale and the naming of the protagonist must be of legitimate concern to the public. And the courts have ruled that legitimate popular "concern" extends to features, sports, and entertainment as well as to reports on public events, governmental issues, and social policy.

Four questions need to be answered before a journalist goes public with potentially embarrassing secrets:

1. *Is the Information "Private"?*   Or has it been made public by being included in official open records or proceedings, like Werner's

past scrapes with the law or a rape victim's name, given in open court? If the information is not in public records and the subject has attempted to keep it secret, as Toni Ann Diaz did, the journalist must decide whether the social interest outweighs the private interest. Whether a subject is a private person or a person with a public role is a factor that has also guided the courts in determining whether information is rightfully private or public.

2. *Is the Information Intimate?* Habits and history that people ordinarily do not display are at the center of serious embarrassment complaints. The Alabama housewife who appeared on the front page of the local paper with her skirt flying and her underpants showing is the epitome. The pancreas disorder that gave Dorothy Barber an insatiable appetite and the sterilization of the unwilling teenager were intimate facts, in the courts' view. William James Sidis's unfulfilled childhood promise and Mike Virgil's macho exhibitions were not considered intimate facts.

3. *Is the Information Newsworthy?* This is the central question. Journalists are divided on whether embarrassing stories should name names and the decision varies from one story to the next. The crucial issue legally is whether identifying the subjects can be shown to be in the public interest. Journalists may be able to deflect some suits simply by making clear in the story why the material and the subjects are significant to the public.

4. *Is the Information Highly Offensive?* The courts consider the character of the facts, the tone, and often the motivation. The Roshto brothers' old convictions shamed them, but the court found that the report was not highly offensive, and that the items were drawn innocently from public records without any intention of hurting them. Some might consider making Diaz's sex change public was highly offensive in itself, but what hurt the newspaper in that case was the "jocular" tone of the column. The jury may also have disapproved of the columnist's use of an anonymous tipster and failure to confront Diaz. Would a report that the first woman president of Alameda Community College was a transsexual have been newsworthy if it had been written in a straightforward manner? Many newspeople and lawyers think it certainly would have been. Which is not to say that that is the "right" judgment, but rather to predict that the law would support it.

6

False Light, Intrusion, and Other Causes of Action

BESIDES embarrassment suits in which people complain about nonnewsworthy revelations of their intimate secrets, there are three other types of "privacy" complaints, called false light, misappropriation, and intrusion.

False light is a hybrid resembling libel but categorized by the courts with privacy suits. Like libel, a false light action is a complaint about a false report. Law books usually say false light differs from libel in that false light does not need to be disparaging—it must simply be false—whereas libel, of course, must be both false and damaging. Theoretically, a person may sue for false light even though the report was not at all degrading, but actually complimentary. In reality, however, false light cases almost always concern unflattering portrayals that have hurt somebody's feelings.

False light—a false impression—can emanate from words or pictures or both. A developing body of law, the essential elements of false light are not yet clear, and it is not known how significant or offensive the inaccuracy must be or how the limits on the action will ultimately be defined. Made-up dialogue and physical descriptions have resulted in false light suits. Omitted facts that would have significantly changed the overall impression of an event or a person if they had been included in the story may be the subject of a complaint. Even the use of a photograph in a context that implies a person is related to a story or represents a problem discussed in a story may become the basis for a suit.

False light suits may be brought instead of or in addition to libel suits. Some states have chosen to restrict all complaints about false publicity to the single remedy of libel and have refused to recognize false light claims. Those states appear to be Missouri, North Carolina, Virginia, and Wisconsin, with the question remaining open in New York. More states can be expected to join them in the future as they address the issue.

A large number of states have recognized false light as the basis for a suit—separate from libel and decidedly more vague in its requirements. A false light suit may have a longer filing period if the state applies its statute governing personal injury suits rather than its libel limitations law. As a relatively new avenue of attack on the press, false light does not have all the precedential baggage that sometimes helps to insulate libel defendants: constitutional privileges, centuries of wisdom on what terms are and are not capable of damaging a person, concessions for "substantial" (rather than purely literal) accuracy, polished jury instructions, and rituals for burdens and standards of proof. In general, plaintiffs may include both libel and false light complaints in the same suit. If they win both, they generally may elect damages for one count.

MADE-UP DETAILS

Fictional Portrait in Nonfiction

The most dramatic false light claims concern invented personal details. A made-up interview with an impoverished widow created the most famous false light case.

Forty-four people died when the Silver Bridge collapsed into the Ohio River at Point Pleasant, West Virginia. In the aftermath of the tragedy, Joseph Eszterhas, a reporter for the *Cleveland Plain Dealer*, covered the funeral of one of the victims: forty-year-old Melvin Aaron Cantrell, who left a wife and seven children.

Five months after Eszterhas's prize-winning coverage of the tragedy, he and a photographer decided to do a follow-up story for the *Plain Dealer*'s Sunday magazine.

They drove to the Cantrell home. Thirteen-year-old William David Cantrell later testified that he had seen the two men approaching across a field and, assuming they were coming to the house, had left the front door open. The boy said that no one invited them inside, but that when they entered, no one asked them to leave, either. Photographer Richard T. Conway took about fifty pictures of the children, who were home alone, while Eszterhas talked to them for the next hour and a half.

Eszterhas's story, "Legacy of the Silver Bridge," called Cantrell's death "a microcosm of the scar which will remain permanent and stark upon the spirit of the people here." Five photographs showed the poorly clothed children and their dilapidated home.

Although Eszterhas had not met with Mrs. Cantrell, he wrote as if he had: "Margaret Cantrell will talk neither about what happened nor about how they are doing. She wears the same mask of non-expression she wore at the funeral. She is a proud woman. Her world has changed. She says that after it happened, the people in town offered to help them out with money and they refused to take it."

Photographer Conway was dismissed from the false light suit because the pictures were found to be true and accurate representations, and he had played no role in writing the story. Eszterhas, however, was held responsible for "a calculated falsehood" amounting to false light. Eszterhas, who had left the *Plain Dealer* by the time of the trial, did not testify. Since he had not talked with the woman and the report could only have been made-up, there seemed to be no question to the court but that it was deliberately or recklessly false.

False light cases are not always governed by the actual malice standard of deliberate or reckless falsity that evolved in *New York Times Co. v. Sullivan*. While actual malice is assumed to govern public plaintiffs' false light cases, at least a half dozen courts have declared negligence—or a simple mistake—to be the standard in private citizens' false light suits, and other states may follow. Many states believed they had to employ the actual malice standard to abide by the Supreme Court's mandate on protecting stories of public concern in *Time, Inc. v. Hill* (pp. 19–21) until that mandate was revoked. *Gertz v. Robert Welch, Inc.*, however, freed the states to fashion their own standards for private figure libel, regardless of the public interest in the story. In so doing, *Gertz* probably opened the way for states to adopt the negligence standard or some other standard in private figure false light cases as well, although the Supreme Court did not directly address the question at the time.

"Poetic License" in Biography

A great deal of made-up dialogue and detail in *The Warren Spahn Story* provoked a false light action by the famous pitcher. Biographer Milton J. Shapiro had not met the Milwaukee Braves hero when he wrote his book for juveniles, using newspaper clips and imagination to piece together conversation, internal monologues, and imaginary events.

Spahn disliked the book's image of him and complained of being cast in false light. The book depicted him as highly excitable, sometimes frantically out of control, and verging on a breakdown. It showed him repeatedly telephoning his wife from out of town in nervous frustration when their baby was overdue. It depicted him as brooding over his father's illness and guilt-ridden that he might have aggravated it, and obsessed with success and his own advancement at the expense of his team. The portrayal did not seem damaging to Spahn's reputation—it did not suggest dishonesty or incompetence, for example—and therefore did not appear libelous, but Spahn considered it objectionable because it was presented as a biography and it was untrue.

Some of the biography was flattering. Two chapters on Spahn's World War II heroism showed him bravely leading troops at the Bridge of Remagen until he was wounded and carried off on a stretcher. Later, the book said, Spahn was awarded a Bronze Star. Spahn said there had been no stretcher and no medal. The author testified that when he had tried to check on the information, the army had told him that although it had no record of having awarded Spahn the Star, "if Mr. Spahn says he got one, then he probably did."

Spahn's false light complaint put a stop to further printing of the biography and won him $10,000 in damages. The case, a rare instance of a suit being brought over a biography, points up the difficulty of reporting on a live person without interviewing him or her. No one owns the exclusive right to his or her life story, and plenty of "unauthorized" biographers manage without personal contact with their subject. However, these people avoid fictionalization; they gather facts from people close to the subject and events and follow the reasonable practice of not making up unflattering or inflammatory information. Making up uncomplimentary facts about a live person is an invitation to a false light suit, or even to a libel suit if the invented information is insinuating or accusatory or damaging to professional reputation.

Novel Shows Real-Life Therapist in False Light

Touching, a novel by Gwen Davis Mitchell about unhappy people seeking emotional fulfillment, described a marathon session of nude therapy in which a psychiatrist helped a group of patients shed inhibitions along with their clothes. The author and her publisher lost a suit brought by a therapist who said he had been the unwilling model for the main character and had been cast in false light.

A loutish psychiatrist, Simon Herford, described as a "bearded, fat Santa Claus type" who cursed and abused his patients, was the protagonist in *Touching*. He had little in common with slender, clean-shaven California psychologist Paul Bindrim, except that they both ran nude therapy programs. Lawyers for the author and publisher said that Bindrim gained weight and grew a beard before meeting the jury.

Even though the novelist said the characters were fictional and had included a disclaimer to that effect in the book, the jury identified Bindrim as the antihero and found he had been damaged by the vulgar portrait of a doctor who cursed and even shoved patients. They awarded Bindrim $50,000 in compensatory and $25,000 in punitive damages.

The most damaging evidence against the author was that there was a real link between Bindrim and the fictional therapist: The novelist had attended Bindrim's nude therapy. Furthermore, she had promised him in writing that she would not write about the session. Mitchell worried about that secrecy agreement while she was working on the book, for which she got a $150,000 advance, but believed that she had disguised all the characters and that the story was entirely fictional. The jury found parallels to the real group, however. They may also have disliked her for cheating on the agreement.

As soon as the hardback appeared, Bindrim's lawyer warned Doubleday that *Touching* violated the author's agreement of confidentiality and, in his view, constituted libel and a false light privacy invasion. Mitchell assured the publisher that it was fictional. New American Library then bought the rights and republished the novel in paper. The California Court of Appeal faulted Doubleday for what it regarded as perfunctory treatment of the lawyer's warning and ruled that failure by the publisher to investigate the claim before authorizing the paperback was sufficient evidence of recklessness to uphold the jury's award of punitive damages.

While the Bindrim case shows that even novels can be judged to be false light privacy invasions, only a handful of novels have run into such trouble and almost all have involved plaintiffs who were known personally by the author—former lovers and ex-spouses, for example—and who were stung by some thinly disguised and deliberately nasty portrayal of themselves. So long as novelists avoid the temptation of borrowing too closely from private life to depict unlikable or immoral characters, libel and false light should not loom as much of a threat to creativity. When drawing from personal experiences, take care to disguise the names, surroundings, and identifying characteristics of protagonists who have been inspired by living people.

Novelizing or dramatizing using public officials and public figures as characters is a common practice and appears to enjoy a great deal of poetic license. Both romans à clef ("novels with a key" in which well-known people are intended to be recognized despite invented names and circumstances) and thrillers of imaginary events involving characters bearing real people's names are common. Numerous spy and adventure stories, dramas and comic gags feature presidents and former presidents, movie stars, former football coaches, and other people in the news.

The writer should make it clear, with a prominent disclaimer, that the work is intended to be fanciful and the characters imaginary. The cautious counselor would advise not making the real-life public figures look worse than they do in life. Fictional dialogue and imaginary events should not be treated by the courts as libelous because reasonable readers would not perceive them as factual and would not think of them as damaging information "of and concerning" a real person. Fictionalization of details about and words of a prominent figure, such as a former president or political figure, should be treated in the law as a privileged statement of opinion, an exaggerated characterization similar to Conrad's political cartoon of Mayor Yorty (p. 120), which was protected as commentary on a public issue.

OMITTED FACTS

Two cases of libel discussed in Chapter 3 are also good examples of a type of false light complaint that might arise from an omission of crucial facts. In the parrot case (pp. 82–85), the story headlined "Saved Parrot, Let Woman Die, Suit Says" failed to mention George Newell's attempts to warn Joan Marie Dini. Newell said it was the omission that created a false impression. In the case of the Memphis shooting (pp. 64–67), Ruth Ann Nichols claimed that the report omitted mention of the presence of witnesses and thereby caused the misimpression that she'd been caught with a lover.

MISLEADING CONTEXT

Photographs have led to some of the most colorful false light cases. Newsworthy photographs are protected, of course, and are not actionable merely because they may be unflattering. But from time to time people sue because they are falsely portrayed in an embarrassing context.

Newsworthiness, in legal terms, is the basis of protection for legitimate editorial uses of portraits taken in public places. Photographs depicting events, themes, problems, and social issues are evaluated by the courts for newsworthiness just as stories are (Chapter 5). An embarrassing picture of a news event does not give rise to a privacy action because it is protected as news coverage.

Occasionally people sue over news pictures, but they lose. A photograph of the arrest of a criminal dressed only in jockey shorts was newsworthy and did not invade his privacy. Glenn Lamar Spradley gunned down a St. Petersburg, Florida, policeman and held a young boy hostage in the boy's home for several hours before giving up in his front yard. From his jail cell, Spradley repeatedly complained to the courts that the television news film of his being arrested in his underwear invaded his privacy, but judges at all levels of the state judicial system uniformly assured him that his arrest was newsworthy and that the five-second film they had reviewed, taken in semidarkness and from a distance, made it "difficult if not impossible . . . to determine what Mr. Spradley is or is not wearing while being arrested."

Human interest photographs are as newsworthy as hot news pictures, in the court's mind, and pictures on such themes as weather and seasons, weekend and holiday pastimes, rush-hour crowds and playing children are protected as legitimate concerns to the public. "Catching" candid shots of people in public may embarrass them, but it does not invade their privacy. A photo of lovers kissing in the park may ruin their marriages (to other people), but they have no legal claim against the publisher. Such complaints do surface sometimes, but getting rid of them is no problem.

Lawsuits based on photographs that can be a problem are false light complaints. The photographs may have been taken in public or with permission, and the subject matter may be newsworthy, but a person in the photo can claim to be unrelated to the context and object to the false impression thus created.

Ruby Clark was neither a prostitute nor a resident of that Detroit neighborhood when she happened to walk in front of cameras filming a news close-up: "Sex for Sale: The Urban Battleground." The ABC network documentary was focusing on a racially integrated middle-class community besieged by pimps and streetwalkers, where customers prowled Woodward Avenue, catcalling and beckoning to virtually any women on the sidewalk.

Footage: A middle-aged white woman, shown full-length, walks by with a shopping bag in each hand. Next, a slightly obese black woman, at least forty, leaves a store, carrying groceries. Now a slim, attractive black woman in her mid-twenties walks by. Stylishly dressed, she has big earrings and long hair piled on top of her head. The frontal close-up lasts three to five seconds.

Narrator, Howard K. Smith: "According to residents, and Detroit police records, most of the prostitutes' customers or johns were white; the street prostitutes were often black. This integrated middle-class neighborhood became a safe meeting place for prostitutes and 'johns.' "

"But for the black women whose homes were there, the cruising white customers were an especially humiliating experience."

Sheri Madison, a black woman resident, being interviewed on camera.

Sheri Madison: "Almost any woman who was black and on the street was considered to be a prostitute herself. And was treated like a prostitute."

Mrs. Clark, a quiet, pretty mother of a two-year-old boy, complained that the effect of the footage and narration was to portray her as a prostitute. Some people who knew her only slightly now suspected her of "moonlighting" as a streetwalker and, she told the court, some of the people in the church choir in which she sang treated her so poorly she had to drop out.

Clark's was a libel complaint, but it was analogous to false light. She argued that she had absolutely no connection to the subject, but that she had been falsely portrayed by the narrative and by the contrast between her appearance and that of the women preceding her.

The trial judge rejected her argument because, according to Clark's lawyer, his own image of a prostitute didn't resemble Clark. Therefore, he dismissed the case on summary judgment without letting a jury consider it. However, the Federal Appeals Court for the Sixth Circuit reversed and ordered the case to be sent to a jury. Just after a jury was chosen, ABC settled by paying Clark $40,000. Her lawyer, Victoria C. Heldman, said: "It was a victory for her, but she didn't feel victorious. She was just exhausted." Heldman said ABC's lawyers "flooded us with paper" and that even though Clark listed twenty-five people who believed she was a prostitute after seeing the documentary, "ABC still felt her complaint was without merit."

ABC's lawyer said afterward that ABC was "absolutely right" and that Clark's complaint was "after-the-fact nit-picking." After settling the case "purely for economic reasons," Detroit lawyer Richard E. Rassel said that Clark had been portrayed accurately: not as a prostitute but as a likely victim, typical of the women who the show said were hounded and abused while walking in the neighborhood. Rassel said he did not believe Clark had suffered.

Heldman and Rassel also settled a second suit arising from the same documentary, brought by a short, balding fifty-year-old white man who complained that he had been misrepresented as a "john" looking to buy sex. Ira Breneman, a chubby, well-dressed businessman carrying a chubby cigar, was caught by the cameras as he left a restaurant and headed back to work with his two lunch companions. The voice-over accompanying a close-up of Breneman said, "The value system with the males having the most power to the exclusion of women is being threatened today, and there is no doubt that men will seek out prostitutes to kind of recapture the old social system." When the same trial judge who originally dismissed the *Clark* case allowed the *Breneman* case to go to the jury, ABC paid Breneman $45,000 to settle.

The *Clark* and *Breneman* cases typify a dilemma not just for television but for print journalists, too. Illustrating stories about social problems with portraits of people who are unrelated to the story may offend them and may convey a misimpression about them.

One such picture, used in a television series on premenstrual syndrome, PMS, showed a woman police officer directing traffic. The four-part news series discussed the hormonal imbalance associated with menstruation that causes some women to behave irrationally, and even violently. The introductory footage to ABC's "Premenstrual Syndrome: Solved? (The PMS Report)" showed officer Kathy Elizabeth Ryan, on duty at Broadway and 65th Street in New York City.

Ryan was not named or referred to in the segment but was just shown on film, as were several other women performing their routine jobs. Ryan complained that seeing her picture on the program would make people think she had PMS. She said she'd been libeled and that her privacy had been infringed.

Dismissing Ryan's case, the New York judge said, "The introduction was meant only to gain the attention of women viewers particularly and alert them that the program would be of interest to them."

The judge considered it "doubtful" that it was libelous to suggest that a woman had PMS because he did not believe that the report, even if it were false, would injure her reputation or make people avoid her or think less of her. He said that PMS was not in a league with "leprosy, venereal disease or other 'loathsome' diseases" that would cause ostracism of the victim (and the false report of which was automatically considered ruinous by ancient libel law). The judge seemed to have drawn his distinction partly from watching the program, which said that PMS "may not be uncommon" and may be medically treatable.

Ryan's libel claim was ousted and her false light privacy complaint defeated. She also failed in her attempt to prove a violation of the state statute prohibiting commercial use of people's names and pictures. The station had included her picture in an advertisement for the program, but that promotional use was excused by the court as merely incidental to the newsworthy editorial broadcast.

An attractive, blue-eyed blond Washington, D.C., bookkeeper complained when her local ABC station used a close-up of her in its report on genital herpes. The crew had photographed her at lunchtime as she crossed the intersection of K Street and Vermont Avenue N.W., near her insurance company office. Later, on the news, the young woman was shown looking in the direction of the camera and then away, as anchor David Schoumacher, in a voice-over, announced a medical treatment for herpes but added, "for the 20 million Americans who have herpes, it's not a cure. . . ."

The jury agreed with Linda K. ("Katie") Duncan that WJLA-TV should not have done it, but awarded only $750. Her lawyer said that the jury failed to "appreciate the impact that those three to five seconds had on her life." But the lawyer for ABC said she had not suffered at all.

One of Duncan's lawyers, Daniel N. Arshack, said that the single, athletic woman from suburban Virginia had suffered because casual acquaintances suspected she might have herpes and insensitive colleagues plagued her with crude jokes. David J. Branson, the lawyer for ABC, said that early in the case he had tried to settle for $2,000 and Duncan had agreed, but that she then switched to new lawyers who demanded $50,000. He said that the five-woman, one-man black jury saw the suit as a put-up job with inflated damages claims.

Print journalists are not immune to the complaints of photographic subjects used in false, unflattering contexts. A widely publicized case, *Arrington* v. *New York Times Co.*, dramatized the problem for the press. An elegant businessman unwittingly became a cover portrait for a story he disliked in *The New York Times Magazine,* "The Black Middle Class: Making It," by William Brashler. Clarence W. Arrington was not mentioned in the story, had not been interviewed, and was offended to have been made a symbol of a prosperous black class the author said had been "growing more removed from its less fortunate brethren." Arrington lost his case because the New York court considered his picture newsworthy and considered him sufficiently related to the story: to the court he appeared black, well dressed, and middle class. Arrington's battle, however, effected a nationwide consciousness-raising among photo editors.

Arrington, a financial analyst for General Motors, was walking along a New York sidewalk when he was photographed by free-lance Gianfranco Gorgoni on assignment for *The Times* to shoot an appropriate cover for the "Black Middle Class" article. Arrington sued *The Times,* the photographer and his agency, and the agency president. *The Times* alone was dismissed from the suit on the ground that editorial use of the newsworthy photograph was privileged.

Copyright © 1978 Gianfranco Gorgoni/Contact. Reprinted with permission.

The court declined to adopt Arrington's arguments that his privacy had been invaded and that he had been cast in false light. Arrington then argued that at the very least a commercial use had been made of his photograph, in violation of state law, when the agency sold the picture to the magazine. The misappropriation law, discussed later in this chapter, regulates advertising and commercial uses of names and photos and was never intended to affect photographers' or agency sales of news pictures and feature photos to editorial publishers. (It has since been rewritten to prevent such misapplication.) But Arrington talked the court into a strained interpretation that kept his suit alive against Gorgoni (the photographer), Contact Press Images, and the president of the agency, Robert Pledge. As this book went to press, Pledge said the suit was dormant.

In another false light suit by a woman coalminer, an old portrait from a photo file was joined to an article about hostility on the part of the men in the mines toward the women who work with them. The *Beckley* (West Virginia) *Post-Herald* had originally taken a picture of Sue S. Crump with her permission for a story on miners preparing to strike. The photographer shot several frames. One was published and the others were filed.

Two years later the *Sunday Post–Herald & Register* (now called the *Register/Herald*) ran a story in its annual "Progress Edition" on the subject of women coalminers entitled "Women Enter 'Man's World.' " It reported that some women had been attacked and beaten in the mines and that one Wyoming miner had been dangled from a 200-foot water tower until she agreed to quit her job. (She quit.) One of the pictures originally taken of Crump was used to illustrate the later story, and she complained that this use falsely implied that she had been among the women miners who had been abused and humiliated on the job. Her false light suit appeared dormant as this book went to press but was still pending in West Virginia State Courts.

Some complaints are more forceful than others, but the lesson of all these cases is that it is journalistically more sound and legally safer to illustrate with portraits of people who actually are related to the story. Remember that false light photograph problems are likely to arise only from contexts that are negative or embarrassing—tax cheats, swingers of the sexual revolution, party-crashing free-loaders. Ideally, choose photographs of people who are interviewed or specifically mentioned in the story. As an alternative, explain the subject and ask permission before using photographs of people who are not really part of the story. Or consider photographs of people who are not identifiable because their backs are turned or shadows completely obscure their faces.

NAMES AND PICTURES WITHOUT CONSENT IN ADVERTISING

Most states recognize the tort of misappropriation, the unauthorized use of a person's name or likeness for trade or advertising purposes. Also called commercialization, the laws are mostly judge-made, but twelve states have enacted statutes: California, Florida, Georgia, Massachusetts, Nebraska, New York, Oklahoma, Rhode Island, Tennessee, Utah, Virginia, and Wisconsin.

The aim of the laws is to give a person control over the commercial exploitation of his or her identity and an ability to limit it to those products or ventures that the person has agreed to endorse. The law does not affect editorial uses of people's names and pictures, only advertising and commercial uses, such as on flyers and brochures, products and labels, cards and calendars, T-shirts and posters.

The law generally has been interpreted to exempt the reuse of news pictures by publishers and broadcasters in their own self-promotions—opening a backdoor for publishers' house ads. Republication of editorial material in campaigns to increase newspaper and magazine circulation or broadcast audience is generally accorded a free ride and is considered to be a protected "incidental" use rather than an unauthorized commercialization.

Sports Illustrated magazine featured a superbowl cover of Joe Namath in its circulation campaign, and the football star sued, complaining that it violated the New York misappropriation statute. Namath's complaint failed when the state court ruled the "incidental" use of an editorial photograph was privileged.

Similarly, actress Shirley Booth lost her suit against *Holiday* magazine, which prominently featured her photograph in its advertising campaign. The magazine had previously published her photograph and profile with consent. The New York Supreme Court said that the reuse was privileged where the photograph was itself unobjectionable and the use in the campaign was to illustrate the typical contents of *Holiday* magazine.

Noncelebrity news photographs are also reusable without consent in "house" advertising by news organizations. The *Baltimore Evening Sun* promoted itself in an advertisement that displayed one of its front pages, which carried a photograph of two children attending Baltimore's Afro-American Festival, "AFRAM." Originally the photograph had been taken with the permission of the mother of one of the children, who had been chaperoning them at the downtown fair. The Maryland Court of Appeals ruled that reuse of the photo in the *Sun's* self-advertising was not an unlawful appropriation of the children's likenesses.

Jacqueline Kennedy Onassis won a misappropriation case against Christian Dior, Inc., and nipped her look-alike's modeling career in the bud. The widow of John F. Kennedy and of Aristotle Onassis got New York Supreme Court to halt a $2.5 million Dior campaign, inspired by Noel Coward's 1933 play *Design for Living* and photographed by Richard Avedon. Real-life celebrities Gene Shalit, the late Ruth Gordon, and Shari Belafonte-Harper had agreed to be in the picture; the J. Walter Thompson Advertising agency had chosen the Onassis "type," Barbara Reynolds, from the Ron Smith Celebrity Look-Alikes Agency. Reynolds was a secretary who the court said "has made this resemblance an adjunct to her career." (See page 174.)

Enjoining the masquerading, the court said, "Let the word go forth. There is no free ride."

Another misappropriation case arose from an advertisement for Au Natural, a concoction to fight cellulite, those "fatty lumps and bumps that won't go away." Herbal Concepts' advertisement showed a woman and child nude, bathing in a stream. They were photographed from behind, and their faces were not visible.

But Susan Cohen and her daughter, Samantha, told the New York courts that they had not consented to the advertisement. They said they had been visiting in Woodstock, New York, one July 4 weekend when they decided to go skinny-dipping on friends' private property. Husband Ira Cohen had caught James Kreiger photographing his wife and child and had told him to stop, they said. Krieger denied it.

The photographer denied that it was the Cohens in the advertisement, which appeared in *House Beautiful, Cosmopolitan,* and *House and Garden,* but the Cohens said that several friends had recognized their backs and behinds. The Cohens had not produced those witnesses as this book went to press, and the case seemed to be stalled.

TRESPASS AND INTRUSION

Trespass and intrusion complaints arise from objections to the conduct of journalists in obtaining information or photographs. Unlike embarrassment and false light complaints, which concern the substance of

The wedding of the Diors was everything a wedding should be: no tears, no rice, no in-laws, no smarmy toasts, for once no Mendelssohn. Just a legendary private affair.

Christian Dior
Clothes for Men and Something for Women

174

the information conveyed, trespass concerns the means used to get the information.

Newsgathering methods that have been held to be intrusive include breaking and entering or using trickery to gain admission to a private area, and secret taping in states where it is illegal.

Trespass is intentional illegal entry onto private property, which violates the owner's exclusive right of property. Trespass cases against journalists are relatively rare. Usually it is enough for a journalist to leave if the owner or person in charge of private property confronts the journalist and orders him or her to go.

Journalists were convicted of trespass for following antinuclear demonstrators over a fence onto the grounds of an Oklahoma power plant. The court rejected their argument for a First Amendment exemption from trespass laws for journalists in the process of newsgathering.

A *Life* magazine reporter and a photographer illegally trespassed when they gained admittance to a private California clinic actually run by a plumber who was practicing medicine without a license. Invited in after saying they had been referred by a friend, they secretly photographed and bugged their consultation with a hidden radio transmitter. The bug was a violation of state law, and their entry under false pretenses was ruled a trespass. The story, however, won prizes and forced the clinic to close.

One Virginia journalist was convicted of trespass when he admitted to gaining entry into prison for a death row interview by misrepresenting himself as an officer of the court. Another reporter was accused of gaining an interview with parents of a teenage suicide at their New Jersey home by introducing herself as being "from the morgue." That privacy and trespass complaint was settled. The journalists who barged in on Dorothy Barber in the hospital (pp. 142–143) and the woman who surreptitiously interviewed William James Sidis in his room (pp. 148–150) might be considered to have trespassed.

Journalists whose assignments require that they get inside private property or another place where people expect privacy, such as in a doctor's office or hospital room, or the living quarters of a nursing home, should identify themselves as newspeople and ask permission. Where reporting can be done in a public place, such as at a parade or in a park or on the street, identifying oneself and asking permission is not legally necessary.

Consumer reporting, such as restaurant reviews and comparison shopping reports, does not usually require that reporters identify themselves and their mission because they are free to enter public places of business, as any member of the public could, for the purpose of gathering and reporting facts. As typical situations involving no trespass and no consents, it is permissible to open several bank accounts with the undisclosed aim of doing a story comparing bank services and fees, and to visit several tax preparers with the unannounced intention of comparing them. Of course, some journalists prefer to operate openly; the decision is theirs.

"Undercover" reporting is not illegal so long as the cover is not a ruse for trespass. For example, it is not a legal violation for reporters to investigate housing discrimination by posing as a racially mixed couple looking for a house. Nor is it illegal for a reporter with a teaching license to take a teaching job with the intention of writing about schools—the teaching credentials permit a rightful entry. By contrast, a photographer with no medical credential who poses as a medical aide in an operating room would be guilty of trespass because the photographer would have had no right to be in the room where the patient was entitled to privacy. Many journalists think undercover work is unethical and choose not to do it. The explanations of the law here should not be interpreted as an endorsement of the practice. The important point is that the law leaves journalists free to examine their own consciences and reach their own ethical solutions.

Photographers have more trespass questions than reporters, perhaps because they have to get in close to get good pictures and many times are in doubt whether they are shooting from places where they have a right to be. Specific questions are best left to local lawyers, but some general instructions here and in Chapter 7, "Questions and Answers," may be helpful.

First, the law treats as two separate questions whether there has been a trespass and whether there is a right to publish information obtained by means of trespass. The privilege to publish the news remains, regardless of whether the newsgatherer's conduct might be punishable as trespass. Second, trespass prosecutions of journalists are infrequent, judging from the small number of cases reported.

In general, it should not be considered trespass to go up to a person's door seeking an interview or photograph, even if the route requires passing over private property to get to the door. Either the owner or a tenant or manager in charge of private premises has authority to invite a journalist in or out. A bold photographer can take pictures on the way out, but once the owner or person in charge orders the photographer to leave the property, he or she must leave if it is possible to do so without danger. No one—neither the police nor the property owner—has a right to confiscate the camera or the film, and anyone who tries should be advised to consult with a lawyer first—both camera and film are private property. Journalists should not place themselves in danger of being hurt or abused by property owners, however, and in a "Your camera or your life" dilemma, plan on a new camera.

Journalists don't have any more immunity from trespass laws than other citizens have, except in a few states where special statutes give them unique status. Where police are engaged in crowd control, as at fires and accidents, journalists must obey police commands. While they are not supposed to be singled out for discriminatory treatment, they usually are not guaranteed specially favorable treatment, either.

Sometimes police and fire officials or other governmental agents invite reporters and photographers to accompany them. But even in the company of officials, journalists on private property may be regarded as trespassers by the courts. Although it is customary in many communities for reporters and photographers to go with police and fire fighters into homes and other private areas, only a few courts have ruled that the officials have legal authority to invite them. Other courts have said that the officials lacked such authority and have held the journalists for trespass. Since the courts are split on this question, even some within the same state, it would be advisable to consult a local legal expert.

Whether an area is public or private is another question best tackled by local lawyers. One key question is whether people inside are entitled to privacy, another is ownership.

People reasonably expect privacy inside a house or fenced yard not visible from the street and inside living facilities, such as in hospitals and nursing homes. Photographers need permission not only to enter those private areas but to take pictures as well. On the other hand, people on the street, in parks, or in a sports stadium have no reasonable expectation of privacy and can be photographed without permission. In between are quasi-public areas that are open to the public for a specified purpose, such as a restaurant for dining or a theater for entertainment. One New York court ruled that photographers shooting inside a restaurant needed permission because the restaurant was a public place for purposes of dining, and patrons dining there should reasonably be allowed to dine in peace.

In addition, the premises were privately owned, and so were not held to be automatically open for filming without permission. Private ownership is a key to whether or not the photographer has free access. Privately owned shopping malls, parking lots, and shop premises are open to members of the public generally, but the owners or managers may ask people to leave at will. Journalists and photographers, like other members of the public, have no inherent right to remain on the premises and should leave if ordered away by the owner or the manager. Various broad protections of the freedom to distribute news—by newspaper vending machines, pamphleteering, and public speaking—are distinguishable from legal restrictions on gathering news, which is a more limited privilege that need not be tolerated on private property.

Public property, including streets, sidewalks, parks, government offices and their grounds, generally are open to the public, including journalists. However, there may be private enclosures within public facilities that are off-limits except by invitation, such as a judge's chamber or a postmaster's office.

Publicly financed institutions are not necessarily open to the public. Schools, hospitals, and jails are examples of public facilities where journalists need permission to rove beyond the public receiving area. There is no inherent right to interview prisoners in jail or patients in their hospital living quarters.

There is nothing illegal about taking pictures in a public place. Pictures of people who can be seen and photographed from a public place may be published without invading privacy. Thus, camera-shy people answering their door only to be caught by a photographer shooting from curbside have not suffered an invasion of privacy. People sitting on their porches or sticking their heads out of their windows or seen through windowpanes are photographable when the camera is positioned someplace where the photographer has a right to be. Individual journalists who shun grab-shots as impolite or overly aggressive should be guided by conscience. The aim of this summary is only to explain that photographing news subjects in public does not constitute a privacy invasion.

The legendary aggressiveness of one photographer, Ron Galella, drove Jacqueline Kennedy Onassis to ask New York federal court to order him to keep twenty-five feet away from her. The self-styled paparazzo specializing in celebrity snaps had hounded and frightened the Kennedy children and their mother for years. While Onassis beseeched the courts, another star with the same problem took direct action. Marlon Brando broke Galella's jaw, infecting his hand in the process.

CONSENTS FOR PHOTOGRAPHS

Written permission to publish a photograph is called a photo release. A valid release can be one sentence by the subject consenting to the publication of the picture, with the date and the subject's signature. The release should specify consent to use the name and picture in advertising if such commercial (as distinct from editorial) use is contemplated. Some form consents recite "consideration," which means payment, but money payment is not needed to make the consent binding. An ordinary release can be short, but some professional and commercial photographers favor detailed documents for multipurposes. An oral consent is as valid as one in writing but harder to prove.

News photographers rarely obtain signed releases, and for news and most feature pictures, of course, no consent is necessary—the privilege to publish is based on newsworthiness, the same as with words.

A photograph of a nearly nude woman fleeing an apartment where she had been held hostage was news. The Florida woman, who had covered her front with only a small towel as she ran to safety, claimed the photograph embarrassed her and invaded her privacy. She lost her privacy suit. Hilda Bridges had been held prisoner by her estranged husband and forced to disrobe to prevent her escape. Newspeople and a crowd waited while police negotiated, but instead of surrendering, Bridges's husband committed suicide.

The newsworthiness of the widely distributed photograph of Bridges being escorted outside by police made it legally protectible, even though it did display much of her body. Intimate photographs, like the Bridges picture, should always be evaluated for newsworthiness with the same standards as those for potentially embarrassing stories, as discussed earlier. An invasion of privacy case will not be sustained unless a photograph is offensive and not of legitimate public interest.

Feature photographs also bear examination for offensiveness and newsworthiness. Most editors avoid sensitive feature photographs where consent is lacking despite the newsworthiness of the pictures. Sensitive subjects include handicapped or disadvantaged people, young children and old people, mentally or physically disabled people of any age, and people who are confined to an institution such as a jail, public residence, or nursing home. To be valid, consent to publish a photograph must come from the subject, if he or she is competent, or from someone authorized to act on behalf of the subject. Some public facilities for the disowned or disabled keep such permissions on file in the office of the custodian.

It is advisable to work with written consents when photographing or reporting on sensitive and embarrassing topics in the feature context. Before using portraits in a story about social or health problems—such as alcoholism, addiction, venereal disease, welfare hardships and delinquents—tell the targets what the subject of the report is and get consent in writing.

When the photograph is not hot news, it is safest to get the subject's written release. Some situations in which written releases are advisable are:

1. The photographer has to get into some private place usually reserved for invited guests.
2. The subject is disabled, confined, or dependent. Newsworthy pictures taken in public places are privileged and can be used without consent, such as pictures of poor street people. However, they should be current pictures, used and captioned straightforwardly. Avoid captions that characterize or interpret in a pejorative way or report more information than is known.
3. The photograph is for commercial or trade purposes.
4. The subject's presence may embarrass him or her, as in a picture of people waiting for screening at a public venereal disease clinic. Many editors prefer to use such pictures only if the subjects are unrecognizable or have consented.
5. The photograph shows more body more intimately than people ordinarily display publicly. Voluntary nude appearances excepted, there does seem to be a courtly antipathy to skin magazines and to exploitation of unwitting, unclothed photographic subjects.

TAPING

It is a criminal offense for a participant to tape record a private conversation without the other party's consent in California, Florida, Georgia, Illinois, Maryland, Massachusetts, Montana, New Hampshire, Oregon, Pennsylvania, and Washington. (Michigan's and Virginia's laws have been interpreted as allowing participants' secret recording.) Some of those states prescribe stiff penalties of fines and jail and also provide for civil suits. When calling interstate, assume that secret taping is governed by the law of the state where the recorder is. Even in states where no such law exists, some news organizations' policies discourage staff from taping without consent.

TORT ACTION AGAINST THE MEDIA
FOR INFLICTING DISTRESS

As if traditional libel and privacy complaints were not enough for journalists to worry about, people offended by the media may attempt to bring yet another type of suit: one for intentional infliction of emotional distress. Plaintiffs may present an intentional infliction charge along with the libel and privacy complaints, either just to have another egg in the basket or to try to overcome some hurdle that they have foreseen awaiting their more traditional claims.

Several states have recognized a claim for the intentional infliction of emotional distress. The elements of this "outrage tort" are extreme and outrageous conduct that intentionally or recklessly causes severe emotional distress. According to the Libel Defense Resource Center's *50-State Survey 1984*, states that accept it as a cause of action appear to include Arkansas, California, Colorado, Florida, Illinois, Louisiana, Maryland, Massachusetts, New Jersey, New York, Pennsylvania, Virginia, Washington, and Wisconsin.

It is extremely rare for a complaint about displeasing journalism to claim behavior obnoxious enough and injury serious enough to qualify as intentional infliction of emotional distress. Bill collectors specializing in intimidating and threatening errant debtors are much more apt to be the target of such an outrage complaint.

An example of a failed complaint of intentional infliction of emotional distress was a construction worker's lament over being included in CBS's "Couples in Love in New York." In their hardhats, a male and a female construction worker strolled along Madison Avenue one spring day, holding hands, oblivious to CBS's cameras.

A woman from the CBS crew approached them with a microphone and asked, "Do you wish to make any comment for our show, 'Couples in Love in New York'?"

Carl DeGregorio's answer, regrettably not quoted in full by the court, was a demand that the film be destroyed. He said that he was married and his co-worker was engaged and it wouldn't "look good" for them to be on the program. CBS used them on the broadcast anyway, not once but twice! After DeGregorio had telephoned and complained about the first broadcast, he contended that the rebroadcast was an intentional infliction of emotional distress.

A New York court dismissed the complaint. The five-second glimpse of the couple, in the context of a ten-minute photographic survey of loving couples in public places was not conduct "so shocking and outrageous as to exceed all reasonable bounds of decency," the court stated. DeGregorio's conventional embarrassment count also lost, on the ground of newsworthiness.

DeGregorio tried to state a claim of prima facie tort, which is another action, recognized perhaps only in New York, for intentional infliction of damage without any motive or justification except to cause harm. The injured person needs to plead and prove actual monetary loss. Obviously, DeGregorio's complaint about "Couples in Love" didn't make it.

One intentional infliction of emotional distress claim that was sustained was brought by evangelist Jerry Falwell against *Hustler* magazine and its publisher, Larry Flynt. Falwell had sued for libel, invasion of privacy, and intentional infliction of emotional distress over a parody of the Campari liquor advertisement. The "ad" featured a made-up confession that the minister's first sexual encounter was with his mother in a barnyard while he was drunk. It carried the disclaimer, "Ad parody: Not to be taken seriously." The Roanoke, Virginia, jury decided that the statement was not libelous because no reasonable person would have believed it or thought less of Falwell on reading it.

Judge James Turk of the U.S. District Court for the Western District of Virginia dismissed the privacy claim from the bench because Virginia does not recognize privacy actions other than as misappropriation cases. But after seven hours of deliberation the jury agreed that Falwell had suffered severe emotional distress, wantonly inflicted by Flynt and *Hustler*, and awarded Falwell $100,000 in compensation and $100,000 in punitive damages (including $50,000 against Flynt personally).

Intentional infliction of emotional distress and prima facie tort are available as additional claims that can be used against journalists in some states. But the traditional suits for libel, embarrassing truths, and false light have remained by far the more significant legal threats to journalists.

Libel and privacy suits are a concern of all journalists. Writing precisely without overblowing, eliding, or insinuating any more than you know will help avoid libel and false light complaints and will be the best defense if a suit is brought. Evaluating sensitive information and pictures for newsworthiness and making clear to readers why material is of public concern will help prevent complaints of embarrassment.

Consulting the editors and a lawyer about a potentially risky or offensive story or picture can help ensure that, when it is published, it will be in a form you are ready to defend.

Citizens depend heavily on journalists for their understanding of events and issues and for the truth about what our government is and is not doing. Journalists give indispensable service and have great power—to make or break careers and alter people's lives, indeed to transform society. The exercise of such power carries the risk of lawsuits by people who have been hurt or ruined by the journalist's work. It also carries the responsibility to report with care and sensitivity.

7

Questions and Answers

A SUIT IS FILED

1. Who gets sued?

The libel plaintiff, the person who brings suit, usually sues everybody who had, or might have had, anything to do with the publication. The publisher, meaning the individual or corporate owner of the publishing company, presumably has the "deep pocket" and is therefore the prime target. However, the writer of the story and the editors who worked on it may be named as defendants along with the publisher.

2. Is the reporter usually sued? The editor?

Yes, it is customary to sue everyone in sight, but, again, this may simply amount to naming various people as defendants on the complaint. The real target is the publisher or publishing company, which is likely to have money and resources.

3. Does the staff reporter have to pay a lawyer?

Not usually. The publisher and the staff generally have a common defense, and the lawyer paid by the publisher handles the case on behalf of all defendants. In rare cases, the publisher and the writer may go separate ways, but not many writers can afford lawyers' fees and a unified defense best protects the writer and the publisher.

4. *Does a book author or free-lance writer need to pay a lawyer when the writer and publisher are sued?*

A publishing contract may specify how the costs of a libel defense are to be allocated. In most reported cases it appears that the writer and publisher mounted their defense together, using the publisher's lawyers. By contract, the writer typically may have to pay as much as half the legal fees for a successful defense.

Occasionally, where the writer has defenses not available to the publisher, the writer may benefit from a separate defense. For instance, if editors created and added libelous material, or deleted a crucial fact from the author's manuscript, and that fact would constitute a defense for the author to the libel charge, the writer might qualify for a dismissal from the suit. If, for some reason, the publisher's lawyer balked at arguing in favor of the writer's dismissal from the suit while the other defendants proceeded, the writer might hire a lawyer to serve him or her, but it is rare that this would be necessary.

5. *What does libel insurance cover?*

Policies vary. The best policies cover some portion of legal fees or all legal fees after a deductible amount as well as all damages up to a specified limit, including both compensatory damages—intended to repay the plaintiff for out-of-pocket losses and to compensate for injury—and punitive damages—designed to punish and make an example of the defendant.

6. *Does insurance cover punitive damages?*

Yes, if the written terms of the policy encompass punitive damages, then those terms represent the insurer's promise to reimburse the insured for any punitive awards that may be assessed by judge or jury. Some states have forbidden insurers from paying punitive damages for intentional injury in the belief that allowing insurers to foot the bill for punitive awards defeats the purpose of punishment unless the culprit is required to pay directly from his or her own pocket. At least twenty-seven states—Alabama, Arkansas, California, Colorado, Connecticut, Florida, Idaho, Illinois, Indiana, Kansas, Kentucky, Maine, Massachusetts, Minnesota, Missouri, New Jersey, New York, North Carolina,

North Dakota, Ohio, Oklahoma, Oregon, Pennsylvania, South Carolina, Tennessee, Washington, and West Virginia—and the District of Columbia have declared insurers' reimbursement of punitive damages to be against social policy and illegal.

While insurance salespeople may assure customers that a given policy covers punitive damages, it would be wise, before buying, to ask for the names of customers whose punitive damages have been reimbursed and call them to confirm.

7. Does insurance cover legal fees?

A policy should cover some proportionate amount of legal fees or all legal fees beyond some threshold. Before buying, ask to speak with customers about their experiences with promptness and completeness of payment.

8. Is libel insurance available to individuals?

Yes. Insurance brokers and companies that sell general liability insurance should be able to recommend a source.

9. Will the publisher's insurance cover the reporter's legal expenses?

Yes. In the usual case where publisher and reporter are defended by the publisher's lawyer, the publisher's policy covers the legal work on behalf of all defendants.

10. Who is liable for damages?

Publisher, writer, and editor have been held personally responsible for libels. Anyone who has participated in the preparation of the story can be sued and held jointly liable. Ordinarily the publisher or its insurer pays.

11. Will insurance pay damages assessed against the reporter?

Yes. Ordinarily the staff reporter is covered by the company policy when the libel arises from assigned reporting. Before buying an insurance policy, discuss its coverage and terms. Ask for clarifications in writing if the terms are unclear.

12. Where can suit be brought?

The person suing has numerous choices. The plaintiff can choose the state of his or her residence, the state where the publishing company is based or does business, or a state in which the publication circulates, even where circulation is by mail. This means that a national publication is vulnerable to suit everywhere it circulates and subject to the longest statute of limitations in its circulation area (see Chapter 1, pp. 27–28). A state court can hear a libel case, or a federal court can take it if the parties have "diversity" of citizenship—as in the case of a New York plaintiff and the *Washington Post*. Some libel principles are a matter of federal and constitutional law and are standardized no matter where suit is brought, at least in theory. However, many aspects of the litigation are governed by state laws and consequently differ from state to state, such as the statutes of limitations, shield laws, or retraction statutes (see the appendixes). A federal court will apply the appropriate state law in deciding a libel case.

13. *When can suit be brought?*

Every state limits the time within which various kinds of legal actions can be initiated. Statutes of limitations prescribing the states' time limits on libel suits are in Appendix A. A suit brought after the expiration of the statute of limitations is dismissed as time-barred. Libel time-bars are notoriously short, which is one sign that the state is eager to limit their number. Twenty-six states require a potential plaintiff to file a libel suit within one year of the publication of the libel. Seventeen states have two-year limits. The longest filing period is Florida's four-year statute of limitations. A publication vulnerable to suit in a given state is subject to that state's limitations period. As noted in Chapter 1, *Hustler* magazine, a national publication mailed to some subscribers in New Hampshire, was ruled amenable to suit there. New Hampshire, which at the time had a six-year statute of limitations, the longest in the United States, later placed a three-year limit on libel actions.

14. *What damages can be demanded?*

For an individual claiming to have been libeled, typical elements of damage are physical and psychological injury and monetary loss. Physical injury may mean pain that required a doctor's visit, aspirin, or Valium. Emotional harm can be just fleeting anguish or embarrassment. One Texas lawyer has said that a Texas libel plaintiff has to prove serious medical problems to collect compensation. "Just worry won't do it in Texas," he said. "The plaintiff pretty much has to worry a hole in the stomach." Mostly, no such strong showing is required elsewhere. Monetary loss includes whatever financial setbacks can be attributed to the libel, such as a loss or cancellation of jobs or contracts. These losses must have been caused by the libel. One woman claimed her moving expenses. She said that on account of the libel "all my neighbors got down on me and we had to move."

A business cannot be embarrassed by a libel. It must prove that the libel caused a loss of income.

15. How are damages proved?

Reputational damage is hard to quantify. Some friends of the plaintiff may come to court and testify that when they read the libel, they wondered if it were true and briefly were uncomfortable about seeing the plaintiff. The plaintiff may testify about feeling humiliated, not wanting to face people for a while and being upset, even consulting a doctor or a therapist. Embarrassment and hurt feelings are counted as elements of injury. Compensatory awards seem more often to be granted on the basis of sympathy with the plaintiff than proof of actual injury, even though that is not the way the law is supposed to work. Juries may feel that a person stung by bad publicity deserves some money.

16. If a restaurant made $1 million in profits in one year, and the following year it closed as a result of a scathing review, can it win $1 million in damages by bringing a libel suit against the publisher of the review claiming the review was libelous?

Even if the review was proven libelous and published with fault (either actual malice or negligence, depending on whether the restaurant was designated as a public figure or not), it would still be necessary to show that the libel killed the business. The defense lawyers would make an effort to prove that the losses were less than claimed and were attributable to causes other than the bad review. It could happen that such a huge business loss would become a damage award in a libel suit, although I don't know of any such reported cases. Restaurants are likely to be classified public figures that must prove actual malice in order to win, and reviewers' opinions ordinarily qualify for the extra protection of the opinion privilege, as discussed in Chapter 4 (pp. 127–131).

17. How much has actually been paid in big, affirmed libel awards?

According to Henry R. Kaufman, general counsel to the Libel Defense Resource Center in New York City, more than two dozen verdicts of $1 million or more had been entered between 1980 and 1985. As of this writing, however, not one had yet been finally affirmed on appeal.

Kaufman said that initial big judgments usually are overturned, while smaller awards generally are upheld.

The largest pre–*New York Times* libel verdict was a $3.5 million jury award to a radio and television personality whose career had been ruined by a blacklisting organization in the mid-1950s. Popular talk show host John Henry Faulk beat AWARE, Inc., at trial in New York City in 1962, but his award was cut to $550,000 on appeal, and only $175,000 was collected. Faulk told his story in *Fear on Trial* (University of Texas Press, 1983).

Elmer Gertz won $460,000. The Chicago lawyer sued *American Opinion* magazine, the organ of the John Birch Society, for calling him a Communist. The case, known for Supreme Court pronouncements about the opinion privilege and each state's freedom to set its own standard for private figure libel plaintiffs, took twelve years and ended in 1982 (see Chapter 1, pp. 22–25). Wade Church, former Arizona attorney general, won $485,000 in damages from Phoenix Newspapers in a suit over an editorial in which he was called a Communist.

The *Saturday Evening Post* paid football coach Wally Butts $460,-000 in damages and costs. He sued over a story accusing him and Bear Bryant of fixing a game (see Chapter 1, pp. 16–19). Coach Bryant reportedly settled for a similar amount. San Francisco mayor Joseph Alioto collected $400,000 from *Look* magazine, which accused him of having ties to the Mafia (see Chapter 2, pp. 37–42).

On appeal at this writing are several large libel judgments, including those against the *El Paso Times, Philadelphia Inquirer, Pittsburgh Post-Gazette, Bridgewater* (New Jersey) *Courier-News* (see Chapter 3, pp. 90–92), the *Belleville* (Illinois) *News-Democrat*, the *San Francisco Examiner* (see Chapter 3, pp. 86–89), and the *Washington Post* (see Chapter 2, 49–56) and a huge false light verdict against CBS and Arnold Diaz.

18. *What amounts have been paid in the biggest settlements in the 1980s?*

Kaufman, of the Libel Defense Resource Center, says that information on settlements is "woefully inadequate," since people frequently prefer not to reveal the amounts. The *Alton* (Illinois) *Telegraph* paid the biggest known settlement so far: $1.4 million. A builder had won a $9.2 million libel judgment against the paper, forcing it into bankruptcy. The settlement enabled the newspaper to reorganize from bankruptcy and continue in business. The *Alton Telegraph* case was unusual because the libel never appeared in the paper. It was "published" in a limited way when reporters trying to verify a tip put their suspicions into a memorandum to law enforcement officials. The memo ended up in bank files, where the builder had several loans, and instantly ruined his credit and, he claimed, caused his business to fail.

The *New York Post* paid $510,000 for libeling a consulting firm that lost business and finally failed after the *Post* falsely accused it of submitting fraudulent bills to New York City's Board of Education. Two *Post* articles stated that Greenleigh Associates made huge improper profits on work for government agencies. The front page headline of the first story was "Probe School Contract Ripoff." A jury had awarded $750,000, and an appellate court affirmed but reduced the damages to $470,000 plus interest. The *Post* filed an appeal but withdrew it and paid a compromise amount of $510,000 to end the suit.

Synanon collected $1.25 million in settlement of a libel claim against ABC and $600,000 in settlement of a libel claim against the *San Francisco Examiner.*

The *Wall Street Journal* settled a case for $800,000 with two government attorneys who complained they'd been libeled by a report that they coerced and threatened an inmate to obtain his testimony.

ABC's "20/20" paid $235,000 to settle the complaint of the head of the Federal Witness Protection Program. He said ABC's editing deliberately distorted his response to questions about witness deaths. Correspondent Geraldo Rivera had remarked on camera that the head of the program was either misinformed or intentionally lying about the deaths.

Steve and Cyndy Garvey collected an undisclosed six-figure amount from "Inside Sports" to drop their privacy suit involving an interview about their marriage and personal lives.

19. *Why would a publisher or broadcaster settle a case?*

Sometimes the risk of losing, combined with the certainty of high legal fees and concern over negative public relations fallout from a trial, are inducements to settle. Sometimes an economic decision is made that paying the plaintiff to drop the case will be less costly than defending, even where the publisher's case is strong and should prevail.

20. *Can the publisher unilaterally settle even if the writer wants a trial to vindicate his or her reputation?*

Theoretically, no. If the writer is a party to the suit, he or she could refuse to settle and could elect to continue alone. Practically, though, most writers are unable to shoulder the expenses of defending and the risk of losing, so they acquiesce in settlements even though they may regard the unresolved questions of liability and fault as a blot on their escutcheons.

21. *What big awards have been reversed in the 1980s?*

Two big judgments altogether vacated were a $26+ million award to a former Miss Wyoming for a fictional *Penthouse* magazine short story, ultimately found not to be libelous, and a $10 million privacy judgment against the Flynt Distributing Company, according to the Libel Defense Resource Center. The reason for reversing the Flynt verdict was the court's finding that there had been no proof of actual malice, as should have been required of celebrity Jackie Collins. Collins had complained that the magazine *Adelina* had misidentified her as being the nude person in a photo.

Two big Texas awards were reversed. One was a $2 million verdict against the *Dallas Morning News.* The newspaper had accurately reported that a public figure had threatened his political enemy, so there had been no libel and no actual malice. In another Texas case, Doubleday won a reversal of a $2.5 million judgment. The Texas Supreme Court determined there was no actual malice in a mistake as to which of two brothers had been indicted.

22. *Which big awards have been reduced?*

Trial judges, or appeals judges, can reduce awards they consider excessive, and as the Libel Defense Resource Center points out, they often do just that. A court cut a $3.5 million judgment against the *El Paso Times* to $600,000 in 1985. The newspaper had lost a libel case to a government prosecutor who, its columnist said, had cheated and lied in presenting a criminal case. A $1.5 million judgment against a publication for a computer audience was reduced to $300,000. There, a report based upon a civil suit was ruled libelous because the noncriminal legal term "conversion" was translated in the story to the lay term "theft," and the court considered the substituted term inaccurate. Carol Burnett's $1.6 million jury verdict dropped to $200,000 when reviewed by upper courts. A $1+ million jury verdict for a teacher was reduced to $100,000. The teacher had sued the *Richmond Times-Dispatch* for criticizing her job performance and treatment of students. (Appeals are continuing in the *El Paso Times* and *Richmond Times-Dispatch* cases.)

BEFORE THE TRIAL

1. What happens in pretrial discovery?

Before trial, lawyers for each party engage in "discovery." By subpoe-
naing and questioning people and examining records, they try to build
and refine their own case and learn the other party's strong and weak
arguments. They also try to "freeze" favorable evidence for use at trial.
Both sides work on collecting evidence relating to whether the plaintiff
should be classified as a public figure or not. Both sides also study the
editorial process that produced the story: the plaintiff in an attempt to
show carelessness or actual malice; the defendant in an attempt to
prove that reporting and editing were adequate. The plaintiff, looking
for proof that the journalists' "state of mind" was hostile or bent on
proving a thesis rather than finding out the facts, will question
newsroom personnel extensively about how the story developed and
will dig into reporter notes and newsroom files (see, for example, the
use of discovery in General Ariel Sharon's case against *Time* in Chapter 2, pp. 43–49). The defendant, looking for proof that the plaintiff
suffered negligible damages, will poke around for facts about the plaintiff's private reputation or business fortunes.

State courts vary in patience and permissiveness, but generally federal courts are liberal about discovery. This can mean years of pretrial
maneuvering. Discovery can be very disruptive and draining for news
personnel, but it is a vital part of trial preparations. Lawyers who are
paid by the hour may find discovery lucrative, and their fees for the
time-consuming digging, researching, reading, questioning, and arguing during this phase often account for a large portion of the defense
cost and are the main reason defense costs are high. *Penthouse* magazine was reported to have paid $4 million in legal fees to defend a libel
suit brought by Rancho La Costa, a California resort. The *Washington Post* and Time, Inc., spent several million dollars each in legal fees
to defend their recent libel cases (Chapter 2, pp. 43–56), as did CBS in
defense of General William Westmoreland's suit, although exact figures have not been made public.

2. What's a subpoena?

A subpoena, which means "under penalty," is a document ordering a
witness to appear to testify, as at a deposition or in court, or ordering
the production of records, or both, at a designated time and place. If
the person is to bring along his or her pertinent files, the subpoena

takes the form of a "subpoena duces tecum" (sup-EE-nah DOO-ches TAKE-em), literally, "you bring with you under penalty."

Once a lawsuit has been threatened or a subpoena has been served, neither party should discard any drafts, memoranda, records, notes, or tapes related to the work. Destroying or losing such material after being notified of a suit or intent to sue will look suspicious and damage the defense. Defense lawyers may find legal grounds to withhold some of the material from the plaintiff, but they should have the benefit of reviewing all of it.

3. What's an affidavit?

An affidavit is a sworn, written statement by a person, who may be either a party to the action or a nonparty. It becomes an official record in a case when it is filed as an open, public record, usually as an attachment to a brief or motion or to papers resisting some motion or argument. The "affiant" is the person who swears that the facts recited in his or her affidavit are true, based on firsthand knowledge or on stated assumptions. The statement made in an affidavit differs from deposition testimony or trial testimony because it is one person's unchallenged version of the facts, not the subject of cross-examination. The words of an affidavit often are drafted by a lawyer.

4. What are interrogatories?

Interrogatories are written questions framed by lawyers and served on the opposing party. In them the opponent is asked to identify which people and places were involved with the subject of the lawsuit and whose files contain pertinent records. Some interrogatories attempt to make the opponent commit to some version of the facts. Information for the answers to interrogatories served on the news organization in a libel suit may come from the individual reporter and editors who worked on the story in suit, but the technical wording of the answers is done by lawyers. On both sides, lawyers drafting the questions and answers may labor over the semantics for so many hours that as a result they render them utterly meaningless.

5. What is a deposition?

A deposition is an interview under oath. "Deponent" (pronounced dip-O-nent) is another name for a witness being examined at a deposition. The defense lawyer may subpoena the libel plaintiff and ask questions about the case, such as whether the libel is actually false and what damage the plaintiff claims. The plaintiff's lawyer may subpoena the reporters, editors, and their sources to answer questions about their knowledge or roles in the alleged libel. A deposition witness appears in the company of his or her own lawyer, who plays an active part by some discreet coaching, objecting to improper questions and asking others that allow the witness to clarify, amplify, or correct what he or she has said. A stenographer produces a typewritten transcript of the deposition, which becomes an official record in the case once it has been signed by the witness and filed in court.

When testifying with defensive preparation and advice from your lawyer, remember that this is no time to vent anger, display personality, crack jokes, or be long-winded. Listen to the question, allow time for an objection, and if none is raised, briefly answer only the question that was asked. Do not volunteer information that wasn't specifically requested. And try not to speculate or guess in a way that may lead to added demands for depositions and documents ("I might have talked with the copy editor"; "I think maybe I saw a memo on this story").

Be on guard as fatigue sets in: ask for breaks, and if the session becomes too long, remember that the deposition session can be adjourned and reconvened another day. It is not possible to be excessively cynical about the uses and distorting misuses in store for the deposition transcript. Frozen and made official, the deposition testimony is a source of powerful and potentially damaging quotes that will surface in motion papers and oral argument.

In court, a deposition transcript has certain limited uses. If someone's story changes at trial or conflicts with what was stated in the deposition, testimony from the deposition can be read at the trial. If a person dies or figures out some way to skip the trial, deposition testimony can be read at the trial.

Depositions may be long and boring and extremely tricky. In addition to having a chance to trip over every word and being badgered and ridiculed for not remembering in detail everything that happened several years and many stories ago, there usually is a chance to produce old, possibly unreadable handwritten notes—if there are any by that time—and read and explain them.

6. Should reporters keep their notes?

Press lawyers disagree, and there may be no right answer. Assuming no company "record retention" policy tells the staff how long to keep notes, reporters themselves should decide on a practice they consider to be useful to them, and then consistently follow it. It might be to save nothing but the published story or to save everything for six months, one or two years, or the length of the longest statute of limitations in the circulation area. It might be to digest the notes after publication, extracting potentially useful names, numbers, and leads and then throwing away the underlying handwritten notes. It might be to throw away handwritten notes but save documentary backup for controversial stories, such as copies of official records relied upon in preparing the stories.

A danger in keeping handwritten notes is that bad notes can become weapons against the reporter in a libel suit if they must be produced. A few states' shield laws permit the withholding of reporters' notes (Appendix B lists the shield laws), but in most states, even those with shield laws, subpoenaed notes must be produced in libel suits because they are evidence of carefulness and state of mind.

Plaintiffs' lawyers love to get hold of reporters' notes. They make for long depositions. Just reading them is tough once they're stale. If they refer to or identify confidential sources, a stream of questions about them and their contribution to the story will ensue. Even if the reporter is not compelled to answer, the unanswered questions make for discomfort and disadvantage.

Notes have a great many gaps to ask about. Names of people never interviewed and leads not pursued. Why not? Telephone numbers never called. Why? Careless? Or biased? Would that untapped source have spoken positively of the subject? Former *Detroit Free Press* reporter Paul Magnusson, writing in *Washington Journalism Review* about his experience in a libel trial, said that his seven notebooks and eighty sheets of paper "greatly prolonged and complicated the trial." The plaintiff's lawyer, repeatedly used the notes, Magnusson wrote, to suggest that "anything not contained in my notes never happened," raise suspicions about anything in the notes but not in the story, and encourage jurors to "speculate about my motives in pursuing the investigation." Magnusson advises destroying your notes before any suit is filed.

Still, a good many reporters are pack rats. Maybe they're all planning to write books someday and can't bear to throw away notebooks (or old boarding passes, used envelopes, or hotels' "Do Not Disturb" doorknob hangers). Anybody with Pack Rat Syndrome should take excellent, thorough, and readable notes. Avoid marginal comments and offensive scribbles, such as doodled nicknames and snide asides. Avoid referring to or identifying confidential sources in the notes. Consider keeping a log of the efforts to get comment from the subject of a negative story.

Probably very little good can come of saving draft manuscripts. Many a change from one draft to the next has no explanation, or if it does, it will be hard to explain to a jury full of nonwriters. Drafts can lead to all sorts of questions about who added what and who subtracted it and why; who wrote the heads and how; who reviewed the copy and for what.

Internal newsroom memoranda talking about the process of a story may also be disastrous to the defense. They may say something like, "Unless we can show he's a lying son-of-a-bitch, there's no story," or "I have nagging doubts about this story. How can it be true?" They may refer to the story by a code name, such as "Gangster." Editors and reporters should commit less of the editorial process to hard copy or, if a paper record is essential, make limited copies and ask that none be saved after the story is published.

7. Do tape recordings of interviews help or hurt in libel defense?

Litigators consulted about tapes say they've been helpful as an irrefutable record of what the source said and as proof that the reporters identified themselves and their purpose. However, eleven states have criminal laws against secret taping of private conversations by a participant: California, Florida, Georgia, Illinois, Maryland, Massachusetts, Montana, New Hampshire, Oregon, Pennsylvania, and Washington. (Michigan's and Virginia's laws have been interpreted as allowing participant taping without permission.) Reporters can be sued for money damages for illegally taping a conversation even though their motivation might have been to ensure accuracy in reporting.

8. What happens in document production?

Either side can discover the other side's documents, tapes, and other records in search of evidence. From the publisher's people, the paper trail usually is made up of notes and backup documentation used by the writer, editor-writer memoranda, draft manuscripts, tape recordings of interviews and telephone conversations, telephone logs, expense sheets, and anything related to postpublication inquiries or requests for correction. These materials might show the factual basis and sources for the story, the care with which the story was put together and who in the newsroom had a hand in it, and whatever work went into getting the other side of the story. A plaintiff's subpoenaed records in a libel case could include material that might have a bearing on truth and on damages. For a newspaper defending a review that criticized the use of bottled salad dressing, the restaurant's purchasing records are available to prove the statement was true; the restaurant's revenue and tax records before and after the publication of the review would also be relevant to its claim that it went from boom to bust solely because of the bad review.

A party may demand to "inspect" records kept by the other side. After the records have been screened by the home team lawyers and all exempt documents have been segregated, opposing counsel are allowed to look over the records and have them copied, at their expense.

People in litigation rarely turn over everything without first arguing over its relevance. Courts have the power to order production or to strike a document request that is objectionable. The records produced thus become evidence in the case and provide a basis for questions to witnesses. Courts may also enter a confidentiality order and have some sensitive documents produced "under seal," typically financial information, where one party successfully argues to keep such data secret. A confidentiality order restricts access to the documents and prohibits public disclosure of the information in them. (An order forbidding the publication of confidential facts about a plaintiff obtained in discovery is constitutional. See the reference to *Seattle Times* v. *Rhinehart* in Chapter 1, p. 29.)

9. *Does personal information about a reporter come out in a libel case?*

Yes, it may. Though information about the reporter has to seem relevant to the case, there is a lot of leeway. A plaintiff might inquire about earlier stories by the reporter that were the subject of corrections, or the reporter's messy divorce and late or delinquent child-support payments might seem to be evidence of unreliability or might show the reporter as being overwrought and distracted during the reporting on the story.

It seems unlikely that a court would allow a reporter's ex-husband to testify that she was an incompetent cook or an insatiable slut unless these observations were tied in with the libel case. However, a reporter's record of speeding, illegal parking, and driving while intoxicated was offered in a trooper's libel case as evidence that the reporter was hostile to police (Chapter 2, pp. 35–37). The "evidence" was permitted but did not affect the case; the newspaper won a summary judgment on the ground that the reporter had a good faith belief in the story, and so had not acted with actual malice.

General Ariel Sharon used *Time* correspondent David Halevy's personnel record to show he'd been reprimanded and suspended for sloppy reporting in the past (see Chapter 2, pp. 43–49). Sharon also argued that the reporter's politics showed his bias against Sharon. Sharon used Halevy's correspondence with an editor to show Halevy's distrust of Sharon's party, which he considered militaristic and fascistic. Incidental use of an editor's snide rejoinder, never meant for public consumption, made *Time* look patronizing toward Israelis.

What does all this have to do with the libel action? Maybe nothing. But the trial tactic is to show bad character; emotions overwhelming and interfering with work; a history of mistakes, corrections, and incompetence; hatred of the plaintiff; and anything else that might prejudice the defense. There is not a lot the reporter can do to hide the past.

A reporter can try to make sure there is no evidence that he or she had been "out to get" the plaintiff. It's best not to talk socially about stories, past or future, or about the people who are or are to be the subjects of stories. Unfortunately, reporters and editors talk about their work all the time, to everybody. So assuming the talk won't stop, never say to anybody that you can't wait to get somebody, do somebody in, or knock somebody off. Not inside the newsroom. Not in a bar or elevator. Nowhere. Don't even joke about it.

10. Are there accepted reporting procedures journalists should follow?

No. There's no list of do's and don'ts and there never should be. Written newsroom guidelines should be avoided. Lawyers get hives even thinking about such a thing. They're afraid a plaintiff's lawyer will make hay with the very idea that procedures had slipped.

11. If the plaintiff can bring up a lot of dirt about the writer, can the defendant at trial bring up dirt about the plaintiff?

Yes. But the dirt has to look as if it has something to do with the defense of the lawsuit—for example, bad facts about the plaintiff that show the alleged libel is true. Or, particularly with a public official or public figure plaintiff, evidence of a reputation that was bad even before the alleged libel, to prove the plaintiff didn't have much of a good name to ruin.

12. *If discovery yields a lot of bad facts about the plaintiff, can a paper publish those while the libel case is pending?*

Yes—unless the discovered material is ruled confidential and produced "under seal," meaning subject to a confidentiality order. (See the answer to Question 8, pp. 196–197.)

13. *Are the reporter's confidential sources safe from the libel plaintiff's discovery?*

Most courts recognize some privilege to shield confidential sources from certain types of inquiries based on the First Amendment or on state law, both statutory and judge-made. But the privilege may not shield the source of defamatory statements from discovery in libel cases. The need to confront and appraise the source may be crucial to the plaintiff's case, particularly where the plaintiff must show actual malice. Refusing to disclose sources of libelous remarks may alienate a jury, and defending without being able to show the quality and reliability of sources may be a losing battle. Partly for this reason, some editors and publishers have policies against running potentially libelous stories based only on confidential sources.

Twenty-six states have shield laws, "shielding" the identities of sources and materials obtained in newsgathering from discovery, but several of those by their terms are inapplicable in libel cases (see Appendix B). A few states have absolute shield laws.

The most common type of shield statute is not absolute; it simply forbids holding a newsperson in contempt for refusing to disclose sources. Governed by this type of noncontempt law, courts still can hobble the libel defense by banning any reference to an unidentified source in arguing the publisher's carefulness and by instructing juries to presume there was no source. If there were no source of an alleged libel other than the confidential source, a publisher could be forced to default.

14. *When do courts respect confidentiality of news sources?*

The journalist's privilege is most protectible where the newsperson is an outsider to other people's lawsuits and investigations. Even in states not covered by a shield law, many courts have excused journalists from testifying as third-party witnesses and from producing their notes or unpublished materials, outtakes, or photos where the evidence is not crucial or could be gathered elsewhere. Balancing the litigant's interest in getting evidence against the journalist's interest in protecting the news process from intrusion, many courts have recognized at least a limited privilege to protect newsgathering sources and materials, founded in the First Amendment.

The limited privilege for the nonparty newsperson is likely to yield, however, if the evidence is crucial and the person requesting it has no other way to get it. There, the balance is considered to tip in favor of the person seeking the information. And where a grand jury investigating crime subpoenas journalists who have committed or witnessed crimes or have unique knowledge of crimes, no general privilege or testimonial immunity exists, absent a clear shield law immunity.

15. *What possibilities exist for having a case thrown out before discovery?*

Courts will dismiss a time-barred case if the defense lawyer makes a motion for dismissal and proves that the plaintiff filed suit too late under the applicable statute of limitations.

If the supposedly libelous statement does not refer to the plaintiff, and the court determines that the statement is not "of and concerning" the plaintiff, then plaintiff loses, frequently even without discovery. For example, surviving family may not bring suit over a statement defaming a dead relative unless the statement also defames the family members themselves. Libel is a "personal" action that can be initiated only by the person libeled and only during his or her life. Whether an action can continue if the plaintiff dies after filing suit varies from state to state.

A broad, collective characterization or statement about a large group is generally not "of and concerning" any individual, either, in a way that gives a viable libel action to any particular person. "All New York City Puerto Ricans are on food stamps" is too all-encompassing and unfocused to permit any individual to claim damage to his or her reputation. Not even a Puerto Rican antidefamation league could sue on behalf of New York City Puerto Ricans; the statement technically does not refer to the league.

A statement such as this one about fifty-three people in town—"all the unindicted police officers in the department were accessories"—is sufficiently focused on identifiable individuals so that one or more of them could sue for libel. A few did.

16. *If discovery shows that the plaintiff has no case, can the press win without a trial?*

If the defense persuades the court that there's no contest, the plaintiff may not get to trial. Before trial the defense can file a motion asking the judge to grant summary judgment, arguing that the significant facts are not in dispute and that the law mandates a judgment. The plaintiff may contest the motion and argue that a trial is necessary to resolve disputed questions. The judge decides on the basis of the motion papers and both sides' briefs, with the help of oral argument.

Summary judgments have been granted in a variety of circumstances, such as where public officials and public figures could not possibly have proved actual malice, or where the statements in issue were nondefamatory terms, privileged opinions, or protected publications of official records or proceedings.

Once the trial starts, summary judgment motions can be converted to motions for a directed verdict and urged at the beginning of the trial, at the close of the plaintiff's evidence, or after all the evidence has been presented but before the jury has begun deliberating. If the judge decides that reasonable minds could come to only one decision based on the evidence, the judge may dismiss the jury and grant a verdict.

AT THE TRIAL

1. *Why does the press lose so often before a jury?*

Newspapers and broadcasters actually have excellent won-lost records in libel when the basis examined is the total suits brought rather than those that go to trial. *Newsday* on Long Island, for example, has lost only two of a hundred cases brought, with only eight cases having been tried, according to lawyer Andrew L. Hughes.

Libel defendants appear to lose more often than they win in front of a jury (although most losses are reversed on appeal or the damages are substantially reduced). One thing to keep in mind is that juries frequently get the worst cases, where there has been a bad mistake in the reporting or editing. To some extent, having weathered the summary judgment motions and defied settlement, the cases that finally end up with juries may be expected to include a high proportion of the press's losers.

On the other hand, some defense lawyers believe juries don't understand the actual malice standard or choose to ignore it and vote their sympathies for victims claiming to have been wounded by negative publicity. Plaintiffs' lawyers sometimes explain the abundant press jury losses with the axiom that the public dislikes the press and perceives newspeople as arrogant, sensationalistic, and powerful. They certainly do their part to portray reporters as gunslingers. Publishing lawyers with extensive jury practice may not be as plentiful as one might hope, and maybe the winning plaintiffs' lawyers sometimes beat them with skill and experience. It's fashionable, too, in some press law circles to denigrate the "plaintiffs' bar" as ambulance chasers in polyester suits. Perhaps some of this elitism and disdain turn the jury off.

For its part, the press should quit writing about how much people hate it and stop all public panel discussions and surveys of public animosity. Ethics and sensitivity certainly should be discussed in-house, but these well-publicized soul searchings telegraph vulnerability to plaintiffs' lawyers.

2. What enables a trial judge to throw out a jury verdict?

If no reasonable jury could have reached the verdict based on the evidence, in the view of the trial judge, then the judge can grant a motion to have the verdict set aside. The decision overriding the jury's vote is called a "judgment notwithstanding the verdict," or "judgment n.o.v." This is what the trial judge did with the jurors' verdict for William Tavoulareas against the *Washington Post* (Chapter 2, pp. 49–56). The United States Court of Appeals for the District of Columbia reinstated the jury verdict by a 2–1 vote in April 1985, then vacated it, then reconsidered it *en banc* in October 1985. The decision had not been announced when this book went to press.

3. If a trial judge denies a motion for a directed verdict and gives the case to the jury to decide, what basis is there for negating the jury's vote afterward? If the judge actually felt that all the evidence was one-way and the law really left the jury no choice, why ask the jury in the first place?

In denying a motion for a directed verdict and letting the case go to the jury, the judge theoretically is indicating that the matter is debatable and the evidence is not completely one-sided. But sometimes even seeing a clear winner and a clear loser, a judge may prefer having the security of a jury verdict to going out on a limb and handing down the verdict unilaterally. So the judge may give the case to the jury hoping for the best and have to override the verdict if it comes in wrong.

4. *Why does the press win most libel appeals?*

Very few libel cases wind up as defeats for the press ultimately after appeals courts have reviewed the trial courts' fact-findings and applied the law. Less likely than jurors to play favorites or to be influenced by emotions, the majority of a reviewing panel must find clear and convincing evidence of a deliberate or reckless libel against a public official or public figure. The Supreme Court reiterated that appeals courts have a constitutional duty to review an actual malice determination as thoroughly as if they were trying the case anew (see the note on the *Bose* case in Chapter 1, pp. 29–31). If the plaintiff has been ruled a private person, the appeals court must agree with that classification, review issues of constitutional privilege, and see that damages are not excessive. Other technical issues are reviewed, too, such as evidentiary rulings, burdens of proof, and instructions to the jury.

5. *Has the actual malice standard succeeded in protecting press freedoms or not?*

It's better protection than the press enjoyed pre-*Sullivan*, but the murky and shifting definitions of public figure make many cases unpredictable.

6. *Does the press win many libel cases on summary judgment anymore, or do most cases go to trial?*

Many courts still dispose of a considerable proportion of libel cases on summary judgment and dismiss others on various legal grounds before trial. Chief Justice Burger suggested that summary judgment should not be favored in press cases and might not be proper for state of mind evidence. But courts appear not to have been swayed by that advisory, contained in a footnote to the Supreme Court's decision in *Hutchinson* v. *Proxmire*, discussed in Chapter 1 (pp. 25–26). As this book went to press, the Supreme Court was reviewing a summary judgment question in *Anderson* v. *Liberty Lobby, Inc.* Jack Anderson, as publisher of *The Investigator* magazine (now defunct), was sued over two articles written by Charles Bermant that called the lobbying organization neo-Nazi, fascist, anti-Semitic, and racist. The procedural question for the Court was: How strong must a showing of actual malice be to defeat a motion for summary judgment? Anderson argued that his motion should succeed unless evidence of malice was clear and convincing.

7. *Who decides whether the publication is protected by some privilege, judge or jury?*

The judge decides that a publication is privileged. It is called a "question of law" for the judge, as opposed to a "question of fact" for the jury.

8. *Who determines whether the plaintiff is a public figure?*

The judge should decide that question.

9. *Who decides that a statement complained of as libelous is just opinion?*

The judge.

10. *Who decides, judge or jury, that a publication is a fair and accurate statement from an official record or proceeding?*

The judge.

11. *What tips for reporter-witnesses come from libel trials?*

Be likable and modest. Find a way to say and show that you care about people, even about those who are the subjects of negative publicity.

12. *What are some of the worst disadvantages to the defense?*

The four worst are: not being able to come up with sources because their identities are confidential; coming up with witnesses who make bad personal impressions, including editors, reporters, and sources; having a hard time explaining why a story belonged in the news in the first place and why it was considered important for the public to know; and arrogance.

13. *What are the biggest pluses in a strong press defense?*

Ability to show that the story is substantially true and fair and that it concerns a subject the public should be informed about, such as dishonest or criminal behavior in business or public life and incompetence among professionals who deal with the public.

14. *How long do libel trials usually take?*

They vary, but a one-week trial of a supposedly simple libel case seems common, and three- or four-week trials of more complex cases are not unheard of. It's time-consuming to parade people to the witness stand and lead them through their stories and the documentary evidence, adhering to technical rules of evidence and interrupting for lawyers' arguments over form and admissibility.

15. *How much time passes from the filing of a complaint through the appeal?*

That depends upon how much discovery is demanded and allowed, and how actively the adversaries decide to pursue one another. If each side jumps in as soon as the suit begins with one or two years of discovery and pretrial motions, a trial and all appeals may take three or four years. The process could be shorter or, more likely, much longer. Recently, the Supreme Court's *Bose* decision in favor of Consumers Union ended fourteen years of litigation on the subject of wandering instruments. Elmer Gertz's now famous case against the John Birch Society took an unusually long route through numerous appeals for twelve years. The *Washington Post* settled a decade-old case with Richard Nixon's friend Charles G. "Bebe" Rebozo.

16. *Why are defense costs so high?*

Many lawyers charge by the hour, and the hourly rates may vary with the kind of work performed and the seniority of the person performing it. Lawyers' fees are substantial, but typically 40 to 60 percent goes for overhead—the lower end in small communities, the higher end in big cities, according to David J. Branson of Washington, D.C. Litigation can consume enormous amounts of time, with research and the writing of court papers, reading material obtained in discovery, planning strategy, preparing witnesses for depositions and trial, trying the case, and filing appeals.

SYSTEMIC CHANGES PROPOSED

1. *Why not outlaw the "contingent fee" to discourage suits?*

Preparing and trying a case on a contingent fee basis allows a plaintiff's lawyer to collect only if the plaintiff wins a money award. The lawyer shoulders all the expenses and foregoes any fee if he or she loses the case. English law forbids taking cases on a contingency, but in the United States, the practice is ingrained and guarded by powerful vested interests. Its advantage is that it makes the courts accessible to everyone with a legal complaint. Lawyers who operate on a contingency basis take on poor people's cases that presumably might otherwise go unheard.

Opponents admit that not everyone can afford legal fees, but blame the contingency lawyers for worthless suits. Some even consider it unseemly for a lawyer to own an interest in the outcome. It is certain that the lawyer's third- or half-interest in the spoils drives up the cost of settlements.

I think it unlikely that the contingency fee will be eliminated here, but reformers may eventually succeed in imposing a ceiling on lawyers' contingent shares of settlements and awards.

2. *To discourage frivolous suits, why not make the loser pay all costs?*

This is the rule in civil suits in England, and from time to time various interest groups "study" it or propose it here. The English rule discourages litigation generally and eliminates frivolous suits, which may make the practice sound appealing, but it probably discourages poor people from using the courts for fear that even a legitimate grievance could result in a legal defeat and bankruptcy.

3. *Is it effective to countersue for damages against plaintiffs and plaintiffs' lawyers who bring frivolous libel cases?*

Sometimes. On the rare occasion in which a complaint has no legitimate legal basis and only harassment value, the defense should seek sanctions against plaintiff and lawyer. Notes on a few cases in which sanctions were approved appear in Appendix D. Some state laws provide for penalties against frivolous suitors, and courts may be persuaded that they have the power to impose such penalties even absent specific enabling statutes. Federal rules require lawyers to swear that their appeals have merit and permit penalties against lawyers for those that are frivolous. These sanctions are considered drastic; they are not imposed where a complaint is merely thin or weak, but are reserved for exceptional, clear cases of abusive, groundless litigation.

4. *Should punitive damages be abolished?*

Yes. Some states have done just that, and it does help to limit libel litigation, partly because lawyers cease to see libel complaints as potentially profitable. Louisiana, Massachusetts, Nebraska, Oregon, Puerto

Rico, and Washington do not permit punitive damages in libel. Michigan disallows punitive damages but permits the plaintiff's compensation to be increased by "exemplary" damages in libel cases where malice is proved. Several states' retraction statutes (Appendix C) limit the availability of punitive damages where a libel committed without malice has been retracted.

5. *Do the news council concept and the newspaper ombudsman represent realistic alternatives to libel litigation?*

At least one survey has suggested that some libel plaintiffs would not have sued if they could have vindicated themselves another way (see Chapter 3, p. 93). A study bill introduced in Congress in 1985 proposed a new type of libel suit that would offer a plaintiff a declaration of truth, if it were proved, but no money judgment. Some news organizations are attempting to establish alternative means of resolving disputes, but there is a good deal of resistance to the concept of outsiders on a council second-guessing the editorial process and judgment of independent publishing organizations. More publishers and broadcasters appear to be airing complaints and corrections, using ombudsmen or editors' notes or making space available for public comment in letters to the editor and op-ed pages.

RECOGNIZING LIBEL AND SLANDER

1. *How can you tell what is libelous?*

Libelous statements have three ingredients: they are false, they hurt a person's reputation, and they cause damage. The false statement— that is, one that either is actually untrue or cannot be proven true— must be of a certain type, which appears to be a factual representation, rather than a statement of opinion. It must be defamatory, meaning disparaging of the person's good name. Typically, a defamatory remark is one that accuses a person of being dishonest, incompetent, or unworthy of the respect of the community for some reason, having the effect of diminishing the esteem in which the person is held by the community. Since reputation is intangible, damage to an individual's reputation is often unquantifiable. The sort of damage libel plaintiffs usually claim is injury to their feelings and loss of other people's respect and friendship.

2. How do you screen for libel?

Any statement in an article being considered for publication that says something negative about a person, group, or business is potentially libelous. Take a close look. Will the statement hurt the person and perhaps cause friends and clients to think less highly of him or her? How do we know this is true? Are there reliable sources for this statement? Are the sources biased in some obvious way? Is the basis for the statement fully reported to the reader? And if the statement is not true, will any privilege protect it? To ward off libel suits, or defend against them when necessary, demonstrate—right in the story itself—factual backup for critical statements about people.

In a related review—not really for libel but for editorial judgment calls—ask, what is the significance of the negative statement to the story? Is this a pot-shot? Has the subject been fairly treated?

3. Is truth a defense to libel?

Truth and accuracy are the best protections there are against libel. This means that reporters' skills and perseverance in digging and sifting, interviewing and documenting are crucial for minimizing lawsuits. The libel law has a few privileges for publishing information whether or not it can be proven true, such as the privilege for reporting material from official records and proceedings, which can be printed regardless of truth simply because it is a matter of official record and the reader is told it is a report of the record (see Chapter 3, pp. 79–92). But by and large, in stories that are critical of people's integrity or the job they are doing, accurate reporting of documented facts goes a long way to avoiding libel suits.

4. It's so easy to sue. Don't people bring lawsuits whether a critical story is true or not?

Anybody can sue for anything. Libel plaintiffs and their lawyers are under no obligation to bring only responsible suits, but where the journalist was responsible, the battle usually will be won by the defendant.

5. What's the opinion privilege and is it really of any use?

If you were playwright Lillian Hellman and still alive, would you sue author Mary McCarthy for calling you "overrated" and a "dishonest writer" and saying on the Dick Cavett television show that everything you write is a lie, including the "a" and the "the"?

As a publisher, would you sue if somebody said you published a paper by paranoids for paranoids? What if that person called you a toady and a hypocrite? A sadomasochist?

If you were a writer for *Sports Illustrated,* would you sue someone who said you were possibly the worst writer on the staff and "not a graceful wordsman"?

All these remarks spawned lawsuits. But aren't they all opinions, and aren't opinions protected? Yes, they are opinions. But in each case the person complaining denied they were opinions and claimed instead that they were libelous "fact statements" that were false and damaging. Therein lies one of the problems with the opinion privilege. In some circumstances, determining what is a statement of opinion and what is a statement of fact seems completely subjective. The other problem is that the privilege for opinions is frail and misunderstood. Its most reliable use is for reporting true facts as the basis for an opinion and then stating the opinion in terms which show as clearly as possible that they represent individual evaluation, conjecture, or subjective comment. For example, "I consider [flags the opinion] the reporter irresponsible [opinion] because this year alone his errors were the basis for five corrections [factual basis for opinion]. With all these tips, the readers are alerted that they have somebody's opinion of the reporter and the facts which provided the basis for it, and they can agree or disagree. For more discussion, see Chapter 4.

6. *So it's not safe to count on the opinion privilege?*

The opinion privilege is a big trap. You can't count on people to be thick-skinned or to have a sense of humor about derogatory personal remarks and criticism of their professional abilities. The reporter needs to take such remarks seriously and do all the reporting necessary to deliver true facts along with the disparaging opinion. It is less and less certain that the opinion privilege will shield casually tossed-off slurs without facts to support them.

7. *What about name-calling? Is that opinion?*

Yes. Usually a brassy epithet is an opinion or characterization that is protected (see Chapter 3, Opinion Indicators 6, 7, and 8, pp. 102–103). For example, the word *mouthpiece* was just an epithet that a federal court in New York decided was nondefamatory. Frank Sinatra's lawyer argued that the word connoted Mafia ties, but the editor who created the headline said he had chosen the word simply because he thought it was snappy.

Reporting that a professor's peers don't consider him a serious scholar, but a mere "activist," embroiled columnists Rowland Evans and Robert Novak in litigation from 1978 through 1985 until they finally won the decision that the statement was a privileged opinion.

Quoting students who called a Stanford professor's course a mick, a gut, and a blowoff got *Newsweek* sued. Calling Kentucky Fried Chicken's gravy "wallpaper paste and sludge" got Harland Sanders (the Colonel) sued. Both *Newsweek* and the Colonel won, but probably neither had expected to be sued for their little quips.

To print opinions that may detract from a person's reputation and get maximum protection for them, work the factual proofs to the last detail and give them to the reader: Here are the facts, and based on them, here's our opinion or the source's opinion. If the disparaging remarks don't warrant that kind of treatment, then think twice before letting the casual approach suffice. This is not a case where half-cocked will do.

8. *At least the editorial page is still protected, right?*

No (see Chapter 4, pp. 114–124). Libelous statements of fact are as risky in editorials and critic's corners as they are anywhere else. What the opinion privilege protects are statements of opinion anywhere they are published. It may be that editorial pages and obvious commentary enjoy a little more leeway because readers naturally expect opinion statements in editorial essays, cartoons, letters, and signed columns, and they are inclined to interpret as opinion whatever they read there. Nevertheless, take care to couch opinions in subjective terms (see pp. 100–103, especially Opinion Indicators 1 and 2), and tell the reader that opinion is being presented (Opinion Indicators 9, 10, and 11). The normal libel rules apply to libelous statements, even in copy clearly labeled "opinion."

9. *What are some examples of opinion statements in news columns?*

Chapter 4 (pp. 103–104) discusses several examples.

If a subject being interviewed says the lawyer screwed the client, find out what facts made the speaker form such an opinion. If the story is newsworthy, then you will want to substantiate it and report it carefully. The conclusion that the lawyer "screwed" the client might or might not be recognized as a statement of opinion, even if it is presented with the true factual basis for the accusation. Remember that lawyers frequently sue for libel, so you should consider having a press lawyer preview the story.

A public official justifies spending taxpayers' money on expensive medical equipment by saying that without it the county will have to continue relying on only one private doctor whose equipment is "obsolete." Report the facts which led the official to conclude that certain machinery is obsolete, and get comment from the doctor who continues to use it.

It may be tempting to skip the facts and quote only the opinion, but the critical statement will be more easily protectible as opinion if reported with the true facts that form the speaker's basis for the opinion.

To report one animal-lover's view that the local pet store's selling of hermit crabs during the winter on Long Island is "just plain cruel," include the reasons: the cold climate will stymie the crabs' reproductive cycle. Omitting the reasons is taking the risk that a court will not recognize "cruel" as opinion. And who wants to have to try proving the truth of the statement that somebody is cruel?

10. *Humor gets more protection than straight derogatory remarks, doesn't it?*

Yes, but. . . . One person's humor may be another's actual malice, so don't think you can get away with something just because you think it's funny.

Radio announcer Johnny Walker cracked a joke at the expense of a local black TV newscaster who, he had heard, was being hospitalized for knee surgery. "Sorry to hear about that knee surgery. Must have fallen down carrying a TV during the blizzard." For that crack: $65,-000 damages!

A TV talk-show moderator did a live interview with the Nevada Republican gubernatorial primary candidate, Bill Allen. He began the interview on camera with a statement like: "Well, Mr. Allen, I thought I'd take this opportunity to let you know that you still haven't paid your bill at this station for political advertising time. Here it is, right here. Your advertising agency, eh-hmmm, sent us a check? Yes, here's the check. It bounced. If this is the way you handle your bills, I wonder how you'll handle state funds." The Nevada jury awarded Allen libel damages of $675,000. A judge cut those damages to $50,000.

A Bangor, Maine, newspaper editorial, in calling for fitness on the police force, said a particular fat cop "makes Jackie Gleason look diminutive." The Jackie Gleason look-alike eventually lost the case and the appeal, thanks to the opinion privilege.

11. What is the "Audubon privilege"?

The "Audubon privilege" is the privilege of neutrally reporting accusations made by prominent figures against one another in a newsworthy public controversy. The privilege is also called neutral reportage. The accusations can be reported without any research or checking to see whether they are true and can be printed even if they are completely false and libelous. In theory, just the fact that they are being made by prominent people fighting over a public issue makes them newsworthy, regardless of truth.

The Audubon "neutral reportage" privilege grew out of public debate over the safety of the insecticide DDT. The Audubon Society publicly spoke out against the use of the insecticide and lobbied to have it outlawed because it believed DDT was responsible for decreasing bird populations. Then a few prominent scientists published a study that concluded DDT was not a threat to birds. The Audubon Society called those scientists "paid liars" in an editorial in the Society's journal. *The New York Times* quoted the Society's remarks in an article about the controversy. One of the scientists sued both the Audubon Society and *The New York Times* for libel.

The opinion privilege could not shield "paid liars" because it was recognized as an accusation of corruption that was libelous, if false. But the Audubon privilege was fashioned by the Federal Court of Appeals for the Second Circuit to shield the entire neutral report of the newsworthy remarks, in the context of a debate between prominent leaders in a public controversy.

The Audubon privilege, never universally accepted, today has been repudiated by some courts and is held in disfavor by others. The Third Circuit specifically rejects it, and the U.S. Supreme Court has not reviewed it. If the privilege can be relied upon at all to shield libelous remarks, the accuser and the opponent must be extremely prominent people, such as candidates for public office or leaders in some controversy of public importance. The less prominent the actors, the less chance of protection from *Audubon*.

12. Is the publisher responsible for libelous letters to the editor?

Yes. Potentially libelous "fact" statements must be verified and should not be published unless they are found to be true.

13. *Can advertising be libelous, and is the publisher responsible?*

Yes. Facts and opinions in advertising need screening. There is no exception generally in the law for libel in advertising, and the publisher remains responsible for everything in the paper. Statements in political campaign advertisements and social issue advertisements (such as those about conservationists' causes) should be verified before they are published.

14. *Can the publisher force an advertiser to pay for the defense of libel complaints and damages stemming from its advertisement?*

Yes. With a valid, written indemnification agreement, the publisher can make the advertiser promise to bear all costs of a libel suit and any judgment arising from its advertisement. The advertiser will have to come up with the money for legal fees and damages or settlement.

15. *Is it possible to sue for the libel of a dead person?*

No. A person must be alive to be libeled and stay alive long enough to file a civil libel suit. If the person dies after filing, some states allow the dead person's estate to continue the suit. The family of the deceased cannot initiate a suit on behalf of the dead person, and they themselves have a libel action only if the damaging statements refer to them personally.

Some criminal libel statutes, discussed below, make it a crime to tarnish the memory of the dead, but they appear to be in disuse and may be invalid, to the extent that they conflict with the Supreme Court's libel decisions citing constitutional grounds.

16. *Are criminal libel statutes a threat?*

Probably not. Most states have or have had criminal libel laws, but have not used them recently. Probably many of those laws could not withstand a challenge to their constitutionality. Standard criminal libel statutes are a vestige of old "fighting words" laws, which make it a misdemeanor or low class felony to provoke a breach of the peace or to disparage the memory of a dead person. Some statutes specifically outlaw impugning the chastity of a lady or the solvency of a bank. Even though criminal libel laws remain "on the books" in many places, they are of questionable validity because they generally place limits on the defense of truth and do not ensure the protections of *New York Times*

Co. v. *Sullivan.* The Supreme Court ruled in *Garrison* v. *Louisiana* in 1964 that the actual malice standard must be applied in criminal libel prosecutions as well as civil suits.

At least seven states have abolished their criminal libel laws: Arizona, Delaware, Hawaii, Indiana, Nebraska, New Jersey and New York. Six others have held their criminal libel laws unconstitutional: Alaska, Arkansas, Georgia, Louisiana, Mississippi, and Pennsylvania. The majority of states have had no prosecutions this century.

I know of only a few states that have reported criminal libel prosecutions in the 1980s: Georgia (voided its statute as unconstitutional); Illinois (upheld its statute, at least when aimed at libels of private people). New Hampshire's criminal libel law was referred to tangentially in 1984 by the United States Supreme Court, although the statute was not at issue in the case. The Court made the remarks in the course of deciding that an out-of-state libel plaintiff could sue an out-of-state publication, *Hustler* magazine, in New Hampshire (see Chapter 1, pp. 27–28). As a basis for approving New Hampshire's jurisdiction over *Keeton* v. *Hustler,* the Supreme Court pointed to the state's interest in protecting people within its borders from exposure to libels, as evidenced by its criminal libel law.

Despite these recent incidents of criminal libel activity, criminal libel is mostly dormant. Colorado and Oklahoma report no criminal libel trials since the 1930s, Florida's latest one was in 1953, and New Mexico and North Dakota last used their statutes in the 1960s.

17. *What is slander?*

Slander is an oral, false reputation-damaging statement made to one or more people about another person. The same statement would be libelous if it were published. Actions for slander are not as common as those for libel, but they do exist. In a libel case, the plaintiff may add a slander count if accusations were made orally as well as in print. Occasionally, libel plaintiffs add a slander count and accuse the reporter of slandering them while interviewing, so it is best to avoid spreading defamatory information in the reporting process. Example: "Our investigation shows that Guy 'The Horse' Todano is a Mafia hit man. What do you know about him?"; or "We are doing a story on street prostitution. What have you heard about Kathy Tine?" Likewise, the source may slander the subject in his or her response to your question. A reporter's notes of the source's remarks can be used as evidence against the source.

18. *Is it possible to slander someone while interviewing for a story?*

Yes. Telling an interview subject that "We already know Jones is guilty; we just need you to verify it" slanders Jones if it's false. A safer opening gambit would be "We're looking into Jones's role in the company, and we'd like to talk with you about what you know."

19. *What is the "innocent construction" rule?*

Words capable of being read innocently must be read innocently and declared nonlibelous under the rule of innocent construction. The judge in a libel case determines whether the complained-of statement has more than one meaning and whether one of its meanings is nondefamatory without taking innuendo into account, without considering how the statement was actually understood by readers, or even how it was intended. Only a few states recognize or appear to approve of the rule: Illinois, Missouri, Montana, New Mexico, Ohio (nonmedia), and Oklahoma. Highly favorable to libel defendants, the rule results in some strained interpretations of language. Illinois once found that "to fix a ticket" was capable of being innocently construed and recently declared "mobster" capable of innocent construction.

THE REPORTING AND EDITING PROCESS

1. *Is it necessary for a newsperson to identify himself or herself and to get permission for an interview?*

Not always. Plenty of news stories would never be written if this were the rule. Newsworthy "consumer" stories, for instance, such as restaurant reviews and comparisons of competing tax preparers or competing bank services do not require the reporter to identify himself or herself. As long as the reporter considers it ethical, he or she should be free to patronize establishments open to the public and to write about the experience (see Chapter 6, pp. 173–178).

"Undercover" work by reporters sometimes accounts for stories about illegal or questionable activities, such as bar and liquor store sales to minors or "steering" by real estate agents to preserve segregation. It is illegal to trespass by breaking in or by impersonating. To get onto private property, a reporter should identify himself or herself and state the purpose of the visit. But where there is no trespass, ethics alone should determine how a reporter goes about looking into some problem of public concern.

Where the story is more a feature than news, and especially where the subject is a private person unsophisticated in dealing with news people, reporters and photographers need to make their identity and purpose very clear. Consent is crucial to publishing an interview and a photograph of a private person about private woes, such as coping with alcoholism or drugs, chronic gambling or delinquent kids.

2. Does consent to an interview or photo need to be written?

Get a written consent before using a person's name or portrait in advertising (Chapter 6, 172–173). A consent for an interview or photograph used editorially may be either oral or written, but if there's a swearing contest, writing is nice because it's easier to prove (see Chapter 6, pp. 179–180).

3. Can consent be revoked before publication?

Yes. If the subject cancels the consent to a story or picture while there is still time to stop it, even if the story is already completely laid out, the editor faces difficult choices. Pulling the story at the last minute makes for a big hole and a mad scramble for filler. If no consent was needed in the first place, because the story is clearly newsworthy and the interview was obtained without trickery, then it may be a reasonable choice to run it anyway—this is what *Sports Illustrated* chose to do with the body surfer story discussed in Chapter 5 (pp. 156–158). But if the subject whose consent is needed cannot be charmed into consenting again, and the story is only marginally newsworthy, running without permission might expose the journalist to a privacy complaint. News interviews of sophisticated subjects should be publishable despite revoked consent provided the subject is of legitimate public concern and has not been hoodwinked by the journalist. If the reporter and editors can consult a lawyer about the impact of a revoked consent, the lawyer may be able to give some useful advice.

4. Is it necessary to get comment from the other side?

No. It's not a legal requirement, but it shows fairness and is exceedingly helpful to a libel defense. Some libel lawyers think it is an extreme disadvantage to defend a journalist who had not made an effort to contact the subject of a damaging story and get comment. Try for comment from the subject no matter what, even if you're positive the person will decline to talk or merely deny the charges. Include the comment in the story or tell the reader that you tried to reach the subject, without success.

5. *What if the subject is unavailable? How many tries are enough?*

There is no magic number. A serious effort to contact the person for comment is enough. Depending on the particular case, it might be sufficient to call the likely haunts a few times and leave unmistakably informative messages. On a story with lead time, drop a note off at the subject's home, office, and club: "We want to talk with you for a story about bank finances before it runs Tuesday. Please call these numbers night or day."

6. *What if the subject won't talk?*

Log the attempts made to contact the subject for comment and try interviewing other people who might supply facts and present some of the points of view from the subject's side of the story. The subject's lawyers, bank colleagues, or family may comment. Other publications' treatment of the subject may provide leads to sources surrounding the subject. Within the time available, all the work done in an attempt to assemble and understand the other side of the story will pay off journalistically.

7. *But in libel law there's no obligation to tell the "other side of the story." Right?*

Technically that's right. But it's easier to avert or to win a libel case on a story that looks fair. The concept of neutrality is more acceptable to people than the vision of a reporter's setting out to prove a thesis.

ACTUAL MALICE

1. *What is actual malice?*

Publishing with actual malice means publishing a libelous statement knowing it to be false or with serious doubts about whether it is true or false (see Chapter 2, pp. 32–62). Actual malice is the standard of conduct that must be applied in a libel case brought by a public official or public figure, as a matter of constitutional law, according to the 1964 Supreme Court decision, *New York Times Co.* v. *Sullivan*, discussed in Chapter 1 (pp. 10–14). Actual malice is also the prerequisite for punitive damages in libel cases, whether the plaintiff is a public or a private person, according to the Supreme Court, if the story is of public concern (see Chapter 1, pp. 22–31).

2. Who is a public official for libel purposes?

A libel plaintiff will be recognized as a public official, and required to prove actual malice, if it can be shown that he or she has been elected or appointed to a significant official position with decision-making or policy-making authority and some actual control. Not just anybody on the public payroll is a public official. Not even every elected official qualifies. Rulings are not always consistent from state to state. A mayor and the mayor's high-ranking deputies, boro and town council members, and officials with purse strings, such as treasurers and tax assessors, are public officials. Judges and commissioners are public officials. A uniformed police officer on the beat, however lowly in rank, has been ruled a public official because the officer is in charge of public safety and law and order and embodies governmental authority.

A person employed in a public job without a title or apparently "important" rank may or may not be defined as a public official. Thus, writing negatively about the job performance of a low-ranking employee on the public payroll may or may not be protected by the actual malice standard, so exercise the greatest care. A teacher in a public school system was ruled a public official by Arizona and Virginia courts, but a private figure in New York, Ohio, and California. In Texas, a court reporter criticized for filing late transcripts was ruled a private figure.

Consultants to government may or may not be public officials, depending upon such factors as the consultants' name recognition in public, access to the press, and whether they actually have policy-making roles in the areas related to the claimed libel.

3. Does passage of time destroy public official status?

It shouldn't if the statements complained about as being libelous concern performance in the public capacity.

4. Who is a public figure?

It's hard to predict who will be considered a public figure because the standards are not clear-cut (see Chapter 1, pp. 22–26). The easiest to spot are big celebrities whose names are "household words" and whose lives are public for virtually all purposes. "Pervasive public figures," as lawyers call these stars, are entertainers, sports figures, high-profile authors, big corporations and prominent corporate business executives, notorious big-time criminals, and well-known personalities. These people have public reputations and news value. Look for voluntary activity in the public sphere and access to the press as signs that a person is a public figure.

Seeking the limelight to influence public opinion or win votes or attract attention can be the mark of a public figure, and if public activities are sustained over a period of years, the person may become a public figure for all purposes. More commonly, though, a person known for a single public stance or activity becomes a public figure only for the limited purpose of comment about that aspect of his or her conduct. The person remains a private figure with respect to publicity about the other aspects of his or her life. This limited public figure status is addressed further in the next question.

It appears that many courts are choking down on public figure determinations and are defining more plaintiffs as private figures, including a medium-sized boat-building company in Massachusetts, a resort casino in California, an Oregon bank, and a New Jersey former bank chairman, all of whom were recently ruled private figures.

5. What's a limited public figure?

A person who is primarily a private citizen but who speaks out or voluntarily assumes a public role in a particular controversy or event may be classified a limited public figure. If the person brings a libel case based on comment about that particular matter, he or she may be defined as a limited public figure, or a "vortex public figure." Look for the voluntary action of injecting oneself into the public sphere, such as making speeches, selling memberships, conducting a campaign, or advertising or writing letters to advocate a point of view.

The sphere of a limited or vortex public figure is narrow and getting narrower. The idea was that people who thrust themselves to the forefront of public controversies in order to influence the resolution of the issues assume the risk of negative publicity by inviting attention and comment, this according to the Supreme Court in *Gertz v. Robert Welch, Inc.* Lawyer Elmer Gertz ultimately was ruled not to be a public figure, but only a private lawyer bringing a case that happened to stir the comment of the John Birch Society, which called him a Communist. The Court ruled Gertz was not out campaigning to influence the public's views and did not seek publicity about his politics (see Chapter 1, pp. 22–25).

6. *What types of people have been ruled limited or vortex public figures?*

People who may be ruled limited public figures are those who have gained some notoriety by leading campaigns—for example, drives for support on issues such as tax reform, conservation, weaponry, and international political stances; charity drives; campaigns to remove somebody from public office; and campaigns to influence zoning laws. Others are people acting as leaders, proponents, or spokespeople of organizations or movements and a corporation making a public offering. People voluntarily performing duties in the public sphere or involved in squabbles about public issues can be ruled public figures with respect to comment about their public activity, but it is impossible to guarantee such a ruling, as seen in the Golden Fleece case (Chapter 1, pp. 25–26), in which a research scientist criticized for work performed with public funds was ruled to be a private figure, and in the horse breeder case (Chapter 3, pp. 90–92), in which a former bank chairman was ruled a private figure in a story about his loans from the bank.

A person who is ruled a limited public figure will have to prove actual malice in a libel case arising from publicity about his or her role in the public sphere. But remember, the person is ruled "public" for the limited purpose of comment about the issue on which the person has "gone public" and not for all purposes. Statements about one's private life or unrelated activity may still be tested, as they would for a private figure, by the negligence standard rather than the actual malice standard. For example, a lawyer urging the recall of the city council president could be a limited public figure as to reports about that activity but a private figure for statements about his default on child-support payments.

7. *How can reporters tell if somebody is a vortex public figure?*

They can't. A lot of problems without direct, local precedent are a gamble. A lawyer's advice may help, but no one has a crystal ball. In general, trying to guess whom the courts would find to be a public figure is rather futile. It's probably more productive to spend the time verifying the facts, scrutinizing the sources, trying to get the other side of the story, and being satisfied that the statement belongs in the story and that it's as defensible as can be.

8. *Is a person arrested for a crime a limited or vortex public figure?*

No, not unless the person was a public official or a public figure before arrest. The act of being arrested will not convert a private person to a public one, even for purposes of reporting on the arrest. The courts are likely to decide that the person did not "volunteer" to be arrested or engage in criminal activity in order to attract press attention. Similarly, filing for divorce or bringing suit against someone is not in and of itself the type of voluntary public act that creates a vortex public figure.

Most people named in ordinary crime stories are private figures, and consequently negligence usually is the standard when those reports give the wrong name, get the charge wrong, or make some other error that hurts somebody's reputation. If the wrong information was taken by the reporter directly from the official written record, it is privileged. But if it's a report based on oral remarks of the police, it generally is not privileged. There, the test in court usually will be whether the reporter was negligent for not checking further. One South Carolina case even held that it was actual malice for a reporter to have relied on a desk officer's oral report instead of personally checking the official written record (see Chapter 3 for more information on the use of police records, especially pp. 64–67).

9. *So, if a reporter makes a mistake on an arrest report and identifies somebody as having been arrested when the person actually was a witness to the crime, that's a negligence case of libel?*

Yes. In most states simple negligence is the test and the press frequently settles this kind of case or loses a few thousand dollars in damages, unless the error came from the written police record. If the paper can claim a privilege for a fair and accurate report of the written police record, then the libel plaintiff should lose. If the reporter got the wrong information from what "police said," the official record privilege often will not be applied and the judge or jury will decide whether it was negligent to take the word of the police. If police deny giving the information to the reporter, it becomes the police's word against that of the reporter and a losing case. Chapter 3 gives examples of libel cases from the police beat.

10. *What is negligence?*

It's carelessness. In libel trials, it means proving that the editorial process was not as careful as it should have been in the eyes of reasonable people. Perhaps the reporter took a disastrous short cut or failed to pursue a lead or was unlucky enough on the crime beat to get the name of the felon right but to pick the wrong address out of the telephone book. The negligence standard is the subject of Chapter 3.

11. *If the libel plaintiff is a private person but the story is of public concern, doesn't actual malice apply?*

The negligence standard is applied in most states when a private person sues for libel, no matter what the subject of the story. Only a few states have a standard tougher than negligence for private plaintiffs who claim to have been libeled in a story about a public matter. In New York, "grossly irresponsible" conduct is the standard. Actual malice is the standard in Alaska, Colorado, Indiana, and Michigan.

12. *Is actual malice a prerequisite to punitive damages?*

Yes. Every state is subject to the Supreme Court's declaration that even private plaintiffs must show actual malice to claim punitive damages if a story is of public concern (see the discussion of *Gertz* v. *Robert Welch, Inc.* and *Dun & Bradstreet* v. *Greenmoss Builders, Inc.* in Chapter 1, pp. 22–27 and 30–31).

13. *How do plaintiffs prove actual malice?*

Either "knowing falsity" or "reckless disregard" is the test. In rare cases, a writer has made up a libel. Officials in charge of Colorado public school ski programs got a reporter to admit that he had no source for his story accusing them of accepting free resort passes and bypassing competitive bidding procedures. In other words, the story was a deliberate lie, and the reporter was ruled to have acted with actual malice.

Reckless disregard is usually the thrust of actual malice proofs, discussed in Chapter 2 (pp. 33–62). Proof that the journalist doubted that the story was true but published anyway is the best evidence of actual malice.

Carol Burnett proved that the *National Enquirer* published false gossip about her despite a warning from the person the *Enquirer* sent to investigate and confirm the story. The jury found actual malice based in part on the trial testimony of the *Enquirer's* researcher, who testified for Carol Burnett. He said he had told the editor before deadline that he had not been able to substantiate the tip about her traipsing around a Washington restaurant and fighting with Henry Kissinger. The *Enquirer* published the story anyway.

Publishing a libelous story accusing coaches of fixing a football game, relying only on the say-so of a convicted check forger, was actual malice. The *Saturday Evening Post* had to pay Georgia coach Wallace (Wally) Butts $460,000 and Alabama coach Bear Bryant an undisclosed settlement award (see Chapter 1, pp. 16–19). Accusing San Francisco mayor Joseph Alioto of mob connections on the basis of contradicted interviews with an inveterate liar was actual malice and resulted in $400,000 damages (see Chapter 2, pp.37–42). Reporting that a presidential candidate was mentally unstable, based on a dishonest and distorted survey of psychiatrists, was actual malice, for which Ralph Ginzburg had to pay $75,000 damages to Barry Goldwater.

Failure to investigate, by itself, does not amount to actual malice, and there is no responsibility to do exhaustive research or even verify information where there is no reason to doubt the statement (see Chapter 2, pp. 35–37). And just the misreading or misinterpretation of a document or an error in judgment by itself would not amount to actual malice, unless the journalist entertained doubts about the truth of the story (see the discussion of General Sharon's suit against *Time* magazine in Chapter 2 at pp. 43–49). The plaintiff has the burden of proving actual malice with "clear and convincing evidence." This means showing an unconcern with the truth or determination to publish despite unresolved questions about the truth.

14. *Is there any forgiveness for mistakes in "hot news," when a story is produced on deadline?*

Yes. Some courts have recognized that time constraints on daily journalists preclude exhaustive research and have considered deadline pressure, among other factors, in excusing reporting mistakes. But just as many courts have not grasped what the rush was all about, particularly on a potentially libelous story. From these courts, the typical opinion asks, "Wouldn't it be more responsible to hold off a day and do more research before rushing to press with a story that hurts a person's reputation?"

In libel cases against weeklies, television broadcasts with long lead times, and books, where the fact-checking has gone awry, it is common for courts to be more unforgiving of mistakes that might have been avoided with more checking, typically with a scolding remark, such as,

"This wasn't even hot news. You had a lot of time to get it right." And one New York court has said that it would apply a higher standard of thoroughness and accuracy in a libel suit arising from investigative reporting, where journalists' initiatives rather than breaking events have produced the news (see Chapter 2, pp. 56–61).

USING PUBLIC RECORDS

The most valuable privilege comes from reporting on official records and official proceedings. Even libelous statements are protected if they come from official records or proceedings and are reported fairly and accurately—"fairly" means neutrally. To rely on the privilege for reporting statements contained in official proceedings or records, where the statements disparage a person, show the reader the context and cite the record or proceeding. Present unproved accusations and ongoing disputes with enough detail to make clear that the truth is still unresolved.

"Accurately" means substantially accurately. The report does not have to be verbatim, but summarize carefully, without distorting or omitting facts that could be considered critical. Be especially strict about accuracy when translating legalisms into lay terms. If lawyers could consider the result inaccurate, the privilege may fail. More guidance on reporting on public records appears in Chapter 3 (pp. 79–92).

What's a "public record" and what's accessible are peculiarly local questions. The answers below are general and beg for consideration by an experienced local lawyer who actually has tackled the authorities and occasionally has won the exciting game of what's public and how to get it.

Police Reports

1. *Are police reports public records?*

Bare incident reports should be public records, although police departments in some places refuse to let reporters look at them. These reports, sometimes called the blotter, should identify suspects in custody and name anybody arrested or charged, giving at least bare details of the incidents. In many places, police also make more detailed reports about the circumstances of a crime, the scene, and the witnesses, and these detailed remarks may or may not be public records.

Increasingly, reporters have said they're unable to get police to tell the value of stolen property or to identify suspects. Police concerns for "privacy" are misguided at times, but negotiating for more information may be the best way to work while avoiding alienating police sources.

2. *Do police have to show the reporter the incident reports?*

The incident reports seem inescapably to be public records, and yet some police don't show them to reporters and insist on reading the incident reports aloud. It's worth fighting for the right to see the record.

3. *What can the reporter do if police insist on telling the reporter what is on the blotter and refuse to show it?*

Negotiate a change in police policy. Consult a lawyer to see if he or she can recommend other action that might get good results. You will not be guaranteed the protection of the public record privilege for information police give orally.

4. *When people call to say the police report was wrong and demand a retraction, what should the paper do?*

Offer to run a correction once the statement is corrected in the official record.

5. *What if the police have confused the criminal's name with the victim's name on the official record? Can the victim bring a libel complaint against the paper?*

Yes, but the victim should lose because the mistaken report is privileged, having stemmed from the mistaken official record. If the victim calls the paper's attention to the mistake, offer a correction once the statement is corrected in the official record.

6. *If a paper generally reports all drunk driving citations but occasionally omits the names of friends of the publisher, do the people whose names are included have a legal complaint?*

No.

7. *After reporting an arrest, must a paper follow up and report the suspect's release if the police decide they made a mistake?*

There's no legal obligation to continue reporting a story. If coverage does continue and the suspect's release is reported, flag the clips in the morgue to prevent anyone from seizing on the original report.

8. *What if the reporter knows the official record is false?*

Actual malice may void the privilege to report the substance of official records, so there may be no privilege for the reporter to deliberately write a false report.

9. *If the reporter does not actually consult the official record but police give the name of the person they've arrested and charged, is that good enough?*

The courts are all over the lot on how to treat an error that is not in the official record but which came from the police, as discussed in Chapter 3 (p. 80). Some courts will uphold the record privilege even where the reporter has not actually seen the record if the reporter has taken the information over the telephone from an officer who is reading from the record or from a police radio hot line instituted by the police specifically for the purpose of informing newspeople. Usually the question to be resolved in a libel suit is whether or not it seems negligent for the reporter not to have personally checked the written official record. If police never show the record but always read it to the reporter, then the reporter should not be considered negligent. If the record is on view but the routine practice of telephoning has been reliable in the past, the reporter should not be considered negligent for following the routine. But, beware! A court may disagree and fault the reporter for failing to look at the record, even if that means requiring a reporter to drive long distances to the precincts. A local libel attorney's advice on the best procedure could be useful. It should help the reporter to be able to testify that, as usual, he or she called the desk sergeant at the regular time, asked the officer to read from the official record, and relied on what the officer said. Some courts have found this procedure adequate despite the fact that it resulted in an error, but other courts have considered it negligent.

In any state, it is risky to rely solely on the word of a police officer while the officer is at a crime scene or if the officer is not apparently reading the official record. Some of what "police say" is libelous, and there is no privilege for the press to quote the unsupported libelous remarks of police. There are too many libel cases over what "police say," and too many times, the police deny saying it.

10. *Where police officers use tape recordings as official records, are the tapes public?*

Probably.

11. *Autopsy records sometimes sit on the shelf for months. Is there some way to speed up access to them?*

Timeliness of autopsy reports may be a requirement in the state record law. If negotiations for quicker access fail, with a lawyer's advice it may be possible to bring pressure upon authorities or bring an action for the release of an overdue report.

Hospital Notices

1. *Are hospital records of births and deaths official public records?*

Yes, in some areas. There may be statutes or regulations governing hospital records, and it would be helpful to research them locally or ask a lawyer which hospital records are public and which are private.

2. *Are hospital lists of admissions and discharges official public records?*

Hospitals do produce such lists in some areas and they are public records. Statutes or regulations may require hospitals to report admission or treatment of accident or shooting victims or may provide for listing all admissions. Some newspapers publish the hospital listings along with police and court dockets. It would be helpful to research the local regulations or to ask a lawyer for specific guidance on which hospital records are public and which are private.

3. *Does it invade people's privacy to report their hospitalization?*

If the admission record is a public one, a report will not invade privacy.

4. *What if they're embarrassed about the reason for their admission, such as for a face lift?*

Even genuine embarrassment should not create a winning lawsuit. Assuming the cause for admission to the hospital is not in the record or in the paper, the bare fact of admission is a protected report based on the record.

5. *Where a paper's routine birth announcements from hospital records give parents' names, should a single mother be left out to spare her embarrassment, since her listing shows she's unwed?*

Practices vary among newspapers. The editor's taste, rather than law, governs decisions here. Assuming the hospital record is public, the report will not invade privacy. It is a mistake to assume a single mother always is embarrassed, but the issue is sensitive and considered scandalous in some communities.

6. *If an unwed mother identifies the newborn's father, should the paper publish his name along with the hospital listing of the birth?*

No, that's too dangerous, unless there's a public record of paternity to rely on.

7. *If an unwed father says he wishes to be identified, should the paper publish his name with the hospital listing of birth?*

The paper may accommodate the father who consents in writing, or it could suggest that he get his name in the hospital listing and publish in reliance on that.

8. *The paper publishes a list which shows that a single person living alone is in the hospital, so a burglar takes that opportunity to clean the person's house out. Is the paper liable?*

No.

Official Proceedings

1. *Given the fairness requirement, is the privilege jeopardized if a paper covers only an exciting fight in a long public meeting and ignores the rest of the agenda?*

No. A fair and accurate rendition of whatever is reported from the public meeting will do. The fairness stipulation does not mean that everything on the agenda deserves coverage.

2. *Is it always safe to publish material from a public record or an official proceeding?*

No. The privilege is just that—a privilege. It's an exception to the general principle that a publisher is responsible for publishing libel. There may be no privilege for deliberately and knowingly publishing lies, even from the public record. In some locales, private citizens can submit text and documents for inclusion in the "public" record, and some of this material is scurrilous! Local news people recognize it and usually decline to publish it, even though it is in the record, not caring to test whether it qualifies for the official record privilege.

3. *Does the record privilege protect reports based on sealed records, such as those filed in a divorce suit?*

If the records are nonpublic, then there may be no privilege. In some states divorce filings are confidential, at least until the matter comes to trial. A local libel lawyer's advice could help here.

4. *Is it legal to report the name of a juvenile who has been charged with an offense, or to publish a photograph identifying a juvenile offender?*

Yes. A state has the authority to close certain judicial records and proceedings to the public and the press. Accordingly, juvenile records may be designated as confidential, and reports based upon them may not qualify for the privilege to report on an official record. However, if a paper can find out the identity of a juvenile offender using legal means, it can publish news about him or her, use a photograph, and rely on a defense of truth. Some papers have policies against identifying juveniles and some identify them only in exceptional cases. Some state statutes have forbidden publishers from identifying juvenile offenders, but invariably such broad prohibitions are declared unconstitutional as prior restraints upon the press (see Chapter 5, pp. 155–156).

5. *If juvenile court proceedings are closed to the public, are a juvenile's arrest and court records public?*

No. A state is permitted to close juvenile proceedings and to seal records, making them nonpublic.

6. *Is it legal to report the name of a rape victim?*

Yes. If the information is not available in a public proceeding or record but can be learned another way, laws cannot forbid its publication.

The press may choose how to treat rape victims (Chapter 5, pp. 155–156).

7. Does the record privilege cover a fair and accurate report of a complaint filed in civil suit?

State practices vary (see discussion in Chapter 3, pp. 80–85). A filed civil complaint is now apparently regarded as an official record in a majority of jurisdictions. The complaint may be entirely one-sided and may make accusations that are not true, but a fair and accurate report of the substance of the complaint should qualify as a report on an official record. In a minority of jurisdictions, though, lawyers counsel media clients that some official action must be taken on a complaint before the complaint can provide a basis for the privilege for fair and accurate reporting on official matters. Even lawyers practicing in the same state give different advice based on their reading and understanding. It is wise to defer to precedent from the jurisdiction or to the advice of an experienced local lawyer where there is no current local precedent.

8. Can a paper immediately report the filing of a civil complaint, without getting comment from the person who has been sued or waiting for an answer to be filed?

Yes, if it's in a jurisdiction where a filed complaint is considered official record (see answer to question 7 above). In a significant story, the journalist may want to try to get comment from the person being sued, but there is no obligation to get comment or to wait for the official answer to be filed. Remember, it is good form to cite to the record: "According to a civil complaint filed today," and to let readers know that there is another side, even simply by adding, "The answer is due in twenty days."

In a jurisdiction which subscribes to the minority position that a civil complaint is not covered by the record privilege until it is acted upon, you should get a lawyer's advice about what other action must be taken upon the complaint before your report on it will be privileged.

9. How protective is "allegedly"?

This poor, overworked word has its place but not in every sentence. When a person is charged but not convicted, "alleged arsonist" is, of course, preferable to "arsonist." But if a crime report is fundamentally wrong and libelous and derives from sources other than written public records, "allegedly" in and of itself will not save the day. "Jones allegedly robbed the bank, police say" libels Jones if he or she is not the accused culprit.

"Allegedly" just means reportedly. If there is a reliable source or good reason to believe that a statement is true, then it's reportable. But there is no protection for just passing along unconfirmed gossip, prefaced by "allegedly."

10. *If a paper or broadcaster reports on some part of a trial but not on every day of testimony, can the fairness requirement still be met?*

Yes. Overall, the effect of coverage should be neutral delivery, to tell people what's going on in the proceedings, and to put various charges and countercharges in context. Sometimes just a sentence or two can effectively summarize the accusation, the defense, and the status of the proceeding.

11. *Does a report of testimony at pretrial depositions qualify for the official record privilege?*

A deposition transcript signed by the witness and filed in the open public file of the action should be an official record. Unless the transcript is signed and filed as an open record (not sealed), a report based on it may not qualify for the privilege.

Also, study the entire deposition transcript so as to make the report on it fair and accurate. If a deposition witness testifies on "direct" examination and later covers the same territory on "cross," both statements may have to be digested and reflected in a fair report. Tell the readers enough about the surrounding circumstances to make them aware the context is litigation and that the witness is involved or interested in some way in the proceedings.

12. *Is an affidavit filed in a case an official record?*

Yes. Give a balanced, accurate report and tell readers the context so they can understand it to be one person's sworn version of facts entered into the file of a case in litigation. Don't report on the affidavit as if the facts in it are true, and don't call it testimony. If the affidavit is under seal and is not a public record, a report on its contents may not be privileged.

13. *What are the most common errors that have undermined the privilege?*

First and foremost, little mistakes, such as the name or address of someone in trouble with the law, or the charge or disposition of the case can undermine the privilege for a fair and accurate report of a public record or proceeding (see Chapter 3, pp. 70–73).

In the eyes of a court, misusing legal terms or translating them into lay terms can void the privilege if the result is inaccurate. It is particularly risky to use criminal law terms in describing the outcome of a civil suit. For example, it is not strictly accurate to report that a defendant is "convicted" or "guilty" in civil litigation. In a contract action, a defendant who is found to have violated, breached, or broken the contract, is held "liable" or "responsible."

Summarizing proceedings in a way that leaves out crucial information may create a misunderstanding. This happens perhaps most often when an old story that unfolded over time is given in summary form as background for a current event. For example, in a new item on police brutality, several past incidents are recited. One thumbnail sketch gives the name of the officer accused of wrongdoing in a past incident but does not mention that he was exonerated.

Misunderstanding or misstating the nature or outcome of proceedings or the sense of an official record may spoil the accuracy or fairness of the report. To save time and mistakes, cultivate friendly experts willing to consult from time to time on stories that seem to require expert knowledge—a lawyer with knowledge of various types of proceedings, a financial expert intimate with technical terms of mortgages and bankruptcy filings (see Chapter 3, pp. 90–92).

Sensationalizing is off-limits, if the plan is to rely on the privilege, because it may destroy the fairness of the story. Watch your copy all the way through the copydesk and the headline process to preserve its balanced, neutral delivery. (See Chapter 3, pp. 82–85, in which a headline was considered to have distorted a report based on a civil complaint.)

14. *What's said outside the proceeding by a lawyer on the case is not covered by the privilege, right?*

In general, no privilege is available for reports of people's remarks outside the proceeding. Naturally, this doesn't mean it's impossible to report on an interview with the parties or lawyers outside the courtroom. It just means that privilege probably won't protect such report-ing, and all the normal libel principles apply.

Old Records

1. *Is it safe to publish an embarrassing fact about somebody from a public record, no matter how old the record?*

The United States Supreme Court has not yet decided this question, but several lower courts have ruled that no privacy action can arise from a fair and true report based on an official record. Bringing up an old conviction (in the context of a lawyer's announcement of his third marriage) did not invade privacy (Chapter 5, pp. 154–155). Neither did a historical item naming the last person to have been punished in Del-aware's stocks. In each case, the court might have considered that good taste or charity should have dissuaded the paper from running the em-barrassing truth, but affirmed the paper's right to publish newsworthy information from old public records.

Assuming the law will leave the press free to decide, news judg-ment is the test of whether to dredge up old negative information about people, as explored in Chapter 5 (pp. 148–155). Ask yourself why the old fact is important to the story and to the public today, and tell the reader right in the story. If the subject is campaigning for office or is an opinion leader or prominent person now, it is important that readers be informed of the person's background and earlier activities. If the current report of the person's past serves some public purpose, what is it? If the item is merely entertaining and arguably just gratui-tously embarrassing, why run it?

True old facts that embarrass should not be actionable, but a false damaging report is libelous, so be careful that old information includes corrective facts or subsequent events which affected the outcome. If an old arrest resulted in acquittal or an old conviction has been over-turned, a true report should include the final result. Many publications have no filing system that consistently couples corrections with the underlying story or follow-ups with the original item. This keeps life in-teresting but may cause libel problems.

2. *Where official criminal records of a prescribed age are "erased" by operation of state expungement laws, are the old facts unprintable?*

No. Facts are still facts. Whether an official record privilege attaches once the record is purged is a conundrum. The record privilege should prevail. However, this is a rather new area and only time and experience will sort out the problems.

PRIVACY

Embarrassment, false light, and trespass are "privacy" concerns for newspeople, as discussed in Chapters 5 and 6. In general, there is a privilege to report true facts if they are newsworthy, even though they are embarrassing. The important question is whether they are legitimately of public interest, rather than just private secrets.

The law gives wide latitude and discretion to the press to decide what to publish. Tastes, styles, and news judgments vary. Where the press can give a credible news reason for going public with somebody's embarrassing secret, there should be no invasion of privacy. Where the press cannot justify an outrageous revelation of a person's intimate secret and appears to be serving only prurient interest, a privacy action may succeed.

In sensitive stories, such as those about people's sexual preferences, bad habits, old convictions, past misconduct, and family life, newspeople need to ask themselves, "Why should this information be made public now?" A reasonable answer tells why the information is newsworthy (see Chapter 5, pp. 135–159). Tell the reader, too, why the information is a story today. A sentence or so about why the story is significant justifies the publicity and explains why the "private" facts are of public importance, even though they are embarrassing to a person.

In addition to wrestling with embarrassment concerns, newspeople are worried about false light. These cases are like libel in that the person complaining believes something about the publicity is false (see Chapter 6, pp. 160–172). Crucial details may disappear in the editing process, causing the finished product to give a distorted impression of the subject (see Chapter 6, pp. 165–166), or a photo used in a negative context may give a false impression that the photograph's subject is connected to the story (see Chapter 6, pp. 166–171). Not every jurisdiction recognizes false light complaints, but the problem they pose is a universal newsroom concern.

Trespass is another action to worry about because newspeople sometimes trespass while trying to get a story or picture on private property. Trespass laws make it a crime to intrude knowingly upon private land. Breaking and entering is a mode of trespass. Impersonation, fraud, or disguise as a means of gaining entry onto private property may also be trespass, as discussed in Chapter 6.

1. *Do public figures have any claim to privacy?*

Yes. Even public figures have privacy rights. The bigger the celebrity, the smaller the area of private secrets that would be considered non-newsworthy.

2. *Are marital problems of a public figure private information or newsworthy?*

For a big celebrity like a president or movie star or national sports hero, nonsalacious facts about the marriage are reportable. Most facets of the life of a star and that of the family are deemed newsworthy within reason. (Extremely offensive exposes that are indecent and shocking are excepted, as discussed in Chapter 5, pp. 139–142.) If the subject is only a limited public figure there should be a clear relationship between the facts about the marriage and the subject's role in public life before marital information is safely reportable. For example, a prosecutor who heads the Bureau Against Violence to Women is found to be a wife-beater. In reporting the story, quote a source's reasoning on why the prosecutor's home life should not remain a private secret, or tell the story in a way that makes the reader understand why you believe the problem should concern, rather than merely titillate, the public, given the subject's public role.

3. *Can the paper name a rape victim? An incest victim?*

Yes. See answer 6 under Official Proceedings, p. 229.

4. *Can the paper name a juvenile offender or publish a photograph of one?*

Yes. See answers 4 and 5 under Official Proceedings, p. 229. Remember, accuracy is at a premium; there generally is no privilege, since there is no public record to rely on.

5. *If the identity of a subject is fictionalized, does that protect against a privacy complaint?*

Yes, provided the disguise renders the subject completely unidentifiable, even by people who know him or her. Where a story about someone's private problems masks the identity of the individual, no privacy complaint can succeed. This means that more than the name may have to be changed, so that the surrounding circumstances are not a giveaway to people familiar with them. Tell the reader that the person's identity and some of the facts have been changed for the sake of privacy.

6. *We publish notices in which one spouse declares that he or she will not be responsible for the debts of the other spouse, naming that person. Does this invade privacy or libelously suggest that somebody's a deadbeat?*

No. The notices do not invade privacy or libel the spouse. Some editors, though, from taste or caution prefer to reword the notices: "Joseph Jones declares that he will be responsible only for those debts which he personally incurs and signs for from now on."

7. *A man killed two women and himself on New Year's Eve in New York City. Many stories about the event included the fact that the man had lived with a certain woman photographer in New York ten years earlier. She disliked the publicity (no one had requested an interview) and said several details had been reported incorrectly. Can she sue?*

If the reports were false and defamatory and the product of grossly irresponsible journalism, there may be a libel action, assuming the photographer is a private person suing in New York. But if the statements were substantially true, there is no privacy claim. The killer's past is newsworthy, and she's a part of it. Of course, it would be preferable to interview her to get her version of the facts, if she'll talk, but her consent to the publicity is unnecessary because of the news value of the information.

8. *How long after an event does it take for a newsworthy person to revert to private life?*

No specific number of years. Factors to consider are how significant the event was when it happened and what makes it a story today (see discussion in Chapter 5, pp. 148–150). A reasonable justification now for recalling old true embarrassing facts will usually mean that their republication will not invade privacy. A desire to commemorate or study history should be a sufficient justification. A current event that brings the person back into the public consciousness may be a justification.

Photographs

1. *Does it invade privacy to publish a photograph of a dead person?*

No. A privacy right is personal and dies with the person.

2. *Readers call up and complain all the time about photographs of accidents in which people were hurt. Is this a legal problem?*

No. A news photo, even one that shows injured or dead people, would not be an invasion of privacy. Whether to run such a photograph is an editorial judgment.

3. *Our paper publishes birthday pictures of children with their names and addresses provided by the parents. If a kidnapper uses this information to snatch a kid, is this a legal problem?*

No, but some editors omit addresses to protect children.

4. *Some of our birthday ads are photographs furnished by a relative or friend. At times, we get ads greeting adults on their birthdays with their old "bear rug" baby pictures from long ago. Any legal problem?*

I don't know of any lawsuits over such advertisements, but if the jokes begin to be a headache, a change of policy may be in order. Remember, almost every state appears to recognize commercial misappropriation as an offense (Chapter 6, pp. 172–173).

5. *Can you photograph a widow at a funeral?*

Yes. Usually, outside in public, but usually not inside without permission, such as in a funeral home or at a religious service.

6. *Can you photograph retarded children without parental consent?*

Outside, yes, as at the Special Olympics, for example, where the children's participation in the events implies that the parents are willing for the public to pay attention. Still, some editors insist on having parental permission for photographs. Inside a school or home, get written permission from a parent of each child photographed. Sometimes public institutions keep such signed permissions on file.

7. *When do you need to get written permission to publish photographs?*

In general, photograph freely outside and avoid trespass, but get permission to photograph inside where permission to enter is necessary and where the person may represent a sensitive subject, such as children or the elderly, the handicapped or disadvantaged (see Chapter 6, pp. 173–178).

So long as outdoor photographs are to be used straightforwardly in a neutral context, no consent should be necessary—provided the photographer is in a place where he or she has a right to be. Fashion shots of pedestrians ("when it comes to pearls, more is better"), weather shots ("today was a day for the beach"), and event pictures (Halloween parade) need no consents. They are "news," and news photos should not require permission.

If a passer-by's photograph is to be used in a negative article about some problem, get the subject's permission specifically for that use, such as for stories on disease, crime, and social problems.

Inside hospitals, jails, group residences, nursing homes, schools, and places of confinement, especially where subjects may be seen as disadvantaged or dependent, get consent from a person authorized to consent for the subject. The manager of the residence is empowered to give the photographer permission to enter, but either the subject himself or herself, or the subject's guardian or custodian, is the person authorized to consent.

8. *Is a consent binding without paying the subject?*

Yes. Some form photo releases cite "consideration," meaning payment, in exchange for the subject's written consent to be photographed, but consideration can be simply the taking of the picture. Some photographers offer to send a print to the subject. Some do offer money.

9. *What should a consent include?*

A professional model release can be long and complex, but news photographers usually find it sufficient and unintimidating to the subject to offer a simple release: Name, address, signature, date, and a statement that the subject gives consent for the publication of his or her picture. If the picture is for advertising, specify advertising in the release. If the proposed use of the picture is sensitive, such as in a story on disease or drugs, specify the use.

10. *Do you need consent for photos in advertising?*

Yes, usually (see Chapter 6, pp. 172–173). Get written permission for the use of a person's name or likeness in advertising or on commercial material, such as brochures, promotions, and calendars.

11. *You see a lot of pictures of the homeless on city streets. Is there a privacy problem?*

No. Generally a newsworthy picture from the street, like a news story, requires no consent. However, be careful not to characterize or overstate in the caption what is known about the person. Don't say or imply that the person in the picture is a welfare recipient or a prostitute unless you confirm it.

12. *Can old pictures be risky if they show a subject in a bad light?*

Old pictures depicting the subject in bad circumstances, such as being arrested or living in jail, probably don't invade privacy, but they should not be used unless there's a current news reason for dredging up the subject's embarrassing past. Chicago's Mayor Washington's campaign was haunted by old mug shots from the days of his conviction for tax evasion, for example, as well as extensive reporting on his past crimes, because the candidate's past was considered of interest to the voters—newsworthy. But avoid rounding up old art for current stories just for the convenience, if the new context might cause the person to complain of being cast in false light (see Chapter 6, p. 171).

13. *If police or fire officials invite the photographer to enter private property with them, is the photographer safe from trespass charges?*

Not always (see Chapter 6, p. 177); the courts have split. Some consider it trespass because the officials had no authority to invite the photographer onto someone's property. Other courts have approved the custom, taking the position that the photographer entered with proper authority. Ask a local press lawyer if there is any direct local precedent for you to rely upon.

14. *When police order the photographer away from an area, is there any recourse?*

Photographers are subject to police authority and have to leave when ordered, unless some special rule gives them special privileges. At the scenes of accidents, crimes, fires, and demonstrations, police have control of the crowds. They are not supposed to single out newspeople for discriminatory mistreatment, but they can direct the crowd. Photographers, like everybody else, must obey (see Chapter 6, p. 177).

15. *Does it invade privacy to publish a picture of a person's house without consent?*

No. The photograph of the exterior of a house is free when taken from someplace where the photographer had a right to be.

Time Limits on Libel Actions in Statutes of Limitations

Twenty-six states allow only one year for the filing of a libel complaint, counting from the day the libel was published. Seventeen states place a two-year limit on libel filings.

A cause of action dies unless filed within the period set by the statute of limitations of the state whose law governs the suit. The purpose of limitations statutes is to rid the courts of stale complaints, prejudiced by faded evidence and scattered and forgetful witnesses. The brief one-year and two-year limits on libel suits are extremely short, compared generally with limits on other types of civil actions, such as the four- or six-year limit ordinarily prescribed for contract actions, and help to limit the number of libel suits brought.

> *One-Year Limit.* Alabama, Arizona, California, Colorado, Georgia, Illinois, Kansas, Kentucky, Louisiana, Maryland, Michigan, Mississippi, Nebraska, New Jersey, New York, North Carolina, Ohio, Oklahoma, Oregon, Pennsylvania, Tennessee, Texas, Utah, Virginia, West Virginia, Wyoming, District of Columbia, Guam, and Puerto Rico.
>
> *Two-Year Limit.* Alaska, Connecticut, Delaware, Hawaii, Idaho, Indiana, Iowa, Maine, Minnesota, Missouri, Montana, Nevada, North Dakota, South Carolina, South Dakota, Washington, Wisconsin, and the Virgin Islands.
>
> *Three-Year Limit.* Arkansas, Massachusetts, New Hampshire, New Mexico, Rhode Island, and Vermont.
>
> *Four-Year Limit.* Florida.

Shield Laws Protecting Journalists' Confidential Sources and Materials

Twenty-six states have shield laws. They vary widely. A few statutes absolutely immunize newspeople from testifying about sources or unpublished information. Some laws merely remove contempt as a sanction for failure to disclose. Other statutes create a conditional privilege that must yield when a competing interest is considered paramount.

Even in states with no shield law at all, courts may be persuaded to recognize a journalist's privilege to shield sources or unpublished information, based on an interpretation of the First Amendment or the state constitution. Generally, a judge-made journalist's shield will be only a "qualified" privilege, which will give way once the person seeking the disclosure has shown compelling need for the information and reasonable but fruitless attempts to obtain it elsewhere. States without shield statutes whose courts have recognized such a qualified privilege include at least Connecticut, Florida, Idaho, Iowa, Kansas, Mississippi, New Hampshire, Texas, Vermont, Virginia, Washington, and West Virginia, according to James C. Goodale, a leading press lawyer with expertise in the journalist's privilege.

Almost all the federal circuit courts have recognized a qualified journalist's privilege, to be balanced against proof that the information is material, necessary, and not otherwise obtainable, according to Goodale. In both the sixth and seventh circuits the privilege had been recognized at the district court level, the ninth circuit was unclear, and the eleventh circuit hadn't yet spoken, according to Goodale's *Communications Law 1985* report published by New York's Practising Law Institute. All other federal circuits had recognized a qualified journalist's privilege.

A list of the state shield laws follows. Some statutes expressly say or have been interpreted to mean that the shield does not apply where a libel defense depends on confidential sources or withheld information. In other words, a libel defendant may not always be free to argue due care and lack of malice while refusing to identify sources of the statements claimed to be libelous. Anyone interested in the details of state shield laws should read full text in the latest, up-to-date state statute books and then should consult a lawyer to learn how the courts have interpreted the laws in civil cases (where the journalist was a party and where the journalist was a nonparty), in criminal matters, and in grand jury proceedings. As the privilege may be a source of tension between lawmakers and judges, it is not unusual to find broadly written legislation narrowly interpreted by courts.
    States with shield laws:

Alabama	Protects sources of published information
Alaska	Source protection yields to "public interest" or to prevent "miscarriage of justice"
Arizona	Needn't testify or disclose source, but libel defense based on secret source may be barred
Arkansas	Protects sources, but may give way if malice is shown
California	No contempt for refusing to identify sources or information
Delaware	Absolute privilege in grand jury; in court proceedings, sources are protected but "public interest" may require disclosure of content
Illinois	Shields unpublished material and sources
Indiana	Protects sources
Kentucky	Protects identity of informants who were sources of published information
Louisiana	Yields to "public interest" in secret source's identity; in libel, reporter must show "good faith" in taking information from confidential source
Maryland	Protects sources of published information
Michigan	Shields disclosure of confidential material to grand jury

Minnesota	Protects sources and unpublished information, but yields to libel plaintiff's crucial need for malice evidence
Montana	Shields any information gathered
Nebraska	Shields unpublished material and sources
Nevada	Shields unpublished material and sources
New Jersey	Shields unpublished material and sources
New Mexico	Yields to party seeking crucial information and source identity if alternatives exhausted (Court rule replaced shield statute)
New York	Shields sources and confidential materials without contempt, but libel defense based on secret source may be barred
North Dakota	Yields if "miscarriage of justice" would result
Ohio	Source protection may yield to crime defendant with crucial need of source to prove innocence
Oklahoma	Shields sources and information until opponent's need prevails; libel defense based on secret source or material may be barred
Oregon	Libel defense based on secret source or material may be barred
Pennsylvania	Protects sources and information
Rhode Island	Libel defense based on secret source or material may be barred
Tennessee	Libel defense based on secret source or material may be barred

Retraction Statutes Reduce
Exposure to Damages

A retraction may be considered in mitigation of damages, and thirty-three states have statutes to govern retractions. Even in states without such statutes, courts can consider the publication of a retraction as one factor in assessing damages. Most of the statutes eliminate punitive damages and limit a libel plaintiff to compensation for monetary loss and injury to reputation if a prompt retraction has been published or broadcast. A catch is that many of the statutes apply only to errors made without actual malice.

Generally, retraction statutes specify what constitutes a retraction and where and how it must be run. They call for "public" and conspicuous corrections under tight time pressure. Some even call for apologies.

The statutes variously define categories of damages, such as "general," "special," "actual," and "punitive" or "exemplary." General damages are compensation for loss of reputation and hurt feelings, and special damages are proven pecuniary business losses. Actual damages (general damages plus special damages) usually are recoverable even after a retraction has been made. Punitive damages (also known as exemplary damages), designed to punish an offender, are the type of award that is typically avoided by a retraction made according to statute.

Anyone interested in details should consult the full text of up-to-date state statutes. The laws limit the plaintiff to a specific kind of damages, as listed below, if the publisher meets a written demand with a timely retraction of a prescribed size and prominence. To understand the list, take Alabama for example: retraction will limit a plaintiff to actual damages unless the publisher acted with actual malice. Next on the list, Arizona: only special damages will be available after a good retraction, except for libels committed with actual malice.

STATE	RECOVERY LIMITED TO
Alabama	Actual damages if without actual malice
Arizona	Special damages unless actual malice (law held unconstitutional by court of appeal in 1985; state supreme court decision pending)
California	Special damages unless actual malice
Connecticut	Actual damages unless "malice in fact"
Florida	Actual damages if honest mistake
Georgia	Actual damages if without malice; must run repudiating editorial if asked
Idaho	Actual damages unless actual malice
Indiana	Actual damages if good faith mistake; excludes election-eve libel of candidate
Iowa	Actual damages if without malice; excludes report of female unchastity and election-eve libel of candidate
Kentucky	Actual damages unless "legal malice"
Maine	Mitigates if mistake or inadvertence
Massachusetts	Actual damages if without actual malice
Michigan	Mitigates all damages
Minnesota	Special damages if good faith mistake; excludes report of female unchastity and election-eve libel of candidate
Mississippi	Actual damages if good faith mistake; excludes election-eve libel of candidate
Montana	Eliminates punitive damages for honest mistake
Nebraska	Special damages unless actual malice
Nevada	Special damages unless actual malice
New Jersey	Actual damages unless "malice in fact"
North Carolina	Actual damages if good faith mistake

North Dakota	Special damages if good faith mistake; excludes libel of female and election-eve libel of candidate
Ohio	Mitigates, but special damages recoverable if actual malice
Oklahoma	Actual damages if good faith mistake; excludes report of female unchastity and election-eve libel of candidate
Oregon	Special damages unless intentional defamation
South Dakota	Candidate for office may not recover punitive damages for good faith mistake; excludes election-eve libel of candidate
Tennessee	Actual damages if good faith mistake; excludes election-eve libel of candidate
Texas	Mitigates
Utah	Actual damages if good faith mistake; excludes election-eve libel of candidate
Virginia	Actual damages (mitigates general and punitive damages)
Washington	Retraction is absolute defense to the publisher-defendant of unauthorized libel committed without publisher's fault or knowledge
West Virginia	Damages mitigated if publisher pleads truth and apologizes
Wisconsin	Retraction mitigates even actual damages
Wyoming	Report of an arrest or judicial proceeding must on request be amplified by follow-up on disposition or plaintiff's explanation

Punishment of Frivolous Libel Suits

To punish those who pursue groundless libel suits in bad faith, many journalists and publishers advocate the filing of countersuits against plaintiffs and their lawyers, demanding reimbursement of defense costs and damages for abuse of process.

Only the rare libel complaint—the extreme case—is likely to be judged to be completely without legal merit and thus a suitable target for a counterclaim (a response within the suit filed by the plaintiff) or a separate countersuit for damages and attorney's fees. The meting out of punishment for litigating is a measure that is reserved only for clear and inexcusable abuses of the judicial process. Courts will not penalize a person merely for bringing a weak libel case, or a marginal case where a flimsy but somewhat cogent argument exists that the plaintiff was libeled by unprivileged publicity. But courts in several states have been persuaded that they have the power, with or without an enabling statute, to fine plaintiffs and plaintiffs' lawyers who use baseless libel claims to harass enemies and stifle debate. Following are three recent examples.

Firm fined for frivolous libel appeal

by BARBARA DILL

LOS ANGELES—A law firm here must pay a $20,000 fine and court costs for pursuing a frivolous appeal of a failed libel suit.

A developer had sued citizens who waged a successful campaign to stop a condominium project with handbills and letters-to-the-editor and appealed decisions which found the handbills and letters nonlibelous.

The firm this month filed a petition with the U.S. Supreme Court for review of the fine. The court has not yet determined if it will hear the case.

The lawyers' five-year pursuit of libel claims had been dismissed on all three levels of the California courts. The California Court of Appeal condemned their persistence as an attempt to inhibit the fundamental First Amendment right of citizens lawfully working through the political process.

The penalty represents a relatively rare instance of sanctions against lawyers engaged in libel litigation. To deter frivolous lawsuits, such sanctions increasingly are being urged by critics of the traditional requirement that each party bear its own costs from trial through appeals.

Publishers and lawyers who advocate suing plaintiffs' lawyers for bringing baseless libel suits hope to shift the burden of defense costs for "nuisance" and harassment suits, thereby taking the profit out of such litigating.

The $20,000 penalty in the California developer's case, *Maple Properties* v. *Harris*, was authorized by a specific state law governing frivolous appeals. The Los Angeles law firm of Levy & Norminton, which handled the case for Maple Properties, was ordered to reimburse the other side's $20,000 legal fees incurred in defending against the builder's appeal of the defamation portion of the action, including both libel and slander suits.

"Defamation" is the term for false, reputation-damaging publication, and it encompasses libel, which is written, and slander, which is oral. Nondefamation claims involved in the same Maple Properties appeal were rejected but not ruled frivolous and not penalized.

Imposing a fine for a "partially frivolous appeal" on the libel claims alone was groundbreaking, according to Beverly Hills lawyer Scott G. Haith. Haith was one of the attorneys who urged the court to separate the legitimate portion of the appeal from the unwarranted appeal of the libel counts. The court allocated $10,000 to Haith's client, Erwin Okun, and the remaining $10,000 to the other defendants, Betty H. Harris and Joann Ruden, for their lawyers' work connected to the libel appeal. In addition, Levy & Norminton was assessed about $5,000 court costs for hearing and deposition transcripts, subpoenas and filing fees.

Okun, Harris and Ruden were sued for writing campaign handbills and letters to newspapers urging the repeal of an ordinance that would have allowed condominiums to take over an industrial zone devoted to municipal services.

Two months after voters dashed Maple Properties' bid to privately develop Beverly Hills' public land in March 1979, the developer brought suit against the three residents whose letters to the *Los Angeles Times* and the *Beverly Hills Courier* had denounced the plan as harmful to the city's interest. The newspapers were not named in the suit.

California's supreme court, the state's highest, reviewed the case in 1981 and directed the trial court to dismiss the libel claims with no permission to amend them because the material was privileged public debate and "could not reasonably be found libelous."

The courts did grant the builder a chance to amend a slander count for further litigation, over a dissent from Supreme Court Judge Mosk who wanted to see an early end to what he called a "misguided" impingement upon the "free exercize of speech, writing and the political function."

"We should discourage attempts to recover through the judicial process what has been lost in the political process," he wrote. All counts ultimately were dismissed, but three years later Maple Properties still was trying to reopen the libel case by claiming to have discovered new facts.

When the court of appeal reviewed the

claims again in August 1984, it found that the so-called new facts were actually old facts which Maple Properties had already presented and which had been rejected. The court then ruled that the appeal was punishable because it was "completely devoid of merit" and had the effect of harassing citizen's constitutionally protected political expression.

Publishers' Auxiliary, January 14, 1985
[The Supreme Court declined to review the case, and the penalty was paid.—BD]

Filer of "groundless" libel suit ordered to pay costs

by BARBARA DILL

SHOW LOW, Ariz.—A first-year lawyer who filed a hopeless libel suit against the mayor of Show Low and a local radio station got an education in First Amendment law and a bill for part of the defense from a court which ruled the suit was "groundless and in bad faith."

The lawyer, Norman H. Kahn, and his client were ordered to pay $8,177 in attorney's fees and court costs.

In his ruling, Superior Judge Richard K. Mangum said Kahn had failed to research defamation law, investigate his client's claim, or discover a retraction made by Radio Station KVSL. This, the judge said, showed a "determination to sue whether right or wrong," which deserved to be punished.

Arizona is one of several states with a law that dictates that anyone who brings a frivolous civil suit must pay the opponent's costs.

The suit grew out of an argument between Ellis B. Qualls, the mayor of Show Low, and David C. Porter, a former mayor and city councilman, over whether the town should build a new city hall or move its offices into an existing building.

After confrontations at public hearings, the two agreed to meet for further discussion at Qualls's office. Shortly before their appointment, Qualls told Porter that an emergency had developed and that he had to leave. The mayor did not return at the appointed time and Porter told others that he had been stood up.

In response, Qualls issued a press release saying that Porter was "telling only half the truth." The mayor added, "Mr. Porter, maybe you are only doing it out of habit."

Porter then brought a $10 million suit against the mayor, Radio Station KVSL, which broadcast the statement, and the municipality, because the statement appeared on city stationery. Porter contended that the statement was false and malicious and that it implied he was a habitual liar.

Libel trial expert James F. Henderson of Phoenix, who represented the mayor and the other defendants, defeated the suit without having to go to trial.

He told the court he had learned through questioning of Kahn, a 1982 graduate of University of Arizona Law School who formerly practiced in Eager, Arizona, about fifty miles east of Show Low, that Kahn had not studied defamation in law school, never handled a libel matter before, and had not read the landmark United States Supreme Court libel cases of *New York Times* v. *Sullivan* and *Gertz* v. *Welch* on what constitutes a public figure.

Henderson told the court it was clear that Kahn had not recognized that his client's prominent role in the debate over the new city hall had made him a public figure and that, as a public figure, he would be required to prove deliberate or reckless lying by the mayor and the radio station in order to win his case.

Henderson pointed out several other mistakes. Kahn had demanded punitive damages against the station despite a statute eliminating them. He had sent the station a demand for a retraction, but then sued without learning that the station had honored it by broadcasting a conciliatory correction from the mayor. He didn't find out about it until months later.

Kahn named Porter's wife as co-plaintiff, even though the complained-of statement made no reference to her, an essential element of any libel claim. Kahn mistakenly believed she was necessary and argued that

Qualls's remarks about her husband upset her so much that she had to see a psychiatrist.

Kahn also ignored red flags from the radio station before the suit. In a letter following his retraction demand, station president Hugh H. Williams advised Kahn that KVSL's coverage of newsworthy statements by public officials was privileged and warned the station would counterclaim for abuse of process if Porter and Kahn tried to muzzle it with a suit.

Williams suggested that Kahn read up on First Amendment law and even cited two cases for his review. Kahn said he did about twelve hours' research and read four to six Arizona cases.

Kahn filed suit but didn't initiate any discovery and withdrew only four months into the case, but with the fight over costs, the case took one year in all.

Henderson and his associate, Terrance C. Mead, had worked ninety-six hours on the case and paralegal Carol Rogers had put in twenty-eight hours. In protracted argument over paying the fees, including a motion for a new trial, Kahn said the penalty was undeserved and the bill was inflated because Henderson's team had done unnecessary work.

Publishers' Auxiliary, July 15, 1985

Lawyer loses libel appeal against lawbook publisher

by BARBARA DILL

NEW YORK—A lawyer here who pursued a libel appeal against a lawbook publishing house for printing a court decision which he said portrayed him as a swindler was assessed double costs and $1,000 damages by the Second Federal Circuit Court of Appeals.

After the lawyer had his home roof fixed, he refused to pay and the roofer sued to collect $656.

The lawyer, Patrick Beary of Jamaica, Queens, won by citing a state law which permits nonpayment for repairs performed by an unlicensed roofer. In his written opinion dismissing the claim of Estates Roofing Company, Civil Court Judge William Friedmann commented, "although the result appears to be unjust, the law is the law."

Noting Beary was not arguing that the work was unsatisfactory, the judge stated the license requirement "cannot be relaxed, although a party should be paid for his completed and satisfactory work."

The Friedmann opinion was published first in West Publishing Company "Advance Sheets," paperbacks containing the full text of recent court decisions which appear periodically until bigger hardbound volumes supersede them.

Beary moved to vacate the opinion and asked West to omit it from the bound volume. He said that he would have proved poor workmanship if the judge had not dismissed the roofer on legal grounds. The judge denied the motion but arranged to remove Beary's name from the opinion, substituting "Homeowner" in West's bound volume.

Suing West for libel, Beary complained that the Advance Sheet negligently portrayed him as a "conniving, contemptible . . . deadbeat" by reason of his "knowledge of the law."

West won summary judgment and the case was dismissed without a trial on the grounds that the judge's opinion was not libelous and was absolutely privileged under state law as a fair and true report of an official proceeding.

Beary argued unsuccessfully on appeal that the law covered only "official" government-printed case reports and not West's unofficial reporting service. The Second Circuit Court of Appeals voted to punish this appeal for "complete frivolousness" under a federal rule on appellate practice.

Publishers' Auxiliary, September 9, 1985

Table of Cases

NOTE: This table lists cases relevant to discussions that appear on particular pages in the text as well as cases mentioned by name in the book.

Index